Splendor on the Diamond

Florida A&M University, Tallahassee
Florida Atlantic University, Boca Raton
Florida Gulf Coast University, Ft. Myers
Florida International University, Miami
Florida State University, Tallahassee
University of Central Florida, Orlando
University of Florida, Gainesville
University of North Florida, Jacksonville
University of South Florida, Tampa
University of West Florida, Pensacola

University Press of Florida

Gainesville ♦ Tallahassee ♦ Tampa ♦ Boca Raton

Pensacola ♦ Orlando ♦ Miami ♦ Jacksonville ♦ Ft. Myers

Rich Westcott

Splendor on the Diamond

Interviews with 35 Stars
of Baseball's Past

05 04 03 02 01 00   6 5 4 3 2 1

LIBRARY OF CONGRESS CATALOGING-IN-PUBLICATION DATA
Westcott, Rich.
Splendor on the diamond: interviews with 35 stars of baseball's past /
Rich Westcott.
p. cm.
ISBN 0-8130-1786-6 (alk. paper)
1. Baseball players—Interviews. I. Title.
GV865.A1 W474   2000
796.357'092'273—dc21   99-086539
[B]

The University Press of Florida is the scholarly publishing agency for
the State University System of Florida, comprising Florida A&M
University, Florida Atlantic University, Florida Gulf Coast University,
Florida International University, Florida State University, University
of Central Florida, University of Florida, University of North Florida,
University of South Florida, and University of West Florida.

University Press of Florida
15 Northwest 15th Street
Gainesville, FL 32611–2079
http://www.upf.com

To Samantha and Harrison,
two little people who provide a big amount of joy

Contents

Acknowledgments

I would like to express my thanks to those who have played a part in the preparation of this book. I am particularly grateful to my son, Chris, for his technical assistance, an invaluable aide in this age of electronic confusion. Thanks also to Bob Armbruster, Frank Barning, Allen Lewis, and Bob Schmierer for the various and important ways in which they contributed to the fulfillment of this book. Last but hardly least, I appreciate as always the patience, understanding, and enthusiastic support of my wife, Lois, whose help in projects such as this is without boundaries.

Splendor on the Diamond

Introduction

The sport's historians generally acknowledge that one of the most glorious eras of major league baseball occurred during the period following the end of World War II. From the late 1940s into the 1960s, baseball was not only an amalgamation of some of the finest players and some of the best teams ever to appear, it was the setting for numerous memorable games and events.

For major league baseball, the decade and one-half after the war were also noteworthy for another reason. During that period, baseball underwent more changes of far-reaching importance than at any other period in its history.

The most significant alteration to baseball's long-stationary structure was doubtless the entrée of African-American players into the big leagues. Soon afterward, Hispanic players began appearing in greater numbers. A players union, which would become a powerful component of the game, was launched. Television began to emerge as a critical force, and night games became more than just occasional occurrences. New parks were built, and new stars emerged among the players. Teams switched cities for the first time in half a century, and ultimately the leagues were expanded to accommodate new teams in cities that had been merely locations of almost unknown minor league clubs. Even baseball cards were mass-produced for the first time, and the way the game was played, administered, written about, and followed underwent alterations.

All of these changes, occurring in the years following World War II, played a major role in transforming the composition of baseball and in shaping its future. The upheaval assured that the sport would never be the same.

Baseball was at the peak of its popularity in that period. At a time when other major sports either were struggling or in their infancy, and at best attracted only small groups of devoted followers, baseball was the dominant game in America. It was truly a national pastime: a grand and glorious game that appealed to men, women, and children, regardless of age, social standing, or geographic location.

There was an appetite then for baseball that perhaps has had no equal in the annals of American sports. That popularity was reflected all across the country in the enormous crowds attending major league games and in the highest number of minor league teams ever fielded. Passionate devotees of baseball, whether performers or watchers, existed in huge numbers everywhere. From small villages to big cities, in barnyards and schoolyards, on vacant lots and playgrounds, and in the streets and alleys of the cities, baseball was the game of choice of an immense segment of the population.

If you were a child of that era and followed baseball, it was an infinitely happy time. The game provided an almost indefinable pleasure. It was majestic. It was heavenly. We loved and worshiped it. And it gripped our attention and generated a level of passion that was unlike anything else we had encountered or ever wanted to encounter.

As young boys, we knew the starting lineups of every team. We memorized statistics and box scores. We hid radios under our pillows at night to listen to the games. We stood in front of stores to watch games on television sets placed in the windows. We collected baseball cards as though they meant something and without regard to what their values might be some day. We read every baseball book we could get our hands on. We cut out baseball pictures from newspapers and magazines and pasted them into scrapbooks or tacked them to our bedroom walls. We collected autographs of the players.

We also played the game at every opportunity, whether it was a hybrid we called stickball, a pickup game among neighborhood kids, or for an organized team. If somebody from your hometown had landed a pro contract, even if it was with the lowliest minor league team, his name would be spoken in the kind of hushed tones usually reserved for deity. And we would bask in his extremely good fortune as though we actually had had a part in it. Best of all, for those of us with the incalculable luck of living in or near cities with big league teams, we went to the games to see first-hand our heroes in action.

If there was one reason above all others that made baseball of that period America's favorite sport, it was the players, those gallant, stalwart, awe-inspiring men who performed with such remarkable talent on the field. More than anything else, they gave substance to the game, made it come alive, and elevated it to a pedestal.

The players were idolized and imitated by kids and admired and discussed by adults. They were the ones whose achievements were the focal points of the game, whose very presence made baseball what it was. They were mesmerizing, virtually bigger than life, and they were the center around which all elements of the game revolved.

Splendor on the Diamond is an attempt to re-create some of the magic that surrounded major league baseball players of an earlier time. It was written to provide a glimpse of some of these players, their careers, their thoughts, and their contributions to this special game and to the special era in which they performed.

Thirty-five players are profiled, all personally interviewed in their homes or at other locations around the country. Although a widely diverse group, collectively they represent in their different ways some of the best stories of one of baseball's best eras. All played in the period after World War II when baseball reached its highest level, their careers having taken place mostly in the 1940s, 1950s, or 1960s (some began their careers before the war). All have easily recognizable names, and all performed outstanding deeds.

Of the players profiled, 12 are members of baseball's Hall of Fame. They range from Warren Spahn, the greatest lefthanded pitcher of all time, to Pee Wee Reese, sparkplug of the great Brooklyn Dodgers teams, to Al Kaline, the youngest player ever to win a batting title, to Monte Irvin, one of the major league's first black players, to Juan Marichal, the finest of all Latin American pitchers, to Harmon Killebrew, one of the most prolific home run hitters ever to swing a bat.

Great hitters such as Eddie Mathews and Billy Williams, outstanding all-around players such as Lou Boudreau, Billy Herman, and Red Schoendienst, and excellent pitchers such as Bob Lemon, Dick Radatz, Bob Rush, and the unfairly maligned Ralph Branca also add their stories to the grand tale of baseball history.

All players in the collection had important careers. Some performed special feats. Jim Maloney pitched three no-hitters, Dick Sisler hit a home run on the last day of the season to win a pennant, Gus Zernial was a home run champion, Elroy Face won 18 games in relief in one season, and Rick Wise hit two home runs while hurling a no-hitter.

Off-the-field achievements of particular interest are sprinkled throughout. For instance, Jim Brosnan became a best-selling author, Lou Brissie was a war hero who came back to pitch after nearly losing a leg, Bobby Avila was the mayor of Veracruz, Mexico, Sid Hudson became a highly successful pitching coach, and Billy Bruton became the right-hand man of Lee Iacocca at Chrysler.

Of course, colorful characters abound. No one had a more colorful—and controversial—career than Jimmy Piersall. The book also includes such other notable personalities as Chico Carrasquel, the first great Venezuelan shortstop, the feisty, fun-loving World Series hero Johnny Podres, Granny Hamner, captain of the Whiz Kids, former college football standout Alvin Dark, and Ned Garver, the pride of the forlorn St. Louis Browns. In addition, there are visits with rock-solid catcher John Roseboro, pioneer reliever Ray Narleski, heavy-hitting Roy Sievers, and wily southpaw Max Lanier.

Six of the players interviewed are now deceased. Their profiles in this collection were in some cases the last stories written about them and therefore serve as a final tribute to their careers and as a vehicle for preserving their thoughts.

In all cases, however, the stories of these wonderful players help to preserve the rich lore of baseball while contributing a written record to the game's history. Collectively, the players tell a fascinating story, not only about their careers and lives but about their sport as it was in a day when the splendor on the diamond reached what was possibly its most enchanting level.

To give this collection some semblance of organization, the book is divided into four parts: Hall of Famers, Especially Noteworthy (players who performed particularly memorable feats), Men on the Mound (pitchers), and Around the Bases (position players).

Hall of Famers ◆ **1**

Lou Boudreau

One of a Kind

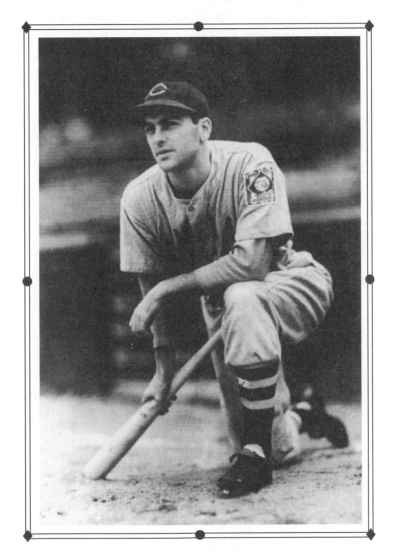

OF ALL ITS many attributes, one of the most endearing qualities of baseball has always been its great variety of interesting performers.

At least until recently, baseball has been a game that has focused more on the participants than on anything else. More than teams, more than records and statistics, more than picturesque ball parks, it has always been the performers who have given the game its enduring appeal.

And unlike so many other sports, cluttered either with robots, zombies, ill-mannered brats, grandstand hotshots, or other such bores, baseball has generally been populated by a vast array of colorful and diverse artists, many of whom seem larger than life. They have come from every corner of society, each one different from the other, and collectively they have produced a unique atmosphere that has been achieved in no other sport.

Every player has seemed to possess a special quality all his own. Some, of course, have been more exceptional than others. But that is the beauty of the game. It has all kinds.

Some, like Lou Boudreau, were one of a kind. In all of baseball, nobody ever fit the same mold as Boudreau. He was unique, a singular virtuoso whose variety of achievements have gone and probably will forever go unduplicated.

Hall of Famer, batting champion, Most Valuable Player, second youngest manager in major league history, World Series winner, exquisite fielder and record-holder, fierce competitor, leader, innovator, the American League's last full-time playing-manager, broadcaster, and college and pro basketball star and coach: the list of Boudreau's accomplishments reads like something out of a Frank Merriwell novel.

Boudreau's career in baseball spanned 50 years. He played in the major leagues for 15 seasons, managed for 16, and was a broadcaster for nearly 27 years. In 1970, the University of Illinois graduate was elected to the baseball Hall of Fame.

"That," says Boudreau, "was the greatest moment of my career. It's the dream of everybody who puts on a baseball uniform to make the Hall of Fame. It certainly was mine."

He certainly had the credentials. In 1,646 games as a player with the Cleveland Indians and Boston Red Sox, he hit .295 with 1,.779 hits, 68 home runs, 385 doubles, 789 RBI, and 861 runs. His slugging average was .415.

The 5-11, 185-pounder won the American League batting championship with a .327 average in 1944. In 1948, when he had his finest season, hitting

.355 and driving in 106 runs, he was named the junior circuit's Most Valuable Player while leading the Indians to the pennant and to victory in the World Series.

He hit over .300 four times and over .280 nine times. He was named to seven All-Star teams. One of the top clutch hitters of his era, Boudreau was especially adept at hitting doubles. He led the league in two-baggers three times (each time with 45), and he hit 30 or more doubles seven times in his career.

As shortstops go, Boudreau was one of the great hitters of modern times, far better than any of his peers at the position. But as good as he was with the bat, Lou was just as good with the glove.

Defensively, he didn't have great speed, but he had a quick start and sure hands, and he was regarded as the most gifted shortstop of his era. He had the uncanny knack of being able to read hitters and to position himself in just the right place.

Boudreau led American League shortstops in fielding percentage eight times, including his first five years as a regular in the majors. He also led in putouts four times, assists twice, and, teaming first with Ray Mack and later with Joe Gordon, he led the league in doubleplays five times. In 1943 and again in 1944 (when he had 134), Lou set American League records—since broken—for most doubleplays in one season by a shortstop.

The Harvey, Illinois, native still has his name connected with other fielding records. He shares the major league mark with Everett Scott and Luis Aparcio for most years leading the league in fielding (eight), and until Cal Ripken came along to break it, he, Aparicio, Joe Sewell, and Eddie Joost co-owned the American League mark for most years leading the league in putouts (four).

Boudreau, whose number 5 is one of three that have been retired by the Indians, still holds the team record with Mack for the best doubleplay combination in Cleveland history with 245. He also ranks third in games played, fourth in at-bats, fifth in doubles, and sixth in runs, hits, total bases, and extra-base hits on Cleveland's all-time list.

As a manager, Boudreau compiled a 1,162–1,224 (.487) record while serving nine years as pilot of the Indians, three years with the Red Sox, three years with the Kansas City A's, and one year with the Chicago Cubs. Exactly half of his 16 teams finished in the first division.

Lou not only won more games (728) but lost more games (649) than any skipper in Indians' history. He ranks 10th in winning percentage on the club's all-time list with a .529, having finished first once, third twice, fourth three times, fifth twice, and sixth once.

Boudreau became the second youngest man ever to manage a big league club when he took command of the Indians in 1942 at the age of 24. (Roger Peckinpaugh, who Lou succeeded in Cleveland, was the youngest at 23 when he piloted the New York Yankees in the last 17 games of the 1914 season.) He was the last man in the big leagues to be a regular player and manager at the same time prior to Pete Rose's performing the same feat in 1985 with the Cincinnati Reds.

The career of Boudreau is filled with so many memorable events that it takes a book to list them all. Several, though, were especially noteworthy.

In 1941, Lou played a key role in the game in which Joe DiMaggio's 56-game hitting streak came to an end at the hands of Cleveland pitchers Al Smith and Jim Bagby.

"That was the game in which Kenny Keltner made two great back-handed stops behind third base," Boudreau recalls. "Joe also hit one in the seventh inning that sent our center fielder [Roy Weatherly] back 357 feet to grab a long, high fly ball.

"In the ninth inning," Boudreau continues, "he hit a sharp ground ball to my left that took a bad hop. In defense of protecting my face, I threw my hand up, made a grab of the ball, and turned it into a doubleplay." That ended his streak, but then he went on after that to hit in 16 more consecutive games.

"DiMaggio was in such a groove during that period that regardless of who pitched or how you tried to stop him, the only way to stop him was by walking him four straight times.

"To us, it was a special achievement to stop his streak. I don't know if you could say we were proud to stop it, but we were happy to be involved in stopping it because it gave us a lot of publicity."

Always known for his quick and innovative mind, Boudreau also had a choice encounter with the league's other fabled superstar of the day, Ted Williams. In 1946, Lou devised "The Williams Shift," a tactic in which he played three of his infielders between second and first bases, leaving only the third baseman to cover the left side of the diamond when the powerful left-handed Red Sox slugger came to bat.

The revolutionary strategy, designed to keep Williams from pounding

Cleveland pitchers, as he had done all season, was not only successful against the greatest hitter of all time, but variations of it were soon appearing throughout baseball. And it became a tactic that is still used against pull-hitters.

Boudreau's greatest brush with fame occurred during the 1948 season when he did virtually everything but sweep the stands after the games. Not only did he manage a team immersed in the heat of a season-long pennant race, but, remarkably, he had his best season on the field.

During the regular season, the Indians' playing-manager set career highs in batting (.355), home runs (18), RBI (106), and runs (116) while leading the league's shortstops in fielding. Lou even played catcher in one game when the Tribe ran short of backstops. Although he lost the batting championship to Williams by 14 points, Boudreau was named the league's Most Valuable Player.

But Lou didn't stop there. With Cleveland and Boston tied for first place at the end of the season, a one-game playoff was necessary. Boudreau, although he had a pitching staff containing such stalwarts as Bob Feller and Bob Lemon, surprised everyone by naming rookie lefthander Gene Bearden to start at Fenway Park. Boudreau slammed two home runs and two singles and drove in four runs as the Indians defeated the Red Sox, 8–3, to capture the pennant.

"If I had to cite my greatest experience in uniform, that year would be it," Boudreau says. "Bill Veeck had tried to trade me in 1947 to the St. Louis Browns, and the fans had rebelled. He changed his mind and called off the deal. That gave me an incentive in 1948. Fortunately, I had one of the greatest years any individual in sports could have, especially because it helped us win the playoff and then go on to beat the Boston Braves in the World Series."

Even Williams applauded Boudreau's magnificent season. "I can't recall ever seeing a player have a better year," he said. "He could do nothing wrong. His hitting in the pinches was uncanny. His fielding was sensational all season. And the inspiration he provided the Indians was what enabled them to win the flag."

"But let me tell you," Boudreau responds. "That may have been my greatest season. But I had a lot of great players, such as Keltner, Gordon, Eddie Robinson at first, Jim Hegan catching, an outfield of Dale Mitchell, Larry Doby and Bob Kennedy, and the great pitching of Feller, Lemon,

Bearden, [Steve] Gromek, [Sam] Zoldak and [Russ] Christopher. It was a great team."

The '48 Indians went on to beat the Braves four games to two in a World Series made memorable by the brilliant pitching of Feller, Lemon, Bearden, Gromek, and Boston's Johnny Sain. The first game was especially noteworthy, not only because Sain pitched a four-hitter to blank the Indians and Feller, 1–0, but because the winning run was scored after one of the most controversial calls in World Series history.

In the eighth inning, with the teams locked in a scoreless duel, pinch-runner Phil Masi was on second with one out when Feller whirled and fired a pickoff attempt to Boudreau at second. Umpire Bill Stewart called Masi—diving back to the bag—safe. Boudreau argued vehemently, but to no avail. Tommy Holmes then singled Masi home with the game's only run.

Was Masi safe or out?

"He was out," Boudreau states emphatically, "and he knew it. But he never admitted it until after the umpire, Bill Stewart, had passed away. He didn't want to embarrass him while he was still alive. That's quite a gentlemanly act on Masi's part."

It had been the Indians' first trip to the World Series since 1920 and would turn out to be only their second Series victory in the 20th century. Boudreau had expected more than that when he was hired. To get to that point, though, he had taken a complicated path that involved basketball and several major decisions.

An outstanding baseball and basketball player as a youth, Boudreau had gone to the University of Illinois where he played each sport with equal proficiency. Before graduating from college in 1939, he had joined both the Indians and a pro basketball team in Hammond, Indiana.

"I played in the old National Basketball League [which later merged with the Basketball Association of America to form the National Basketball Association] with Caesar's All-Americans," Boudreau recalls. "We played in a league that had Oshkosh, Sheboygan, Minneapolis, Fort Wayne, Akron, Detroit, and a lot of other midwestern cities. One of my teammates was John Wooden.

"Meanwhile, I was a third baseman in baseball. I had played that position all through high school, college, and my semipro years. In 1938 I signed with the Indians, and after finishing the year in the minors as a third baseman, I joined them in spring training. Oscar Vitt was the manager. He said, 'Kid, we've got a third baseman over there who's a youngster who's going to be a great one. That's Ken Keltner. You better look for another position.'

"The Indians sent me over to Plant City to join the Buffalo team. Steve O'Neill was the manager, and Greg Mulleavy, a former White Sox player and later scout for the Dodgers, was the shortstop. He took me under his wing, and taught me how to play shortstop."

Boudreau hit .331 for Buffalo, then as now a member of the International League. The Indians recalled him in August 1939, and he hit .258 for them and in one game made 12 assists at shortstop. That winter, he spent his second season playing pro basketball.

"But I had to make a choice," Boudreau says. "The Indians wanted me to stop playing basketball. Finally, my father made the choice for me. He said, 'There's more of a future for you, and you would last longer in baseball than you would playing the tough game of basketball on all those hard courts.' And he was right."

Lou stepped away from the hardwood as a player, but it wasn't a total separation. He returned to his alma mater in 1940 where he took an off-season job as freshman basketball coach. Many of his players, including future NBA star Andy Phillip, went on to form the nucleus of the famed Illini Whiz Kids, a group that won 35 and lost six over a two-year period in the early 1940s.

"That was the greatest basketball team ever to perform for the University of Illinois," Boudreau says. "My job was to coach the freshmen and help recruit. One assignment took me to Granite City to talk Phillip into coming to Illinois. Andy was also a great baseball player and had worked out with the St. Louis Cardinals. But eventually, we got him to come with us. He became an All-American and went on to a great career in the pros."

All the while, Boudreau was getting established as a rising star in the American League. In his first full season in the majors in 1940, the 22-year-old shortstop hit .295, made the All-Star team, and for the first of five straight years led American League shortstops in fielding percentage. In 1941, his bat slipped to .257, but he led the league in doubles and was again selected to the All-Star squad and got two hits.

That winter, Boudreau crossed another big bridge in his life. "I was now 24 years old, had graduated from the University of Illinois, and was their freshman basketball and baseball coach," he says. "That fall, Cy Slapnicka, our general manager at Cleveland, had a heart attack. They moved Roger Peckinpaugh, who was manager, up to the GM job. That left an opening.

"I sat down after basketball practice one day and wrote a letter to Alva Bradley, the Indians' president, explaining to him that I had taken my high school basketball team to the state tournament three successive years, which set a record, and that I also played college basketball and baseball and was captain in both sports, which set a precedent at the university. I said I thought I could handle the Cleveland Indians.

"I wrote the letter, sent it, and then I realized what I did. I was frightened. I went out to the basketball court and saw the head basketball coach and athletic director, Doug Mills, and talked to my baseball coach, Wally Red-ker. I asked them, 'Is there any way I can get that letter back?' They said, 'Forget it. Mr. Bradley will file it like they do all complaint letters.' My letter had no sense to it.

"So, I relaxed a little. But only for two days. Then I received a tele-phone call from Mr. Bradley. They called me off the gymnasium floor to take the call. I talked with him, and he said, 'Come on in. We want to inter-view you.'

"Now, I was more scared than ever. Once again, I was told to go ahead, gain the experience. Nothing will happen. So that's what I did.

"I was interviewed by 12 directors and Mr. Bradley for about 45 minutes. Then I was told to wait in a conference room. When they called me back, I heard this story:

"A Mr. George Martin, chairman of the board of Sherwin Williams Paint Co., 84 years of age, changed 11 no votes to 11 yeses. He was the only yes on the first vote. He said that in the last dozen years Cleveland had had eight managers and had become a graveyard. He talked them into starting over with a young manager and a young player who had a bright future.

"They went for it, and on the next vote all 11 no votes voted yes. I became manager with the stipulation that I would hire older coaches to help me with the responsibilities.

"I thought about it over the winter, and I concluded maybe I could manage, not only with the knowledge I had of my ballplayers, but that I could manage by example. So, whenever I would give myself up by hitting the ball to the right side of the diamond with a man on second with less than two outs, or if I gave myself up and sacrificed in a particular spot, I would bring that up to the players. I would say, 'I'm doing this. I'm diving after balls and giving 110 per cent, and I'd like to have you do the same.'

"At first, the players didn't accept that," Boudreau says. "But I would send an older coach with great experience, like Burt Shotton or Bill Mc-Kechnie, over to the individual. They would tell the player to do it the correct way or you're not going to play. If the player complained or argued with the coach, the coach would tell him to see #5, Boudreau. But they never came over to me. So I think the older coaches helped me tremendously the first few years."

In his first year as manager in 1942, the second youngest skipper in big league history gave a pointed demonstration of what he meant by "setting an example." The Boy Wonder upped his batting average to .283. Voted for the first time the American League's starting shortstop in the All-Star Game, Boudreau led off the game by belting Mort Cooper's second pitch into the upper deck in left field at the Polo Grounds to help his team to a 3–1 victory.

The '42 Indians finished fourth. They moved up to third the following season, then fell back and scuffled for a few years before finally leaping to the pennant in 1948.

As a player, Boudreau was hitting his peak. In 1943, his average climbed to .286. In 1944, he won the batting title with a .327 mark—which included a league-leading 45 doubles—beating out Bobby Doerr (.325) and Bob Johnson (.324).

"It went down to the last day of the season," Boudreau recalls. "I got one hit and that enabled me to win the race, which had gone back and forth all during the final week of the season."

The following year, Lou hit .306, but he missed a big chunk of the season when his ankle was broken by Boston's Dolph Camilli sliding into second to break up a doubleplay. Over the next four years, Boudreau's batting average went .293, .307, .355, and .284. His 1946 season included one game in which he drilled five extra base hits (four doubles and one home run), which tied an American League record.

"It was hard to play and manage at the same time, but I enjoyed it," Boudreau says. "It gave me an incentive. I had responsibilities, and I was interested in doing the best I could. I always tried to manage by example, and that made me bear down, made me take care of myself a little better, and made me study the pitchers, the count and the hitters more. Overall, I would say that managing made me a better player."

After the Indians finished fourth in 1950, Lou—now no longer a regular in the lineup—was handed his release by general manager Hank Greenberg. Cleveland fans were furious at the Indians for axing their hero. One week later, however, Boudreau signed as a player with the rival Red Sox.

"I signed with Boston because of Joe Cronin [the Red Sox general manager and former shortstop]," Lou says. "He was one of my idols. I liked him very much. I would've made more money with the Washington Senators and Clark Griffith, but I decided to go with Joe. I liked Fenway Park. I liked the fans in Boston. I intended to go there for two years."

Boudreau, however, stayed for four. After playing one year as a reserve infielder and hitting .267, Lou was asked to replace the incumbent manager, his old minor league pilot Steve O'Neill.

Boudreau's Bosox never contended for the pennant, and after one sixth-place and two fourth-place finishes, he was relieved of his duties at the end of the 1954 season. Almost immediately, Lou got a job as manager of the A's, who had just moved from Philadelphia to Kansas City.

Boudreau tried to revive his moribund club, but it was hopeless. In three years, his A's finished sixth once and eighth twice. After the 1957 season, Lou was again handed his walking papers.

"At that point, I went into broadcasting," he says. "Jack Brickhouse asked me to come into broadcasting Cubs games with him. Then in 1960 Charlie Grimm decided to give up managing the Cubs. He was reading a magazine at three o'clock in the morning in his hotel room with the lights off, and he just figured he had had enough and quit. I was brought from the radio booth down to the field, and Charlie went up to the radio booth."

Under Boudreau, a hapless Chicago team finished eighth in 1960. The next year, he was replaced by a team of coaches who took turns serving as manager.

"In 1961, Mr. [Phil] Wrigley went to the college of coaches, which I didn't agree with," Boudreau says. "So that became my last year of managing."

Boudreau went back to the press box where he continued to broadcast Cubs games until 1987. Today, Boudreau, the father-in-law of ex-pitcher Denny McLain, is officially retired from baseball, but he still takes an active interest in the game and follows it closely from his home in Dolton, Illinois.

"When I played, we all had seven or eight good men in the lineup, who were consistent, good hitters," he says. "When you have guys like Williams,

DiMaggio, Tommy Henrich, Phil Rizzuto, George Kell, you know it was a great era.

"We had great teams, too. Boston, New York, Cleveland, Detroit, Philadelphia—they all were good ball clubs. It was definitely a great era for baseball."

And it was enhanced by one Lou Boudreau. There was nobody quite like him.

Billy Herman

Master Second Baseman

Billy Herman

DOWN THROUGH THE YEARS, there has been no shortage of outstanding second basemen adorning the diamonds of big league baseball. Some of the most decorated names gracing the list of legends at Cooperstown have been guardians of the keystone sack. And scores of others rank just behind that hallowed gathering.

Indeed, more than most positions, second base has always been a popular domicile for good, if not great players. It has never been a spot where mediocrity abounded.

One of those who commands a place among the best at the position is Billy Herman, a Hall of Fame veteran of 15 big league seasons and one of the finest all-around artists with the bat and glove in a long list of second base masters.

One of the 14 modern second sackers in the Hall of Fame—a group that includes such players as Eddie Collins, Nap Lajoie, Charley Gehringer, Jackie Robinson, and Rogers Hornsby—William Jennings Herman attained his lofty status with a sparkling career that reached its zenith during 10 memorable years with the Chicago Cubs.

From 1931, when he arrived late in the season, until early in 1941, when the Cubs dealt him away in a stunning trade, Herman was the anchor of a stellar Chicago infield. An adroit hit-and-run specialist, he was not only a skillful batter but also an outstanding defensive player. And he was one of the game's most talented base-stealers.

He was smart, too. Casey Stengel once called Herman "one of the two or three smartest players ever to come into the National League." After his playing days ended, Herman parlayed his intelligence into a long tenure as a big league coach and manager.

Billy not only had brains. He was a sparkplug, a hustling player who helped his teams to four pennants. And he was durable: Eight times he played in 152 or more games in a season, five times without missing a single game the entire campaign.

During his playing career, which also included three and one-half seasons with the Brooklyn Dodgers, one-half year with the Boston Braves, and one year as playing-manager of the Pittsburgh Pirates (he also managed the Boston Red Sox for two seasons), Billy had a batting average of .304. He had 2,345 hits in 1,922 games while driving in 839 runs and scoring 1,163. Never a power hitter, he lashed just 47 home runs but slugged 486 doubles, a number that ranks among the game's top 50 all-time leaders in that category.

Herman hit over .300 eight times in his career. Three times he pounded more than 200 hits in one season, leading the league with 227 in 1935. In 1932, he was one of six rookies in National League history to have 200 or more hits.

Billy, who hit .433 in 10 All-Star games, was equally adept in the field. In fact, he was perhaps more proud of his defense than any other phase of his game.

"My strongest point in my mind was my defense," Herman claimed. "I always thought it was my glove that got me into the Hall of Fame."

He had a point. Herman led National League second basemen in fielding percentage three times, in putouts seven times (one was a tie), and in doubleplays and assists three times each. Currently, he holds the major league record among second basemen for most years (five) with 900 or more chances. He also still holds National League marks for most years (seven) leading the league in putouts and most putouts (153) in a 154-game season. He shares NL records for most putouts in one game (11) and most putouts in a doubleheader (16).

The fact that he got to so many balls, often making diving stops that for most players would have been impossible, also accounts for a dubious record. Herman led the second sackers of his league in errors four times, another record he shares. In 1933, he booted 45, and three other times he was charged with 35 or more errors in a single campaign.

"You have to have a certain amount of quickness in your hands and feet to be a good second baseman," said Herman. "I got to balls that a lot of other people couldn't have gotten to.

"But I was also very fortunate as a fielder. I played alongside two of the game's finest shortstops. In Chicago, Bill Jurges was the shortstop, and he was about the best defensive shortstop anybody ever had. Pee Wee Reese was the shortstop in Brooklyn. I helped him when he came up, and he turned out to be a great shortstop."

With Jurges, who broke in with the Cubs the same year as Herman, as his doubleplay partner, Billy was the big cog in an infield that helped Chicago to three National League pennants in the 1930s. Herman's 1941 Dodgers also won the NL pennant. As a coach on four other Brooklyn pennant-winners and one more with the Milwaukee Braves, Herman totaled nine trips to the

World Series. Of that total, only the 1955 Dodgers won the World Series, beating the New York Yankees in a memorable seven-game classic.

"At least, I had one World Series winner," Herman mused. "That was better than none. It seemed like we were always losing the World Series to the Yankees. We lost to them in 1932, 1938, and 1941 while I was a player, and in 1952, 1953, 1956, and 1958 while I was a coach. Of all those World Series I was in, the only time my team didn't play the Yankees was when we played Detroit in 1935.

"In 1932, we lost in four straight, and we were totally overmatched. They had [Babe] Ruth and [Lou] Gehrig, and we had a bunch of kids. About nine guys on that Yankee team went to the Hall of Fame. They were downright awesome. It may have been the best team in the history of baseball. It was no disgrace losing to a club like that.

"Our 1935 team that lost in six games to the Tigers was the best team we had. Talent-wise, it was outstanding. Our 1941 team with the Dodgers was excellent, too. It came pretty close to being as good as the 1935 Cubs team."

The Cubs of the mid-1930s featured a heavy-hitting array that included Chuck Klein, a young Phil Cavarretta, Augie Galan, Gabby Hartnett, Stan Hack, and Frank Demaree. Contrasting with that group was the '41 Dodgers, featuring Dolph Camilli, Dixie Walker, Joe Medwick, Pete Reiser, and the unfortunate Mickey Owen.

Both teams had excellent pitching staffs, Chicago leading with 20-game winners Lon Warneke and Bill Lee, plus Larry French and Charley Root. Brooklyn went to battle with 22-game winners Kirby Higbe and Whit Wyatt as well as Hugh Casey and Curt Davis.

It was with those 1930s Cubs powerhouses that Herman really made his mark. And even more than 60 years later, Billy's name has weathered the test of time in the Cubs' record book. Among the club's all-time leaders, he still ranks in the top 10 in doubles and runs. He also holds club records for most at-bats (666) and most doubles (57) in one season.

Herman, who lived in Palm Beach Gardens, Florida, for more than 30 years before he died in 1992, was oddly enough not always a second baseman. In fact, in high school in his native New Albany, Indiana, he wasn't even a regular. Billy was a reserve infielder on his schoolboy team and attracted absolutely no attention until pitching his church team to a league championship.

"Mostly, though, I was a shortstop and a third baseman as a kid,"

Herman recalled. "After I went into professional baseball, they told me to forget about being a pitcher. They asked me if I could play second, I said, 'Sure, I'll play anywhere.' So I switched to second and stayed there until the end of my career, when I played a little bit at first and third."

Herman arrived in pro ball in a rather direct fashion. At the age of 18, he invested a dime in a round-trip bus ticket to Louisville to attend a tryout with the Colonels, an American Association entry.

Billy got a contract and was assigned to Vicksburg of the Class D Cotton States League. After hitting .332 in 106 games in 1928, he was called up to Louisville at the end of the season. But the Colonels sent him out to Dayton of the Central League for the 1929 season. Herman responded by hitting .329.

This time when he was brought back to Louisville at the end of the season, Herman stayed. After hitting .305 and .350 over the next two seasons, his contract was purchased by the Cubs for the flattering sum of $60,000.

Herman arrived in Chicago in August. His first game was one he'll never forget. "I made a big mistake," he said. "We were playing the Cincinnati Reds. The pitcher was Si Johnson. I got a hit my first time up. He didn't like that very much, and the next time I came up, he tried to stick one in my ear. He did a pretty good job of it, too."

A Johnson fastball aimed at Herman's head crashed directly into his skull. Knocked unconscious, he had to be carried off the field, a frightening end to his major league debut.

"They played like that back then," Herman recalled. "There were no hard hats like there are now. You had to have a hard head instead."

Herman soon made it back into the Cubs' lineup and, playing in 25 games, finished the campaign with a .327 batting average. The next time he faced Johnson, he slammed three hits.

The following season, the 5-11, 180-pound youngster proved he belonged. Playing in all of Chicago's 154 games, Herman hit .314, in the process slugging 42 doubles, third best in National League history for a rookie. His 206 hits also made him only one of six NL players ever to collect 200 or more hits in his first season.

"It was hard, though," Herman recalled. "In those days, they just gave you a bat and ball and told you to go out and play. You learned the hard way. Nobody helped you. You had to teach yourself."

Herman encountered the sophomore jinx in 1933 as his average slipped to .279, but he had some memorable days in the field. On June 28 that year, in the first game of a doubleheader against the Philadelphia Phillies, he made 11 putouts. In the second game, he registered five more to give him a record 16 for the day. The next day, he reeled off 12 assists in a 12-inning game.

The next year, Herman's bat came back to life, and in four of the next five seasons his average was over .300. From .303 in 1934 during a season in which he had a 20-game hitting streak, Billy soared to .341 the next year while leading the league with 227 hits and 57 doubles. Playing in all 154 games again, he had 83 RBI and scored 113 runs, one of five times he scored more than 100 runs in one season. He also led the circuit's second basemen in fielding percentage, assists, putouts, and doubleplays. His 520 assists, though not a record, make modern figures pale by comparison.

"No question, that was the best all-around year I had," said Herman, who was fifth in the league in hitting, but was perhaps unjustifiably nudged out of MVP honors by teammate Hartnett, owner of a .344 batting average in 116 games. Herman finished fourth in the voting.

Over the next five years, Herman continued his blistering pace, hitting .334 in 1936, followed by averages of .335, .277, .307, and .292. In 1936, when he had his second straight year of 57 doubles and was third in the MVP voting, Herman collected 93 RBI. He had a career high in home runs in 1937 with eight and led the league in triples in 1939 with 18.

Along the way, Herman had five or more hits in six different games. On one of those occasions, he belted two triples, two doubles, and a single in the Cubs' first night game, an 8–4 win in 1935 over the Reds at Crosley Field. In 1936, he clubbed a single, a home run, and three doubles to set a major league opening-day record for most hits in a 12–7 win over Dizzy Dean and the St. Louis Cardinals.

When the Cubs beat the Cardinals, 10–3, to clinch the pennant in 1938 (two days after Hartnett's legendary "Homer in the Gloamin"), Herman led the attack with four hits. That fall, the Cubs again fell to the Yankees in the World Series in four games.

Billy, who was also the only player ever to ground into three doubleplays in one game on two different occasions, said he never paid much attention to what he was hitting. "I never was much for statistics," he claimed. "Oh, I knew at the end of the year what I'd hit. But I never knew where I stood in relation to the other hitters. All I knew was whether or not I was doing my job.

"Of course, there were certain kinds of pitchers who gave me a lot of trouble, and I would remember them. I always had trouble with the right-handed, sinkerball pitchers. Thank God, there weren't a lot of them around. Guys like Bucky Walters, Hal Schumacher, and Hugh Mulcahy gave me trouble. I never really knew how to hit the sinker.

"On the other hand, I didn't mind guys like Carl Hubbell and the Dean brothers. In fact, they used to joke about the way I hit Hubbell. They said he was my 'Cousin Carl.' With those guys, I knew what was coming and how to hit it."

One thing Herman didn't know was coming was his trade in 1941. The Cubs thought they had a youngster named Lou Stringer ready to take over at second, making Herman expendable. Brooklyn general manager Larry McPhail felt Billy was just the man the Dodgers needed to become a contender.

A deal was struck. Early in the 1941 season, Chicago sent Herman to the Dodgers for infielder John Hudson, outfielder Charley Gilbert, and $40,000.

"There had been a lot of talk when Hartnett was let go at the end of the 1940 season as manager that the Cubs would make me the manager," Herman remembered. "But they brought in Jimmie Wilson instead. He didn't seem to care for me. I always thought he wanted to get rid of me because of my managerial prospects.

"I was surprised when the trade actually happened. But I didn't really care. I just wanted to play. McPhail called me at two in the morning and told me he'd just traded for me. I said, 'Who the hell would make a trade at this time of the night?' He said, 'I would.' I went to Brooklyn and played that day and went four-for-four.

"In a way, though, I hated to leave Chicago," Herman added. "I really enjoyed it there. The fans were great. They were more quiet than they are now, but they were really behind you. Once I made two errors, and they gave me a big ovation to get my spirits up. Brooklyn fans were something else. They were much more avid than the Cubs fans. But between the two, they had to be the greatest fans in baseball."

The wily veteran immediately solidified the Dodgers' infield, and—hitting .291 the rest of the season—helped Brooklyn capture its first flag since

1920. Unfortunately, Herman tore a muscle in his rib cage during batting practice before the third game and missed most of the final three games of the Series, which the Dodgers lost to the Yankees, four games to one, with the help of the infamous passed ball by Owen on a Hugh Casey pitch to Tommy Henrich.

After hitting .285 for the full season in 1941, Herman slumped to .256 in 1942. But he wasn't down for long. Billy caught fire in 1943 and wound up hitting .330 and placing second to Stan Musial in the batting race.

Billy spent 1944 and 1945 in the Navy in World War II. He rejoined the Dodgers in 1946 and was hitting .288 after 47 games when Branch Rickey sent him to the Boston Braves for an unknown catcher named Stewart Hofferth. Rickey was anxious to unload Herman because of his $20,000 salary and because he had Eddie Stanky primed to play second.

Herman hit .306 in 75 games with the Braves, finishing the year with an overall mark of .298. His double in the last game of the season helped the Braves defeat the Dodgers, 4–0, dropping Brooklyn into a tie for the pennant and forcing a playoff with the Cardinals, which the Dodgers lost in a best-of-three series.

It was apparent he could still play, even at the ripe old age of 37. But Herman had another idea. He wanted to manage.

The Pirates, seeking a skipper, focused on Herman and finally landed him in a trade in which they received four players for two of theirs. Along with Herman, the other key player in the deal was Bob Elliott, who went to Boston and in 1947 became the league's Most Valuable Player.

Meanwhile, Herman became a playing-manager for Pittsburgh. Playing sparingly, he hit .213. Worse yet, the Bucs finished tied for seventh place with a 62–92 record. Billy was fired with one game left in the season.

"I just sort of stumbled into managing," Herman recalled. "But being a playing-manager was the toughest job you could get."

As veteran big leaguers often did in those days, Herman went back to the minors in 1948 as a reserve player with Minneapolis, then a member of the American Association. Near midseason, he took over as manager and piloted the club to a fifth-place finish.

After being out of baseball in 1949, Herman returned the next year as a reserve infielder with Oakland of the Pacific Coast League. He hit .307 in 71 games. The following year, he signed as manager of Richmond of the Piedmont League but quit at midseason.

Herman rejoined the Dodgers in 1952 as a coach and, serving under managers Chuck Dressen and Walter Alston, stayed through the 1957 season. When the Dodgers moved to Los Angeles in 1958, Herman switched to Milwaukee where he spent two more years as a coach. He then joined the Red Sox in 1960.

At the end of the 1964 season, Boston pulled Herman from the coaching ranks and made him the manager. Billy's Bosox blundered their way to a 62–100 record and a ninth-place finish in 1965. In 1966, they were in 10th place with a 64–82 mark when Herman was relieved of his duties late in the season.

"In a way, I enjoyed managing, and in a way I didn't," Herman said. "If I could have managed the way I wanted to, it might have been a lot better."

With a career managerial record of 189–274, Herman returned to the coaching lines, working one year with the California Angels and two with the San Diego Padres before retiring from baseball.

Soon, though, he was back in the spotlight. In 1975, Herman was elected to the Hall of Fame by the Veterans Committee. "It was the biggest thrill I ever had," he said. "I think I had a good career, but nothing topped that.

"I hadn't really thought about being in the Hall of Fame. But then I starting seeing guys go in, and I said to myself, 'Hell, I played as good as him.' I was hoping I'd get in, but it was still a big surprise when I was elected.

"When I got inducted, I don't know, I just can't explain the feeling. If you don't choke up over something like that, there's something wrong with you.

"I had waited a long time, and I didn't really think I'd ever get in. But then it happened, and it was just an experience you can never fully appreciate unless you've gone through it."

Billy Herman, though, deserved to go through it. After all, he was one of the finest players at a position heavily stocked with fine players.

Monte Irvin

Champion of Racial Equality

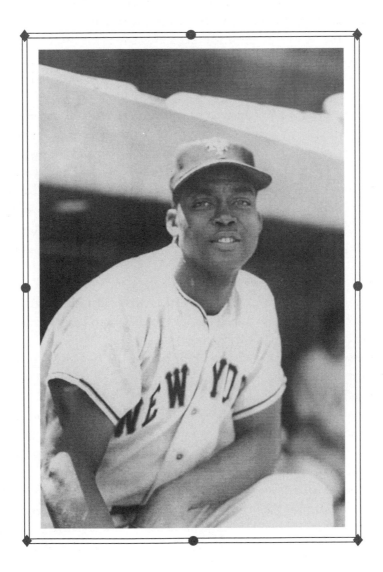

MORE THAN 50 years after baseball provided for the entry of black players into the major leagues, one can still not overlook the significant contributions of Monte Irvin.

A pioneer who helped to usher professional baseball out of its Neanderthal quagmire and into the modern era, Irvin was an integral part of the national pastime as both a player and an executive.

On the field, he was one of the great black players who formed the bridge between the Negro Leagues and the major leagues. Irvin had been a star player for the Newark Eagles before becoming one of the first blacks signed to a major league contract. He went on to have a brief but brilliant career in the majors, playing seven years with the New York Giants and his final season with the Chicago Cubs.

Later, he became a key figure in the office of the baseball commissioner, serving as director of community relations, as a member of the public relations staff, and as a liaison between the commissioner and the players.

Irvin was elected to the baseball Hall of Fame in 1973. "That," he says, "is the greatest experience any baseball player can ever have. It's like finally getting your degree to become a doctor or like your first child being born, or the feeling you have when you get married. It's just a wonderful, wonderful feeling. You never expect anything like that to happen to you, but when it does, it's just beautiful."

Although otherwise now retired, Irvin served for a number of years as a member of the Veterans Committee, which elects older players and others into the Hall of Fame, including those from the Negro Leagues who never had the chance to play in the big leagues.

"It is a good feeling to see some of the pioneers of the Negro Leagues get inducted into the Hall," Irvin says. "I never thought it would happen, but it has, and I'm delighted about it."

In that context, Irvin also expresses delight that major league baseball saw fit to make special note in 1997 of the 50th anniversary of Jackie Robinson's breaking the barrier that had segregated white and black players.

"I think about that all the time," Irvin says. "Sometimes, I ask myself, 'What would've happened if Jackie had failed?' But that question is moot because he didn't fail. And what he did helped everybody. He helped blacks. He helped whites. He made it better for all athletes in all sports, particularly the black athletes. So, we're very grateful to him for what he did. He did an outstanding job of pioneering."

That pioneer almost was Irvin. For a number of reasons, many people thought that Monte would be the first black player to join the major leagues. Although born in Columbia, Alabama, he had grown up in Orange, New Jersey, and had played on integrated teams in high school. He had spent two years at Lincoln University in Oxford, Pennsylvania. He was an outstanding player. And he was extremely even-tempered and outgoing. In short, he possessed all the qualities perceived to be necessary for baseball's first African-American player of the 20th century.

"Major league baseball had scouted me way back in 1936," Irvin reveals. "The owners said, if they ever start to take black players, Monte Irvin is our man.

"But I don't want to take anything away from Jackie. He was a super baseball player, very electrifying, thrilling on the bases. He was intelligent, he could talk, and he was a leader. When Jackie said something, the players, the owners, just about everybody listened."

Irvin had begun his professional baseball career in 1939, signing with the Newark Eagles for $150 a month. "It was the same team that produced Ray Dandridge, Don Newcombe, and Larry Doby," Irvin remembers. "I came up as a shortstop. Funny thing was, Doby came up as a second baseman, and we both wound up in the outfield.

"We had a star shortstop on the team named Willie Wells. One day, after I had reported to the team, I was going out to shortstop, and Wells pulled me aside. He said, 'Monte, you're a fine athlete, but I think your position is in the outfield. If you want to play as a regular, you better go out there because this position belongs to me.' I said, 'Willie, I don't care where I go, as long as I play.' It turned out, he gave me the best advice anyone ever gave me."

Irvin quickly became one of the top players in a league crammed with outstanding players. In eight seasons with the Eagles, his unofficial batting average hovered around .350. That included, he says, a .420 mark one year.

In 1946, Monte led Newark to the championship of the Negro World Series. He scored the winning run in a 3–2 victory in the seventh game of the Series as the Eagles defeated the Kansas City Monarchs.

Around that time, Irvin, like numerous other black stars, had begun to attract the serious attention of major league teams. After the Brooklyn Dodgers signed Robinson, they began signing other black players, one being Irvin.

Newark Eagles owner Effa Manley, however, cried foul, claiming that Irvin, unlike some of the other players, was not a free agent and was the property of her team. She threatened to take court action. Branch Rickey and the Dodgers backed down.

Manley then offered to sell Irvin to the New York Yankees, who responded that they were not interested. Then she approached the Giants, who were interested.

"I finally signed a contract with the Giants while I was in Cuba playing winter ball in 1948–49," Irvin says. "The Giants signed Hank Thompson [who in 1947 had been signed, then let go by the St. Louis Browns] and me at the same time.

"We reported to the Jersey City club in the spring of 1949 at Sanford, Florida. We played at Jersey City, and then we were called up in July [at the time Irvin was hitting .373]. Hank was a second baseman and an outfielder. I played first base, third base, and the outfield. He wound up at third with the Giants, and I wound up in left field. It was all very thrilling. In fact, one of the greatest thrills of my career was when I reported to the Giants' clubhouse in July of 1949."

Blacks were still not immune to the racial taunts of opposing players, fans, or even the press, although it had now been two years since Robinson first stepped onto a major league diamond.

"We still faced some of the same problems as he did," Irvin recalls. "But he really got the butt of it. What we faced was not nearly as tough as what Jackie faced. By the time I came along, people had gotten kind of used to us, so it wasn't as bad for us as it had been for Jackie when he came up."

Hitting big league pitching wasn't so easy, though. Irvin hit just .224 in 36 games. The following year, he found himself back at Jersey City. After 18 games, he was hitting .510 with 10 home runs and 33 RBI. The Giants, embroiled in a hot pennant race with the Dodgers and Philadelphia Phillies, could hardly contain themselves.

Irvin was called back to New York and finished the year hitting .299 with 15 home runs and 66 RBI. This time, Monte was in New York to stay.

"I particularly remember one game that year," Irvin says. "I was struggling a little bit. We were playing the Cubs, and Dutch Leonard was pitching. He was very tough. He threw that knuckleball. Just getting a base hit off him was enough, but I hit a bases-loaded home run. The ball was hit to right field, but I didn't care. As I rounded the bases, I was saying to myself, 'If you can hit a home run off of Dutch Leonard, as tough as he is, you must be a pretty good hitter.' That gave me some confidence, and I went on to have a good year."

The following year turned out to be the crown jewel in Irvin's big league career. While hitting .312, he socked 24 home runs, scored 89, and led the National League with 121 RBI. And the Giants won the pennant after storming from behind to tie the Dodgers for first place during the regular season and winning a best-of-three playoff.

Irvin's home run in the eighth inning put the lid on a 3–1 Giants' win in the first playoff game. Then, after Brooklyn roared back with a 10–0 romp in the second game, Bobby Thomson's dramatic three-run homer in the bottom of the ninth gave New York a 5–4 victory and the pennant in the deciding game of the playoffs.

"That victory was the greatest thrill I ever experienced," Irvin says. "I'll never forget it or that 1951 team. It was just a great thrill playing down the stretch and catching the Dodgers after being 13½ games behind them in August. Then Bobby Thomson hit the most memorable home run that's ever been hit. Whenever I see him, I think that he made us an extra $5,000 that year. Just to have been part of that great event is mind-boggling to me.

"We had a great team. It took love, it took dedication, and it took talent to catch the Dodgers. We had all three, plus a lot of luck. We dedicated ourselves to seeing how close we could come. Leo Durocher kept egging us on. We really complemented each other on that team. One player would pick up the others, and we just kept going. I have fond memories of every member of that club.

"Of course, not only did we have a great bunch of guys, we had the best manager—one of the greatest managers who ever lived. He's in the Hall of Fame. When you talk about managers, his name's always one of the first ones you mention. Ask the question among baseball people—who was the best manager?—and all of them say Leo Durocher.

"He was a great strategist. He knew how to handle the players. He knew how to give you confidence. He knew who to pat on the back and who to kick in the butt."

He also brought in a player who was to make a lasting impression not only on Irvin but on the entire game of baseball.

"It was in May 1951 when Willie Mays came to us, and started us on the way to the pennant," Irvin remembers. "We were floundering around in fifth place, and he reported to us when we were playing the Phillies in a three-game series. Durocher brought him into the clubhouse and introduced him around. You could tell just from looking at him and from his actions that he was a super, super player.

"When we went out to the field, and he took outfield practice and started to throw, you just knew that we had a star in our midst, even though he was only 20 years old at the time. And it turned out just that way. The only difference was, we did not know that he was going to become the great home run hitter that he became. We thought he'd be a good hitter, but we didn't know he would be extraordinarily strong the way he was."

The young Mays was placed under the special care of the veteran Irvin. What transpired was one of the high points of Irvin's career.

"I think the mere fact that I was instrumental in getting Willie started on the right track was one of the the proudest accomplishments of my career," Irvin says. "He was a diamond in the rough, and by being with him, I taught him a few things that I knew. Then his natural talents took over, and he became a great star. I've never been around a youngster with that much talent. He could do everything."

Although Irvin hit .458, the Giants bowed four games to two to the Yankees in the '51 World Series. But that wasn't nearly as damaging as what happened to Monte the following spring. A few days before the season-opener, in an exhibition game in Denver against the Cleveland Indians, Irvin broke an ankle sliding into third base. He did not play again until late July.

"That injury really cut my career short," Irvin says, wincing at the memory of the accident, which was so terrible that several players broke into tears as Monte lay writhing on the ground.

"If it hadn't been for that, I probably could have played four or five years longer than I did," he says. "I was 38 at the time [the record book says he was 33], but there was no reason I couldn't play to 43 or 44 because I could still hit and I could still run. Breaking that ankle cost me a lot of money,"

Chosen for the National League All-Star team that year despite his injury, Irvin returned to finish the season with a .310 average in 46 games. Then, reasonably healthy the following year, he bounced back with a .329 mark with 21 home runs and 97 RBI. He followed that with a .262–19–64 slate in 1954 as the Giants again went to the World Series.

This time, led by a remarkable catch by Mays in deep center field in Game One and the clutch-hitting of Dusty Rhodes, the Giants swept the Series, defeating a Cleveland team that had set an American League record with 111 victories during the regular season.

"Cleveland had that great pitching staff [including future Hall of Famers Bob Lemon, Early Wynn, and Bob Feller] and had won all those games, so beating them was a great thrill," Irvin says. "The keys were Mays making that great catch off a 460-foot drive by Vic Wertz and Rhodes' pinch-hitting. Dusty came in and got a big hit every time he was called upon. Mays saved it, and Dusty won it."

Irvin hit only .222 in the Series. The next year, the Giants moved veteran first baseman Whitey Lockman to left field to make room for rookie Gail Harris at first. Irvin was relegated to the bench and got into only 51 games (hitting .253) before being abruptly shipped out to Minncapolis, the Giants' Triple-A farm club.

Proving that he could still hit, Irvin bashed opposing pitching to a .352 tune. After the season, he was drafted by the Chicago Cubs. He was the Cubs' regular left fielder for much of the 1956 season. He hit .271 with 15 homers while driving in 50. But it turned out to be his last year in the majors.

Irvin finished his big league career with a lifetime .293 average. In 764 games, he drilled 731 hits, including 99 home runs, while collecting 443 RBI and scoring 366 times. He had a .475 slugging average.

"You're never totally satisfied," Irvin says of his career. "I wish I had come up sooner so I could've played 10 or more years. I'd like to have hit six or seven hundred home runs. I think I was capable of doing that if I'd have come up sooner. You're not frustrated or bitter, but you do wish you'd gotten a chance a little earlier. But you can't look back. You just have to be grateful for what you've got.

"I was originally a dead pull-hitter, but after getting out of the Army, I had to start all over again. So, I'm sorry that people never did see me when I could really play. I wish they had."

There were plenty of pitchers, though, who saw enough of Irvin. And plenty that Irvin saw more than enough of, too.

"Ewell Blackwell was a real tough pitcher," he says. "So was Don Newcombe. Robin Roberts was very, very tough. Bob Rush, Warren Hacker,

Harry Brecheen, Warren Spahn, Gene Conley—all those guys were tough. But you hung in there, and somehow or other you managed. It's just a good thing those guys didn't pitch every day."

These days, Irvin has retired from his job in the commissioner's office. He lives in Florida where he spends much of his time "having a good life," playing golf and tennis, fishing, and visiting friends.

"I retired from the commissioner's office in 1984 after 16 years there," he says. "It was a great experience, and I really enjoyed the work. I got to know a whole different aspect of baseball. I got to deal with the game on a different level, and I think I was able to make a contribution. I had to wear a lot of hats, but all were very enjoyable."

Irvin is proud that he had a chance to play in the era in which he did and that he could put something back into the game. "I treasure every moment I spent in the major leagues," he says. "I played for a great owner (Horace Stoneham) and in a great park. The Polo Grounds was wonderful. What I really liked about it was, it was deep, so Willie could really run after balls. You learned to play the angles of the wall and how to play the caroms. If you pulled the ball, you got a home run. Unfortunately, I hit to right and to left-center. I hit more home runs on the road than I did at the Polo Grounds."

Although he was one of the first black players to enter the major leagues, Irvin regrets that so many black stars before him were deprived of the opportunity to perform at baseball's highest level. "If they had started to take black players about 10 years sooner, they would've really gotten some superstars," he says. "Guys like Josh Gibson, Cool Papa Bell, Buck Leonard, Willard Brown, Barney Brown, Johnny Williams, Bill Byrd, Ray Dandridge, Willie Wells, Quincy Trouppe. There were so many outstanding stars. You could just go on and on.

"Take Doby, for instance. Doby only spent a short time sitting on the bench in the big leagues. He came up in 1947, and by 1949 he was an All-Star. It showed the caliber of players we had in the Negro Leagues.

"Roy Campanella was that way, too. So was Newcombe. Both of them became in a matter of a year or so star ballplayers. That's what kinds of talent we had. Minnie Minoso was the same thing. He was a great star in the Negro League, then spent a little time with the Cleveland Indians and Chicago White Sox, and then became a real star.

"From my standpoint, I was very fortunate to have played with all those guys," Irvin adds. "Now, when I look back, I have some great memories of all the great guys I met, great guys I played with and against. It was just super. And for me, I had the benefit of playing with the best in the black leagues and the best in the major leagues. Not too many people can say that."

Not too many can say they played the game any better than Monte Irvin, either. He was a star in two leagues and a man who made a valuable and lasting contribution not only to the game of baseball but to his fellow players.

Al Kaline

A Superb All-Around Talent

IT IS THE rare breed of baseball player who throughout his career is able to perform all of the five basic skills of the game well. In a sport in which specialists abound, the one- or two-dimensional player has been the norm, especially of late. Few players have had the ability to run, field, throw, hit for average, and hit for power with equal effectiveness.

Al Kaline was one of those few. For 22 years, he demonstrated the kinds of all-around skills that throughout baseball history have seldom been displayed by an individual player. A 6-2, 180-pound right fielder, Kaline, the cornerstone of the Detroit Tigers' franchise, could, as they say, do it all.

Nine times he batted over .300, winding up his career with a .297 average. He hit home runs in double figures 20 straight years, finishing with a career total of 399. He won 10 Gold Glove awards and twice led the league in fielding, once posting a 1.000 average for the season. He also led the league twice in assists by an outfielder, and during his entire career he averaged fewer than four errors per season. And he stole 137 bases and scored 1,622 runs.

During a glittering career that was capped by his election to the Hall of Fame in 1980, Kaline slammed 3,007 hits and drove in 1,583 runs while playing in 2,834 games—the 12th highest total in big league history. He won a batting title, was twice runner-up in the MVP voting, was named to 18 All-Star teams, and was the batting star in a World Series. Twice he was named American League Player of the Year by *The Sporting News*.

Few players did as many things well on an everyday basis and for such a long time as the first player, and one of only four, whose number has been retired by the Tigers. For Kaline, though, excelling came easily.

"I've been very lucky in my life," he says. "As a kid growing up, the only thing I wanted to do from the start was to become a professional ballplayer. It just seemed like everything worked out for me. Whatever I did in my life—playing, broadcasting, making the Hall of Fame—it just seemed that everything always fell into place for me."

Now, more than four decades after he broke in with the Tigers, things are still falling into place for Kaline. He is a popular television broadcaster for the Tigers—in 1999 he was entering his 24th year in the booth. He also does public relations work for a pizza company, whose president, Thomas Monaghan, owns the Tigers. And he appears frequently at card shows and old-timers games around the country.

Foremost among Kaline's long list of credits as a player was the batting title he won in 1955 when he hit .340 and led the league with 200 hits in his second full season in the big leagues. At 20, he was the youngest player in baseball history to win a batting crown, one day younger than Ty Cobb was when he won his first title in 1907.

The memory of his best season still looms fresh in Kaline's mind. "I had had a very good spring training," he recalls. "I hit well over .400. In my first game of the season, I got three hits in Briggs Stadium, including two triples.

"Everything just seemed to carry on from there. Shortly afterward, I hit three home runs in one game, including two in one inning [he is one of eight American Leaguers to have hit two homers in one inning] against the Philadelphia A's. I just missed my fourth home run by inches.

"Everything was working. I had confidence. I saw the ball well. And the pitchers didn't respect me because I was so young. They'd rather pitch to me than the older guys behind me. Also, I could run very well.

"Actually," he adds, "I never had trouble hitting the ball even coming into the big leagues. I could always hit the ball, although it wouldn't always be with authority. But I didn't strike out much. I didn't care who I faced. It was one of those things where everything just seemed to fall in for a base hit."

For such a young player, Kaline's stunning entry into the ranks of the American League's hitting elite was eye-opening but not at all surprising. Al appeared destined to become an outstanding hitter well in advance of his winning a batting title before he was old enough to vote.

"As a kid growing up in Baltimore, I was a pitcher, an infielder, and an outfielder," Kaline says, "I played mostly in the outfield. I enjoyed playing a lot.

"I always liked to hit, I had two idols, Ted Williams and Stan Musial. I wasn't a great baseball fan in that I went to many games. We had the International League in Baltimore at the time. I'd go out to watch the Orioles once in a while, but I'd much rather play baseball than watch it. But I would always look in the newspaper to see how Williams and Musial did every day."

Kaline played four years of high school and American Legion baseball. Eventually, word got around that the skinny Baltimore youth was a hot prospect. Pro scouts began flocking to his games.

"About my junior year in high school, I started playing in a semipro league," he remembers. "It was a pretty good league, and it helped me tremendously.

"I began hearing that there were some teams interested in me. It turned out that two teams went after me hot and heavy. They were the Philadelphia Phillies and the Boston Red Sox. Boston wound up offering me a much larger bonus than the one I eventually got from Detroit, but they were up front with me. They said they were after a shortstop, and if they were able to sign him, they would sign him and not me. They signed him. His name was Billy Consolo.

"I almost signed with the Phillies, but they wanted to sign Tom Qualters, a pitcher for a big bonus [$100,000], which they did. So I ended up signing with Detroit, which worked out great, I had a chance to play fairly quickly in the big leagues. I did pretty well in the beginning, so I stayed in the big leagues the whole time."

After graduating from high school, Kaline reported to the Tigers at mid-season in 1953 as a wide-eyed 18-year-old. He had neither minor league experience nor much experience at dealing on his own with the world in general.

"I had never been away from home for any length of time," he says. "The only time I had ever been away was to play in a couple of tournaments, but then I was always with a lot of close friends and teammates. But this was much different. I had to live in a hotel by myself, and I didn't have any friends because most of the players on the team were so much older. Fortunately, a lot of the older players liked me right off the bat, and they would invite me out to their houses and I'd do things with them on the road.

"It was mainly guys like Johnny Pesky, Pat Mullin, Steve Souchock, and Don Lund. They were very friendly with me and really helped me a lot."

Kaline's first day with the Tigers, though, was particularly trying. He remembers it clearly. "I joined the ball club in Philadelphia," he recalls. "I had taken the train up from Baltimore with my dad and the scout, Ed Katalinas, who signed me.

"Well, I was late getting to the hotel, and got there just as the bus was leaving. Now, you know, the bus is never late leaving the hotel. They don't wait for anybody. But when I got there, Freddie Hutchinson, our manager, said, 'Go check in and we'll hold the bus for you.'

"I checked in, then got on the bus. You should have heard the groaning by the veteran players. Here they were, waiting for this 18-year-old kid with pimples all over his face, and they normally wouldn't even wait for a superstar. I walked down the aisle, and I was scared to death. I've never been that scared in my life. I didn't know anybody.

"Finally, Ted Gray, who was our player rep, grabbed me and said, 'Sit down kid. I want to talk to you.' On our way to the ballpark, he discussed some of the things I should know, like tipping the clubhouse man, catching the bus, and curfews—all the little things you have to know when you're in the big leagues."

Soon afterward, the youthful Kaline got his baptism on the field. It came against the Philadelphia A's at Connie Mack Stadium (formerly called Shibe Park).

"I got in as a pinch-hitter in my first game," he says. "I think it was the seventh inning against a pitcher named Harry Byrd. He was having a good year. I'll never forget him. He was such a big man; big shoulders and about 6–2. I hit the first pitch, a semi-line drive to center field."

Kaline appeared in 30 games in his first season, hitting .250. The Tigers finished sixth, losing 94 games, which turned out to be a break for the raw rookie.

"The one good thing for me, although not for the team," Kaline says, "was that it was a real bad ball club. They were not going any place. In fact, the day before I signed, they had lost a game in Boston by a score of 25 to something. So I got a chance to play, which I wouldn't have had with a contender."

Kaline became a regular in 1954. The following year he won the batting title, then hit better than .300 in six of the next eight years.

In 1959, he led the league with a slugging average of .530, and in 1961 he was first in doubles with 41. And twice he finished second to teammates in the batting race, trailing Harvey Kuenn in 1959 and Norm Cash in 1961. Al hit .327 and .324, respectively, in those seasons.

Kaline drove in more than 100 runs three times, reaching a high of 128 in 1956. Seven times he hit 25 or more home runs in one season, his best being 29 in both 1962 and 1966.

His 1962 season was limited to 100 games when he fractured his right collarbone making a diving catch for the final out in a 2–1 victory over the Yankees on May 26. He didn't return to the lineup until July 23 and still had

29 homers and 94 RBI that year. He also hit two home runs in one game 23 times and slammed two homers in All-Star games.

While Kaline was winning applause with his bat, he was also dazzling the fans with his defensive play. At no time did he ever commit more than nine errors in one season, and his arm was as good as any outfielder's in the league.

"I enjoyed that part of the game very much," Kaline says. "I knew the first day I worked out with the team that I could field as well as anybody and I could throw with anybody they had. That made me feel real good because I knew I wouldn't be a complete waste.

"I didn't know how I was going to hit, being a youngster at 18, and having never been in the minor leagues. I'm sure they didn't know how I was going to hit, either. But I had all the confidence in the world that once I got into the game defensively, I could play.

"I just loved to play. I loved to run. I loved to throw. I was a kid who always wanted to be on the ball field. Even when I first joined the Tigers, I was always out on the field. When the veterans were taking extra practice, I was always out shagging balls. I took a lot of pride in my defense. I knew I couldn't do it all the time with the bat—nobody can—but there was no reason in the world you can't do it every time when you're playing in the field. That's the way I approached it.

"Quite honestly," Kaline adds, "I think the batting title I won was more of a fluke than anything else. What I'm more pleased about was my defensive ability. I was a much better defensive player than I was an offensive player.

"I feel that I helped more people by being a good defensive player. I was a good offensive player—let's face it. But I never had any slumps in the outfield. I had slumps as a batter, but not as a fielder."

Actually, Kaline never slumped much as a batter, either. His lowest average as a regular was .272, and that came when he was trying to regain his stroke after breaking his wrist the year before.

Kaline had broken the wrist during the 1968 season. He missed six weeks. When he came back, the Tigers put him at first base, and Al wound up the season hitting .287 and helping Detroit to its first pennant in 23 years.

His presence, however, caused a major story at the time and a lineup problem for the Tigers. Manager Mayo Smith was faced with a seemingly unsolvable problem as the World Series approached. He had three outfielders who had played well, and now he had Kaline, too. Who would play where?

"I knew Smith was going to have a problem on his hands," Kaline recalls. "The writers had started to talk about how Kaline should be playing. So I went to Mayo and said, 'I know you have a great problem, but you've got to play the guys who got you here and not me because I didn't play that much.'

"That sort of made him feel good. He said, 'I'm glad you feel that way, but we're going to try to get you into the lineup.' He said, 'How about working out at third base?' because he knew I was a good athlete, and there aren't a great number of plays at third. So I started taking infield practice. Then, almost as if fate meant it to be this way, Willie Horton got hurt and couldn't play. Smith said, 'Al, you've got to go back to the outfield.'

"We still had 15 to 20 games left. So I got into the lineup, and I started to hit the hell out of the ball. I was tearing it up, hitting about .400 over a three-week period, and driving in a lot of runs and hitting home runs. I even scored the winning run when Denny McLain won his 30th game. Then all of a sudden, Smith makes another decision. He's going to move Mickey Stanley, who was our best athlete, in from center field to shortstop.

"Horton went back to left, Jim Northrup moved from right to center, and I went back to right. And I stayed in right for the duration of the Series."

It was a Series that was noted not only for the three wins posted by Detroit lefthander Mickey Lolich—which completely overshadowed the mediocre work of 31-game winner McLain—but also for the near-flawless fielding of Stanley at shortstop and the hitting of Cash and Kaline, which helped the Tigers down the St. Louis Cardinals.

Al, who had waited 16 seasons to get into the World Series, hit .379, leading his team with 11 hits and eight runs batted in. He poled a two-run homer in a 7–3 Tiger loss in the third game and slammed a two-run single that put Detroit ahead to stay in a 5–3 win in the fifth game. In the sixth game, won by the Tigers, 13–1, Kaline drove in three runs with two singles during a record-tying, 10-run inning, then homered off Steve Carlton two innings later.

Detroit wound up winning the Series in a stirring seven-game set after being down three games to one. For Kaline, it was a perfect climax to a memorable year.

"Getting a chance to play on the only pennant-winner I ever played on was one of the top thrills of my career," he says. "It was the first and only year I played on a team where everybody had one goal—to win the pennant. The year before, we had gotten beat on the last day of the season, and we dedicated ourselves in '68 to winning.

"We had a veteran ball club. We didn't have a lot of young guys. And we had a fine manager. Mayo Smith was a super guy to play for. He was a great strategist, and he was the kind of guy who'd let you play.

"We had a lot of good teams around that time," Kaline adds, "Of course, we had faced the Yankees all those years when they were winning everything. So it was good to turn the tables a little bit."

Although the Tigers would not have another Series winner until 1984, long after Kaline had retired to the broadcasting booth, Al had some memorable moments left.

In 1971, while playing in 129 games in the outfield and five at first base, he fielded a perfect 1.000, a feat that has been performed by American League outfielders playing in more than 100 games only 16 times in the history of the circuit. Over a 242-game span between 1970 and 1972, Kaline set a league record (since broken) for most consecutive games without an error.

Kaline scored five runs in one game in 1971. And in 1974, at the age of 39, he poled his 3,000th career hit, a double off Baltimore's Dave McNally. It made him at the time only the 15th player in big league history to reach the 3,000-hit mark.

One level that eluded Kaline, however, was 400 home runs. He finished just one short. "At the time, it really wasn't a big deal," he says. "At least, I didn't think it was. Quite honestly, if I'd known it would be some kind of a major feat, I probably would have hung around and gotten the 400. But I wasn't too concerned about records. Our PR department obviously didn't think it was a big deal because there wasn't a lot made of it."

So Kaline retired from the Tigers after the 1974 season. He had been with the club for 22 years. Only Brooks Robinson with Baltimore and Carl Yastrzemski with Boston spent more years (23) in baseball with the same team.

At just a few months shy of age 40, Kaline says he was more than ready to retire. It was hard, though, to leave the game, and to terminate a career after playing in a very special era. Nevertheless, Kaline left with few regrets.

"I would have liked to have played on better teams," he says. "But I always prided myself as a guy who could get the job done in tight situations. I was always a real good player in All-Star games, always got hits. I did real well in the World Series I played in, too.

"I always thought I was a guy who could rise to the occasion. I would've welcomed the chance to play on teams that were in contention going into September. But it didn't happen very much.

"But I played in a great baseball town. The fans were great to me. The only thing I regret was, I didn't play on better teams.

"Otherwise, there's only one thing I would change. I wish they had the Nautilus and things like that when I played. I would've been a lot stronger and hit more home runs. When I played, lifting weights was against the rules. They didn't want anybody doing that. I can see some of the kids coming in today who are 20 or 21 years old, and they're developed like they're 26–27 years old. They're much stronger."

But, Kaline is quick to point out, they're not all necessarily better. "When I played, all the players belonged in the big leagues," he says, "whereas now you have a few players on each team who probably shouldn't be there.

"There are really some super players right now—better than the ones in the era when I played. But there are also a lot of players who have no reason to be in the big leagues other than the fact that there's expansion.

"I think the teams are diluted now. You don't see the good pitching day in and day out that you used to see. There are some great pitchers now, but the whole staffs are not as strong as they should be."

Kaline saw plenty of good pitchers when he played. "Early in my career, when I was a real good player, Early Wynn and Bob Lemon were extremely tough on me," he says. "That whole Cleveland staff was tough with [Mike] Garcia, [Bob] Feller, [Ray] Narleski, and [Don] Mossi. But Wynn and Lemon were the toughest.

"When I was washed up, and I'm not taking anything away from him, Nolan Ryan was the toughest. He could throw hard, and he was just wild enough to be effective."

Kaline sees baseball these days from the press box where he works some 50 Tigers telecasts per year. It's a job that he never envisioned having. Circumstances came together, however, and in 1976 he made his debut on the airwaves. The job became full-time a year later.

"It was the weirdest thing," Kaline remembers. "I had retired from base-ball and had a small business. I was happy doing that. One day, I got a call from the station. They wanted me to try it. I said, 'I really don't know whether I want to do it or not.' They said, 'Let's work a deal out where you can do a few games, and see if you like it.'

"I did 10 games the first year. I wasn't really crazy about it. I didn't really do a good job. I was always a real quiet guy and always a person who would never say something about another player. That was my code. Even if I had a string of hits off a pitcher, I'd always say, 'Oh, he just made a lot of bad pitches to me. He wanted to make good pitches, but he just threw them in the middle of the plate.'

"It was always my philosophy that I never wanted to be the one to say, 'This guy's terrible,' and maybe cost the guy a big league job. So I had a lot of trouble my first couple years of broadcasting because I could never bring myself to say, 'This guy made a mistake. He didn't do this or he didn't do that.' But I realized that those are things you have to say, and I grew to like broadcasting, mainly because it kept me in the game a little bit."

Kaline's place in the game was permanently guaranteed in 1980 when he was elected to the Hall of Fame in the first year he was eligible. To him, it was an honor that ranked above all others. He remembers exactly how he felt on that memorable day he was inducted.

"It was the most awesome feeling I ever had," he says. "You walk into the room where all the other Hall of Famers are sitting, waiting to go out before they introduce you, and all of a sudden you think, 'Do I belong to this group?'

"Here are all the people you used to read about and watch and copy. Now, here you are in the same breath, going to be included with all these great players.

"It's the ultimate honor," he concludes.

But it was one that Kaline richly deserved. He was, after all, one of those unusual players who did everything well. Few others have had such out-standing all-around talent.

Harmon Killebrew

Home Runs Were His Specialty

IT NEVER TOOK a rocket scientist to tell what Harmon Killebrew did for a living. One look at his broad shoulders, massive chest, and arms as thick as tree limbs, and it was easy to figure that this man with the incredibly sturdy upper body spent his time bashing baseballs.

Oh, those poor baseballs! Did they ever take a beating! No baseball was meant to withstand the kind of punishment Killebrew dished out. When Harmon laid his bat against a baseball, it was one of the great mismatches of modern physics.

At the peak of his career, Killebrew stood six feet and weighed a muscular but compact 210 pounds. With a relatively short and controlled stroke, he would pound a baseball just about as often and as far as anybody who ever lugged an ash limb to the plate.

It is, of course, no exaggeration to say that the man given the nickname of "Killer" because of the way he smote baseballs ranks as one of the greatest of the game's home run sluggers.

Killebrew's 573 four-baggers, amassed over a 22-year period between 1954 and 1975, represent the fifth highest total in big league history. Only Hank Aaron, Babe Ruth, Willie Mays, and Frank Robinson blasted more balls out of the park than Harmon.

In a career that began with the Washington Senators, moved in 1961 to the Minnesota Twins, and ended with the Kansas City Royals, Killebrew hit more home runs in the American League than any other righthanded batter. Only Ruth had a higher total of homers in the junior circuit.

"The number one thing I'm proud of," says Killebrew, "is that I'm the American League's number one righthanded home run hitter in history, and I'm second to Babe Ruth in the league. I'm extremely proud of that."

Killebrew won six American League home run crowns. Eight times he hit 40 or more home runs in one season. Over a 14-year period between 1959 and 1972, Killebrew never hit fewer than 25 round-trippers a season, except during the injury-plagued year of 1968. During that time, he averaged 38 homers per year.

He hit 11 grand slams. Forty-six times he homered two or more times in one game. He hit 11 home runs in extra innings and 10 pinch-hit balls out of the park. Three times he won 1–0 games with homers.

Currently, Killebrew has the fourth best home run ratio in big league history. He hit a home run every 14.22 trips to the plate. Only Ruth, Mark McGwire, and Ralph Kiner have done better.

Elected to the Hall of Fame in 1984, where he joined such other renowed K-men as Kiner, Chuck Klein, and Al Kaline, Killebrew—whose number 3 was the first one retired by the Twins—also had a career slugging average of .509, which ranks among the game's top 50 players. In addition, he is among the all-time leaders in extra base hits with 2,057, RBI with 1,584, walks with 1,559, and strikeouts with 1,699.

Killebrew, who twice won two legs of the triple crown and three RBI titles, had his finest season in 1969. That year, he led the league in home runs (49) and RBI (140)—both career highs—while scoring 106 runs (also a career high) and batting .276. His feats powered the Twins to the American League West Division title and earned him the honor of being named the league's Most Valuable Player.

"I'd have to say that was my best year," says Killebrew. "It was a very satisfying year because the year before, I had had a serious injury when I hurt my leg in the All-Star Game. To come back and have the kind of year I did meant a great deal to me.

"Of course, a lot of guys on our team had good years that season," he adds, pointing out Tony Oliva (who hit .309 with 24 home runs), Rod Carew (who hit .332), and Rich Reese (who hit .322). "They helped me a lot. There's no question about that. With them in the lineup, the other teams couldn't pitch around me."

Throughout most of his career, Killebrew, who nine times drove in more than 100 runs, had a strong supporting cast. Initially, the support came from sluggers such as Roy Sievers, Bob Allison, and Jim Lemon. Later, big clouters such as Jamie Hall, Earl Battey, and Rich Rollins joined the lineup. Killebrew, who still looks very much like the guy who used to squash enemy pitches for a living, recalls those days with special relish.

Since his retirement as a player, Killebrew has remained busy with a variety of business and baseball interests. After leaving Kansas City following the 1975 season, he rejoined the Twins as a color analyst on television. He did that for three years, then joined the Oakland A's in the same capacity. After four years in Oakland, where he also served as a part-time batting instructor, Killebrew spent one year on television with the California Angels, then returned to the Twins broadcast team until leaving after the 1988 season.

Harmon also runs an insurance business in Boise, Idaho, where he now resides, and an auto dealership in Ontario, Oregon. Sometimes, he appears at old-timers games and gives spectators a fleeting glimpse of the way he used to bash baseballs.

That is a habit Killebrew acquired at an early age. "I was a power-hitter, even as a kid," he says. "I started to play baseball in the second grade. I always wanted to be a major leaguer. I didn't have any idols. I just liked all the players, although I admired Ted Williams as much as anybody.

"I guess I was a little crazy. I just liked to play all the time. I even liked to play doubleheaders.

"I learned early on the good fundamentals of hitting. I had power, but I had to refine it. It was something I had to work at and develop, but I knew I wasn't going to be a great average hitter or base-stealer, so I concentrated on power.

"Then, early in my career, I had a conversation with Ralph Kiner. At that time, I used to hit the ball all over the park. He said, 'Kid, if you're going to hit with power, you need to get on top of the plate and pull the ball.' I tried it, and it worked pretty well, although I never consciously tried to hit a home run every time up. I just tried to go with the situation. If I hit a home run that helped win a ball game, it was very satisfying to me. If it didn't help win a game, it was just another home run to me and didn't mean that much."

Killebrew was originally a third baseman when he was signed as a bonus baby by the Senators. Even though he grew up in a remote section of the country where few scouts bothered to travel, Harmon had no trouble attracting attention.

"A lot of scouts came to watch me play when I was in high school," says the Payette, Idaho, native. "At the time, we had a U.S. senator from Idaho whose name was Herman Welker. He was a big baseball fan and used to go to Griffith Stadium all the time. He told the Senators' owner, Clark Griffith, about me. Griffith sent a scout, Ossie Bluege, out to watch me. Bluege signed me, and because of the bonus rule at the time, I had to report right to the Senators."

Although he was a mere 18 years old, Harmon was forced to enter the big leagues without benefit of minor league training. He languished much of his first season (1954) on the bench, appearing in just nine games and getting four hits in 13 at-bats.

"They had Eddie Yost at third base, so they switched me to second," Killebrew recalls. "I remember the first game I played in was at Comiskey Park in Chicago. I was used as a pinch-runner."

Killebrew did get to start a game late in the season. "I had two singles, a double, and two RBI, and we beat the Philadelphia A's at Connie Mack Stadium, 9–2," he remembers.

In 1955, playing mostly at third base, Harmon hit just .200 while appearing in 38 games. But he did get his first major league home run.

"I'll never forget it," he says. "It came off Billy Hoeft of the Tigers at Griffith Stadium. Frank House was the catcher. When I came to the plate, he said, 'Kid, we're going to throw you a fastball.' I didn't know whether to believe him or not. I hit it out—it was one of the longest home runs I ever hit. As I crossed the plate, House said, 'That's the last time I ever tell you what pitch is coming.'"

Playing in the big leagues as a fuzzy-cheeked 19-year-old with a team of grizzled veterans that included Mickey Vernon, Yost, Clint Courtney, Pete Runnels, and Sievers was no easy task for the young future slugger. He finished the season with four home runs.

"I was nervous," Killebrew recalls. "I thought it was going to be easier playing in the big leagues than it was. I found out very quickly it wasn't going to be easy. There were so darn many things you have to learn, and the only way you could do that was by playing every day. I had to go back to the minors to learn them."

Partway through the 1956 season, Killebrew got what he needed. The Senators sent him to Charlotte, then of the South Atlantic League. There, he hit .325 with 15 home runs.

Killebrew spent the following season with Chattanooga of the Southern Association and led the league with 29 home runs while hitting .279 with 101 RBI. He ended that season and began the next with Washington but wound up with Indianapolis of the American Association and then went back to Chattanooga for the balance of the 1958 campaign. Indianapolis, Killebrew explains, was a farm club owned by the Chicago White Sox. He was sent there because the Senators had no Triple-A club.

After hitting 63 home runs in 336 minor league games, Killebrew returned to the majors in 1959 with all the subtlety of a Washington political scandal. In his first full season in the big leagues as a regular, Harmon led the American League with 42 home runs while driving in 105 and batting .242.

Killebrew had only one more season in Washington before the Senators moved to Minnesota to become the Twins. But the years he spent in the nation's capital were ones that he will always cherish.

"Washington was a special place to play in," Killebrew says. "You saw people you never saw anywhere else. I saw presidents, vice presidents, members of the cabinet, congressmen. Ike [President Dwight D. Eisenhower] once asked me to sign a ball for his grandson David. I told him I'd sign one for him if he'd sign one for me. He did, and I still have it. It's one I really treasure."

After the 1960 season, the Senators moved to Minnesota, and Killebrew quickly became a fan favorite in his new home. After hitting 42 and 31 home runs during his two seasons in spacious Griffith Stadium in Washington, Harmon's home run totals over the next 12 years were 46, 48, 45, 49, 25, 39, 44, 17, 49, 21, 28, and 26.

He won home run crowns in 1962 (48), 1963 (45), 1964 (49), 1967 (44), and 1969 (49). In 1962, he won two legs of the triple crown (also leading the AL with 126 RBI), and he repeated the feat in his MVP year in 1969. Killebrew also led the league in RBI in 1971 with 119.

Killebrew never hit .300 during a full season, but he had two seasons over .280, including the 1961 campaign when he hit .288, a career high. Six times he hit .270 or above.

"One of the things people talk about was that maybe I could have hit for a higher average," Killebrew says. "To me, the most important thing was driving in runs. I wasn't so concerned with my batting average."

Over the years, Harmon was shifted from third base to first base to left field. He finished his career with the Twins back at first, a position he played in 969 games. He appeared in 792 games at third base and 470 games in the outfield.

While never noted either for his glove or his speed (he stole just 19 bases in his career), Killebrew made an indelible mark on the game with his home runs. Many of them were particularly memorable.

"Your first home run is always one you remember," Harmon says. "But I have special memories of my 500th home run, my last home run, and the home runs I hit in the All-Star Game.

"I was the first righthanded batter ever to hit a ball over the roof at Tiger

Stadium. I hit it off of Jim Bunning. I think I still have the longest home run ever hit in Baltimore [at Memorial Stadium]. I hit that over the center field fence off of Milt Pappas. I also hit the first ball ever hit into the upper deck at the old Metropolitan Stadium in Bloomington. That was off of Lew Burdette."

In 1963, Killebrew hit four home runs in a doubleheader at Fenway Park, including three in one game. One year earlier, he and Allison had both hit grand slams in the same inning against Jim Perry. In 1964, Oliva, Allison, Hall, and Killebrew hit consecutive home runs, and in 1966, Oliva, Don Mincher, and Harmon hit three straight homers.

While playing in 11 All-Star Games, Killebrew hit three home runs. He slammed a pinch-hit homer in 1961 at Candlestick Park in a 5–4 American League loss. He added a two-run homer in the 1965 game at Bloomington, which the AL also lost, 6–5. And he hit one out in 1971 with one man aboard to help his team to a 6–4 victory at Detroit.

Harmon hit .308 in 26 All-Star Game at-bats. He also hit two dingers in League Championship Series games and one in a World Series. His two LCS clouts came in the 1970 playoffs when the Twins were swept by the Orioles for the second year in a row. The World Series homer occurred in the fourth game in 1965 as the Twins were losing to the Los Angeles Dodgers and Don Drysdale, 7–2. Harmon hit .286 in the seven-game Series, won by the Dodgers.

"That was an unusual year for me," Killebrew says, referring to the '65 season. "I had dislocated my elbow. At the time, I was leading the league in home runs and RBI. I was out until the end of the year and played in only 113 games. So I was real happy to get back and to get into the World Series.

"It was a good Series. In the first two games, we beat Drysdale and [Sandy] Koufax. We all figured, we beat their best, so we're going to sweep the Series.

"The third game, Claude Osteen beat us. Then Drysdale and Koufax came back to beat us before we finally won the sixth game behind Mudcat Grant. Then Koufax, pitching with two days' rest, beat us in the seventh game, 2–0."

While the 1969 season was Killebrew's crowning achievement, he continued to be a force in the American League until the 1973 season, when injuries finally started to take their toll. By then, Harmon had become almost exclusively a designated hitter. The 1974 season turned out to be his last one with the Twins.

"During the winter, [Twins president] Calvin Griffith said he was not going to send me a contract, that he wanted me to become a coach," Killebrew recalls. "I said, 'I think I can still play.' So I talked to several other clubs, and Kansas City seemed to fit in with my personality, and I went there as a DH. I spent a year there, but it didn't work out. I only played against lefthanders, but I still had 14 home runs and 44 RBI. After the season, I retired. I had to. My knees were really bad."

Killebrew finished with a career batting average of .256. He had 2,086 hits, including 290 doubles, while driving in 1,584 runs and scoring 1,283.

While no pitcher ever handled Killebrew thoroughly, one in particular gave him more trouble than the rest. "I could hit most pitchers, but Stu Miller was the toughest," Killebrew says. "He had such an uncanny way of changing speeds. And his motion was incredible. It was so different than anybody else's. I think I got two hits off him in the five years I faced him."

In 1984, Killebrew's glittering career was climaxed with his election to the Hall of Fame. He was the first Twins player elected to the baseball shrine.

"It is still hard for me to believe I'm in the same company with guys like Babe Ruth and Ty Cobb," Killebrew says. "Getting elected is the ultimate thing that can happen to a player.

"When I was going to be inducted, I said I wasn't going to be emotional. But I was very emotional, as it turned out. That was the culmination of everything in my career."

What a career it was. When it came to hitting home runs, Harmon Killebrew was among the best in baseball history.

Bob Lemon

Ace of Some Great Indians Staffs

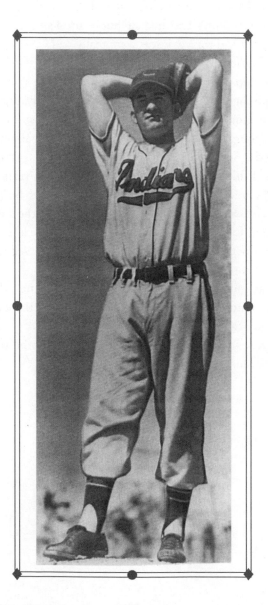

BASEBALL HISTORY IS filled with the tragic stories of players whose careers were either shortchanged or destroyed because they were seized from the diamonds by World War II.

There is at least one story, however, in which a player's career reaped immeasurable benefit because of his military service in that war.

If it hadn't been for the time he spent in the U.S. Navy, Bob Lemon might never have turned into a Hall of Fame pitcher. He might have had a career in which he toiled mostly as a minor league outfielder or infielder, perhaps occasionally rising to the big leagues as a utility man, but for the most part performing as a mediocre position player on an uncharted journey through professional baseball's whistle-stops.

His story began in 1938 when 18-year-old Lemon was signed by the Cleveland Indians to his first professional contract. "I was signed as a short-stop-outfielder-pitcher right out of high school," Lemon remembered. "I had pitched some in high school. The scout who signed me told me to write down pitcher on the contract. I got a bonus of $300, which I blew on a used Model-A Ford.

"I really didn't get to pitch in the minors," added Lemon, who died early in 2000. "I played the outfield and infield."

From 1938, when he broke in with Springfield, Ohio, of the Mid-Atlantic League, until 1941, when he played for Wilkes-Barre—and led the Eastern League in runs (109) and hits (169) while compiling a .301 batting average— Lemon pitched in just two games. The native of San Bernardino, California, spent the rest of the time at shortstop, third base, and the outfield.

Called up to Cleveland at the end of the 1941 season, Lemon played in five games at third base. The situation was repeated in 1942 when Bob hit .268 with 21 home runs as a third baseman–shortstop for Baltimore of the International League, then appeared in five games at the end of the season with Cleveland.

Military service intervened in 1943, and for the next three years Lemon was in the Navy. The first two years, he was stationed on the West Coast, where he played third base on a Navy team. In 1945, he was assigned to Hawaii and played in a high-class service league that was filled with major leaguers.

Lemon was good enough to make his league's all-star team as a third baseman. But along the way, he also did some pitching for the team, managed by Billy Herman, then a Brooklyn Dodgers infielder.

"A number of the guys I played with and against told me I couldn't make it in the major leagues as an infielder or an outfielder," Lemon recalled. "But I was pitching a lot of games and had a natural slider. A lot of players told me I should stick with pitching."

Several of them, including catchers Bill Dickey and Birdie Tebbetts, were so convinced that Lemon's arm—and not his bat—could be his ticket to the big leagues that when the war ended, they sought out Cleveland manager Lou Boudreau and urged him to give Lemon a chance on the mound.

With veteran Ken Keltner firmly established at third base, Boudreau himself ensconced at shortstop, and a flock of talented outfielders in the organization—including a young and up-and-coming standout named Dale Mitchell—the idea made sense.

"We needed pitchers anyway," Boudreau recalls. "Besides, I knew Bob had a great arm because of the way he threw from third base. So I figured, why not? It was worth a try."

When Lemon made the team in 1946, he did so essentially as a pitcher. "I got off to a bad start with the bat, and they sent me down to the bullpen," he remembered. "I wasn't too hot about the idea." Bob pitched in 32 games, most of them in relief, and posted a 4–5 record with a 2.49 ERA in 94 innings.

Lemon still got in some time in the outfield, too. He appeared in 12 games and, in fact, was the center fielder when Bob Feller pitched a no-hitter on April 30 to beat the New York Yankees, 1–0.

The 6-0, 180-pound Californian hit just .180 that year. The following year, he upped his average to .321 and played in two games in the outfield. But, despite his lack of minor league mound experience, the strong right-hander (he batted lefthanded) had now essentially made the conversion to pitcher.

Lemon was still working mostly out of the bullpen in the early part of the 1947 season. "Boudreau had me working with Mel Harder, our pitching coach," Bob recalled. "Finally, Harder told Boudreau, 'He's ready.' So they gave me my first start. It was against Boston. I remember it well because it was my father's birthday. I went six or seven innings, and we won. That was pretty much the end of my being a reliever." Lemon finished the season with an 11–5 record and a 3.44 ERA while working in 167.1 innings in 37 games.

The '47 season, however, was a mere warmup of what was to follow. In 1948, Lemon—with all the suddenness of a midsummer tornado—catapulted into the upper levels of the American League's pitching elite with one of the great seasons in the years immediately following the war.

Leading the league with 10 shutouts, 20 complete games, and 293.2 innings pitched, Lemon registered a 20–14 record while placing second in the league to Feller in strikeouts with 147 and second to teammate Gene Bearden in ERA with a 2.82.

On June 30, Bob fired a 2–0 no-hitter at the Detroit Tigers, striking out four and walking three. It was the American League's first no-hitter in a night game.

"That game was a special thrill to me," Lemon said. "It was one of those nights when everything went right. I remember Mitchell made a helluva play in left field [when he made a leaping, one-handed catch against the wall of George Kell's line drive down the line]. The last batter was Kell. He tapped one back to me. I was afraid I'd throw it away, but I got it over to first to end the game."

Lemon teamed with 20-game winner Bearden and 19-game winner Feller to pitch the Indians to their first American League pennant in 28 years. The season was particularly noteworthy because five teams were in the pennant race most of the way, and it took a special playoff to determine the winner. Bearden beat the Red Sox, 8–3, in a one-game playoff for the flag after the two teams had finished the regular season tied for first place.

In the World Series, Lemon continued his sparkling season with two wins over the Boston Braves. Bob beat the Beantowners, 4–1, with an eight-hitter in the second game. In the sixth and deciding game, he clinched the World Championship for the Indians with a 4–3 victory, again allowing eight hits over seven and one-third innings before being relieved by Bearden.

It was a truly amazing season for Lemon, and Bob was rewarded for his efforts when *The Sporting News* selected him the outstanding pitcher in the American League (an honor tantamount in those days to winning the Cy Young Award). It would be the first of three such awards for Lemon, who was the choice also in 1950 and 1954. In those same three years, *The Sporting News* also chose Lemon to its major league all-star team.

"The 1948 season was a very special one for me," Lemon said. "So many good things happened that year, both to me and to the team. I think you'd have to go some to top the '48 season from an overall team standpoint. We had a good season, but so did Boston, New York, Detroit, and Philadelphia. There was great competition throughout the league. The funny thing was, we always seemed to have more trouble with the other teams like Washington and St. Louis. In fact, one year in around that time, we had 11 extra-inning games with the Senators.

"It was a good era. Of course, that was before expansion, and before the other sports got big," Lemon said. "All the good athletes were playing baseball in those days because it was about the only sport where you could make any money. Today, a lot of good baseball players are probably playing football and basketball."

For Lemon, the 1948 season not only rendered the ultimate justification for his being switched to the mound, it launched him on a streak that would eventually take him to the Hall of Fame.

Lemon posted three straight 20-win seasons, then four more over the next six years. No other Cleveland pitcher has seven 20-win seasons.

From 1948, Lemon went to 22–10 in 1949 and 23–11 in 1950 while leading the league that year in wins, complete games (22), strikeouts (170), innings (288), and hits (281).

After dropping back to 17–14 in 1951, Bob went 22–11, 21–15, 23–7, 18–10, and 20–14 over the next five years, three times leading the league in complete games (once with a career high 28) and twice leading the junior circuit in wins and innings pitched.

Bob pitched in four All-Star games, taking the loss in 1952 in a rain-abbreviated, five-inning match in Philadelphia. Twice he combined with teammates to give the Indians three 20-game winners—in 1952 with Early Wynn (23), Mike Garcia (22), and Lemon (22) and in 1956 when Lemon, Wynn, and Herb Score each won 20.

In 1954, Cleveland—with 111 wins, an all-time American League record for a 154-game season—was back in the World Series as Lemon's 23–7 mark led the way. The Indians' pitching staff that year, which included Wynn, Feller, and Garcia, has often been cited as one of the best in baseball history.

Nevertheless, the Indians were swept in four games by the New York Giants in a World Series made famous by the pinch-hitting heroics of Dusty Rhodes.

"Our 1954 team was the best I ever saw," said Lemon, who lost the Series opener, 5–2, and the fourth game, 7–4. "Unfortunately, the thing that takes away from it was our getting swept in the World Series. We just didn't get timely hitting, and the Giants did."

Timely hitting eluded the Indians over the next two seasons, too, as they finished second to the Yankees both years. Lemon, though, continued to pitch well until his career started winding down in 1957.

Bob was 6–11 that year. The following year, he worked in just 11 games, and went 0–1. It turned out to be his final season as a big league player.

Lemon, who pitched in 12 games during the 1958 season with San Diego of the Pacific Coast League, finished his major league career with a 207–128 record and a 3.23 ERA. He appeared in 460 games, pitching 2,850 innings, allowing 2,559 hits, striking out 1,277 and walking 1,251. Bob completed 188 of the 350 games he started and hurled 31 shutouts.

"I had a pretty good curve, slider, and sinker," Lemon said. "The slider is a breaking ball that you can control. I had one for a 3–1 count, one for a 3–2 count, and so forth. They broke differently, depending on the count.

"Probably the toughest hitter I faced," Lemon added, "was Minnie Minoso. He'd stand right on top of the plate. You could hit him any time you wanted. I didn't want to hit him, though, because he was a friend.

"Joe DiMaggio, Ted Williams, George Kell—anybody who hits like they did has to be tough. I tried to stay down on Williams.

"Basically, though, you just went out there and tried to do your job. It was a lot easier when we added [Ray] Narleski and [Don] Mossi to our pitching staff. With them in the bullpen, you could go as hard as you could because you knew they'd come in and get the job finished."

Although he emerged as a Hall of Fame pitcher, Lemon hardly had a one-dimensional career. With 37 career home runs, he has the second highest total of homers by a pitcher in big league history, ranking one behind Wes Ferrell. Bob's seven home runs in 1949 (he homered twice in one game against the Chicago White Sox) ties for second place on the all-time, one-season list.

Because his early days as a position player taught him how to wield a glove, Lemon was also an accomplished fielder when he was on the mound. Currently, he holds American League records for pitchers for most years leading the league in putouts (five), assists (six), and chances (eight) and for most career doubleplays (78).

After his playing days ended, Lemon held a variety of positions in baseball, including pitching coach with the Indians, Philadelphia Phillies, California Angels, Kansas City Royals, and Yankees. He also served as a scout with the Indians, Atlanta Braves, and Yankees.

Along the way Lemon turned to managing. He spent seven seasons in the minors at the Triple-A level as a pilot and in 1966 was named Manager of the Year when he led Seattle to the Pacific Coast League championship.

Lemon spent all or parts of eight seasons as a major league skipper with Kansas City, the White Sox, and the Yankees. His career regular-season record was 430–403.

Bob piloted the Yankees to two American League pennants—in 1978 defeating Kansas City in the playoffs and in 1981 downing the Oakland A's. His Yanks won the '78 World Series in six games with the Los Angeles Dodgers but lost the '81 fall classic in the same number of games with L.A.

"Every once in a while I think about those years, but I really wouldn't ever want to manage again," said Lemon, who lived in California after retiring from baseball.

"The game has changed since I played," he added. "There's not the camaraderie now that there was. When I played, you rode on trains, you had roommates, and six or seven guys would always go out to dinner together. You were a lot closer to your teammates."

The apex of Lemon's career as a player was reached in 1976 when he was elected to the Hall of Fame. "Going into the Hall of Fame was my proudest accomplishment," he said. "Every player who goes in there is at the top of the curve. It's a great feeling.

"I've had so many good things happen to me, it's hard to ferret them all out," Lemon added. "Almost anything a player, coach, or manager could do has happened to me. I've had so many wonderful moments.

"But going into the Hall of Fame was the epitome of them all. I was very fortunate. My mother was still alive, and she was able to see it. That was a great feeling."

And it was all made possible because of Bob's stint in the Navy. Score one for the military.

Juan Marichal

No Hispanic Hurler Was Better

IT WAS ALWAYS the windup that you noticed first with Juan Marichal.

Shut your eyes, and you can almost see it today. Forward dip, then a big, smooth rock backward as the arms come fully extended above the head. And then the highlight of the delivery—that incredibly high kick with the left leg jutting straight out and up. While Marichal's right shoulder seemed to be nearly scraping the ground, his left foot appeared to be pointing out some distant star.

As the leg landed back on the ground, Marichal's long right arm would come swooping across the top of his body in a huge overhand arc. Eventually, the ball would be released toward the plate in one final grand burst of energy.

There were few prettier sights in baseball than Juan Marichal's delivery. It was poetry in motion, as gorgeous in its own way as a cover girl's face, as stunning as the Grand Canyon. As baseball movements go, it was the perfect 10.

Ironically, it did not come with the original merchandise. And, if you listen to its owner, it eventually resulted in damaged goods.

"My first two years in pro ball, I pitched nothing but sidearm," Marichal reveals. "My last month in Class A ball in Springfield, the manager asked me why I pitched that way. I told him that there was a guy in the Dominican Republic who pitched that way. His name was Bombo Ramos. I was a shortstop originally. But after I saw him pitch, I wanted to be a pitcher, just like him. So I learned to pitch sidearm the way he did.

"The manager [Andy Gilbert] asked me if I wanted to learn to throw overhand. I said, 'Why?' He said it would make me more effective against lefthanders. I said, 'Okay.' So he took me to the bullpen, and I worked on throwing overhand. I found I could throw the ball harder that way, so I stayed with it. That's how I developed the delivery and pitching motion I used for the rest of my career. The only trouble with it was, it took two or three years off my career because it took so much out of my arm."

In his prime, though, the Hall of Fame righthander's arm was magnificent. Over a 16-year big league career spent mostly with the San Francisco Giants, Marichal registered a 243–142 record with a 2.89 earned run average in 471 games. He won more games than any Hispanic hurler until Dennis Martinez passed him in 1998.

Juan could throw hard, he had an assortment of pitches, and he had razor-sharp control. In 3,509.1 innings of work, Marichal struck out 2,303 batters while walking only 709. He was one of the top control artists in big league history, walking just 1.82 batters per nine-inning game, according to *The Great All-Time Baseball Record Book.*

"A lot of people said that because of my high kick, I didn't look at the batter," Marichal says. "But that wasn't true. I always had my eye on the plate. And I was relaxed when I pitched. That was the key.

"When you have confidence, you relax. When you relax, you can do anything you want with the ball. That's why I was such a good control pitcher. I pitched relaxed. I knew that no matter how bad I was, I was going to be there on the mound, and I was going to do my best.

"My managers gave me confidence, too," he adds. "One time, I gave up 15 hits against the [New York] Mets. Herman Franks kept me in the game. At one point, he came out to the mound, and said, 'How do you feel?' I said, 'Bad.' But he said, 'I have to keep you in because you're the best I've got.' I stayed in and wound up getting the win."

Marichal did not have an overpowering fastball, but the pitch was effective because he complemented it with so many other offerings. "I think the slider was my best pitch against righthanders," he says. "Against lefthanders my best pitch was the screwball. Candlestick Park was a lefthanded hitters' park, and I always faced lefthanded lineups, so I had to come up with that pitch. I started fooling around with it in 1960. About that time, we had a pitcher named Ruben Gomez. He threw one of the best screwballs I ever saw. I learned from him how to throw the pitch, and by 1962 I had a pretty good one."

It turned into such a good pitch that it helped Marichal win 20 or more games six times. Twenty-five times he struck out 10 or more batters in one game. He pitched a no-hitter, he won 10 straight games twice, he was selected to nine All-Star teams, including eight in a row, he won seven complete games by scores of 1–0, and he won six opening day games, at the time a National League record.

A history of the Giants includes some of the greatest pitchers of all time. Names such as Christy Mathewson, Carl Hubbell, Rube Marquard, Joe McGinnity, Gaylord Perry, and Sal Maglie are among the many legends who have toed the rubber for the Giants. Marichal ranks near the top of that distinguished group.

On the Giants' all-time list, only Mathewson won 20 games in more seasons than Marichal. Only Mathewson pitched more shutouts and struck out more batters than Marichal. Only Mathewson and Hubbell won more games or pitched more innings in Giants uniforms than Marichal.

From 1962 to 1969, Marichal's record was 18–11, 25–8, 21–8, 22–13, 25–6, 14–10, 26–9, and 21–11. Over that period, he pitched in fewer than 262 innings just once, four times working in more than 300 frames.

Marichal led the National League in wins, innings pitched, shutouts, and complete games each twice and in won-lost percentage, earned run average, and hits allowed once each.

It might be hard extracting a best season from Marichal's glittering record. But a leading candidate would be the 1968 campaign when he posted a 26–9 record with a 2.43 ERA while leading the league in wins, complete games (30), innings pitched (325.2), and hits (295). As he did in 1966, Juan won 10 straight games that year.

Marichal's particular patsies were the Los Angeles Dodgers. His lifetime record against them was 37–18. He had a 24–1 mark against the Dodgers at Candlestick Park.

"I always felt like I wanted to beat them," Marichal says. "I loved to pitch in front of a lot of people, and every time we played the Dodgers, we had a full house. That gave me a lot of incentive."

Playing in front of full houses was a long way from the streets of Laguna Verde in the Dominican Republic where Juan made his own baseballs by wrapping old silk stockings around pieces of rubber and then binding them with adhesive tape. Born Juan Antonio Sanchez Marichal, the Dominican Dandy, as he was later sometimes called, grew up in a baseball atmosphere. But he never expected it to lead him to the United States.

"I was in the Dominican Air Force back in the 1950s," Marichal says. "I pitched for the Air Force team, and was doing real well. A scout named Horacio Martinez used to follow me everywhere. He wanted to sign me with the Giants. We agreed that when I was ready to become a professional player, he would sign me."

Marichal signed in 1957 for a $500 bonus. The following summer, he was assigned to Michigan City of the Class D Midwest League. "It was some kind of experience," recalls Juan. "It was the first time I'd ever been out of the Dominican, and I didn't know one word of English. I even had a hard time eating."

Juan had an easier time on the mound. Leading the league in wins, innings pitched, and ERA, he posted a 21–8 record with a 1.87 ERA while striking out 246 in 245 innings.

Moved up in 1959 to Springfield of the Eastern League, he again led the circuit in wins, ERA, and innings while adding strikeouts to his crown. Juan went 18–13, fanning 208 batters in 271 innings and recording a 2.39 ERA.

In 1960, Marichal began the season with Tacoma of the Pacific Coast League, and he had an 11–5 record when he was called up to the Giants in midseason. His first big league game was nothing short of sensational.

"I was called up on July 10," Marichal remembers, "but I sat on the bench and watched for a while. They told me I was going to pitch against the Phillies when they came to town."

That day finally arrived. Marichal, not quite 22, pitched a one-hitter, beating the Phillies, 2–0. The only hit for the Phils was an eighth-inning single by Clay Dalrymple.

"The Phillies sent up Dalrymple to pinch-hit in the eighth," Marichal recalls. "Tom Sheehan was our manager. He came out to the mound and said, 'This guy's a good fastball hitter. Throw him nothing but curves.' The first pitch I threw him was a breaking ball, and he hit a line drive for a single."

Although his no-hitter was broken, Marichal could have easily gotten the impression that pitching in the big leagues wasn't very difficult. After all, he was still an impressionable youngster who had won 50 games in two and one-half years in the minors, and in his big league debut he had the hitters in his back pocket.

"I didn't let myself think it was easy," Marichal says. "Just because I pitched a one-hitter, I never thought pitching in the big leagues was going to be easy. There were only eight clubs in the league at that time, and they were all pretty good."

So, too, was this 6-0, 190-pound Latin with the big, easy motion. By the time his first big league season was over, Marichal had won six of eight decisions and was considered an up-and-coming young mound star.

In his first full season, Marichal was 13–10. He followed that with an 18–11 mark in 1962 as the Giants won the National League pennant and went to the World Series against the New York Yankees.

En route to a loss to the Yanks in seven games, the Giants sent Juan to the mound in the fourth game of the Series. After four innings, the Giants had a 2–0 lead, and Marichal had allowed just two hits.

"I was pitching real well," says Marichal. "In the top of the fifth, we had men on first and third with no outs, and I came up as a hitter. Whitey Ford was pitching, and the count went to three and two. On the next pitch, I was supposed to squeeze. Tom Haller started racing home from third, but Ford threw me a slider. The ball was going to hit my foot. I had to try to bunt, but the ball hit me right in the finger. My whole fingernail came out. They had to take me out, and I missed the rest of the Series. That was one of my greatest regrets."

While the Giants went on to win that game, 7–3, it turned out to be Marichal's only World Series appearance. Juan, however, had no shortage of memorable outings. In fact, two of them surfaced the next season.

In one of the great pitching duels in baseball history, Marichal and Warren Spahn matched shutouts for 15 innings. Willie Mays' home run in the 16th inning finally gave Juan and the Giants a 1–0 victory. "To me," says Marichal, "that was one of my greatest games. I was lucky that I won the game."

On June 15, 1963, Marichal won another 1–0 game, this time with a no-hitter against the Houston Colt 45s. Juan struck out five and walked two to beat Dick Drott.

"I didn't have anything on the ball that day," Juan says. "I had no speed. All I had was control. But all of a sudden in the last two innings, my fastball came back, and I struck out four of the last six batters."

Marichal finished the 1963 season with a 25–8 record. That launched four straight 20-win seasons, which put Juan squarely on a level with Sandy Koufax, Bob Gibson, Don Drysdale, Jim Bunning, and Jim Maloney as the dominant National League pitchers of the era.

Marichal added another laurel in 1964 when he won his second All-Star Game. Juan had been the winning pitcher in the 1962 clash when he hurled two hitless innings in a 3–1 NL victory. In 1964, he got the win after Johnny Callison ripped a three-run homer in the bottom of the ninth for a 7–4 NL triumph.

Marichal's finest All-Star Game moment happened in 1965 when he was the National League's starting pitcher and gave up just one hit in three innings. He was named the game's most valuable player in his team's 6–5 victory.

Juan also started the 1967 All-Star Game and again yielded just one hit over three innings. Overall, working in eight All-Star tilts, Marichal gave up only seven hits in 18 innings while striking out 12 and walking two. He had a 0.50 ERA.

Over his first five years in the big leagues, Marichal won 103 games, the eighth best total in big league history. Then, as later, he pitched most of the time against rugged mound opponents. "I always had to pitch against the best pitchers," he says. "Most of the time, the other teams would save their 20-game winners for me.

"Every guy who came up to the plate with a bat was dangerous, too," Marichal continues. "You always had to be careful.

"I faced some very good hitters, but one of the toughest was Roberto Clemente. He played the game so hard. He always went onto the field to win. After him, I'd say the next toughest hitters were Pete Rose and Billy Williams."

With his easy delivery, relaxed attitude, and a sometimes playful look on his face, Marichal was occasionally perceived as one who took the game lightly. In truth, however, Juan was a fierce competitor who hated to see his teammates give less than their best.

"I sacrificed myself very much to be a major league pitcher," Juan says. "I was crazy about the game, and I always tried to be in top shape. I used to go to bed early. Not too many players did that. They wanted to play the game, but then they wanted to go to the disco. They'd come to the game the next day and give 80 or 90 percent.

"I always thought you had to give 100 percent. If you didn't give 100 percent, you shouldn't be out there.

"I loved to be home. I loved to rest. I loved to give 100 percent. That was the only way to do it. Often, my teammates would be out all night. I knew it. And then the next day, they'd make an error behind me. It would make me feel real bad."

Marichal's fiery nature got carried away in 1965 when he hit Dodgers catcher John Roseboro over the head with a bat. After Marichal had been brushed back by L.A. pitcher Sandy Koufax, Juan and Roseboro exchanged heated words. When one of Roseboro's return throws to Koufax whistled inches from Marichal's ear, Juan retaliated by swinging the bat at the catcher. A melee followed. Eventually, Marichal was fined $1,750 and suspended for nine days.

Marichal prefers not to discuss the incident now. "Johnny and I have become good friends, and it's been so long since it happened that I don't want to bring any memories of it back," he says. "Roseboro was very kind to me after the incident. The next time we came to L.A., the fans were ready to jump all over me, but he told them to forget what had happened."

Marichal had his last big year for the Giants in 1969, when he checked in with a 21–11 record and led the league with eight shutouts and a 2.10 ERA—his career low. Over the next four years, he went 12–10, 18–11, 6–16, and 11–15.

In December 1973, Marichal was sold to the Boston Red Sox. Saddled with arm problems, Juan pitched in only 11 games in 1974, compiling a 5–1 record. That fall, he was released. The Dodgers signed him the following spring, and he worked in two games before deciding to retire.

Marichal returned to the Dominican Republic where he owned a 1,000-acre farm. Eight years later, the inevitable happened. Juan was elected in 1983 to the Hall of Fame.

"It was a surprise to me," he says. "I didn't get elected the first or second time, but it was a great feeling going in on the third time. Bob Gibson had said he didn't think he was better than me. Coming from the best pitcher I ever faced, that made me feel good."

Juan's induction was packed with emotion. As the first Hispanic player elected to the Hall of Fame through the regular selection process, Marichal seized the occasion to send a message to his countrymen.

"It was the first time anybody spoke Spanish when he was getting inducted," Marichal boasts. "I just wanted to say how proud I was. As the first Dominican elected, it meant a lot to me, and it meant a lot to my countrymen.

"I played the game because I loved it. I never thought about money. When I started, I didn't know anything about the Hall of Fame. But I was very fortunate.

"The whole thing reminded me of my first game. I warmed up in the bullpen. When they announced my name, it was a great feeling. I ran all the way in from the bullpen to the mound. When I heard my name announced at the Hall of Fame, I had the same feeling. I never thought a person who grew up in my hometown would become a professional baseball player, much less a member of the Hall of Fame."

In the years that followed his induction, Marichal—whose number 27 has been retired by the Giants—tried diligently to help more players from his country reach the ranks of professional baseball. Along the way, he served for a time as director of Latin American scouting for the Oakland A's and supervised a rookie, 12-team summer league in the Dominican Republic in which 19 major league teams participated.

In recent years, Marichal has served his country as the minister of sports. In 1998, he was named to the 15-member Hall of Fame Veterans Committee. Juan was an active participant in the massive celebration that took place when Chicago Cubs slugger Sammy Sosa returned home to the Dominican Republic after the 1998 season.

"Everything I have—I have a beautiful family, a beautiful house—I owe to baseball," Marichal says. "It has given me a wonderful life."

That, of course, is only fitting. A wonderful life for a wonderful pitcher.

Eddie Mathews

One of the Best Third Basemen

BECAUSE IT IS A position that has ordinarily been reserved for players who could hit the long ball, third base has been a spot where legions of power-hitting titans have roamed.

In the years since the home run became a dominant force in baseball, sluggers of all shapes and sizes have manned the hot corner. Some had the added ability of being able to field. And a few of them even counted among the finest long-distance clouters in the history of the game.

Eddie Mathews was without question a certified member of that group. The slugging lefthanded batter was the finest long-ball-hitting third baseman of his era and the first at that position in baseball history to hit 500 home runs in a career.

Until Mike Schmidt came along, Mathews was usually considered the game's greatest third baseman. Brooks Robinson was a better fielder, and Pie Traynor hit for a higher average. But nobody before him played the game with such overall skill, and certainly no third sacker had hit home runs like he did.

The Hall of Fame beckoned Eddie in 1978, and he became only the ninth third baseman to enter the baseball shrine. No one questioned whether he belonged there. After all, he ended his 17-year career with 512 home runs, which presently ties him with Ernie Banks for 13th place on the all-time list. In 2,391 games, he hit .271, lacing 2,315 hits, driving in 1,453 runs, and scoring 1,509.

Mathews led the National League in home runs twice (in 1953 and 1959). He was named to nine All-Star teams. He was *The Sporting News* major league All-Star third baseman four times. Twice he was runnerup (in 1953 and 1959) in the Most Valuable Player voting. And he shares with Schmidt the National League record for most consecutive years (nine) with 30 or more home runs in a season.

His playing career began in 1952 and ended in 1968. During that period, he spent most of his time with the Milwaukee Braves, but he also played briefly with Braves teams in Boston and Atlanta and with the Houston Astros and Detroit Tigers. Mathews is the only man to have played with the Braves franchise in all three cities.

A resident of Del Mar, California, Mathews was born in Texas but grew up in California. The 6-1, 190-pounder was signed to a Boston Braves contract by former major league outfielder Johnny Moore in 1949.

"I'll never forget how I signed," recalls Mathews. "When I was in high school, a number of scouts tried to sign me. They were offering big bonuses, but there was a rule in those days that if you got a bonus, you had to go right to the major leagues. I didn't really want to do that.

"Johnny Moore was a very persuasive man and a very nice guy. He explained to me that the Braves were trying to start a youth movement. They had won the pennant in 1948 with a team made up mostly of older players. I saw that signing with the Braves would be an opportunity to play every day in the major leagues pretty fast.

"Moore came to my senior prom to sign me. There was some kind of rule that you couldn't sign the same day you graduated, so he waited around at the prom, and then signed me after midnight."

Mathews spent the rest of 1949 and the next two years in the minors, playing in 1950 in Atlanta, then in the Southern League, and dividing the 1951 campaign between Atlanta and Milwaukee, then in the American Association. How ironic that both cities would become part of the Braves' three-city tour of the National League.

Eddie was promoted to Boston in the spring of 1952. Once there, he quickly displaced the veteran incumbent, Bob Elliott, as the regular third baseman.

Although it turned out to be the Braves' last season in Boston, Mathews served notice that he would be one of Beantown's most lamentable losses. He slammed 25 home runs, including three in one game, the first time in major league history that had ever been done by a rookie. He hit just .242 and led the league with 115 strikeouts, but he had big league star written all over him.

Mathews remembers an incident in Philadelphia that helped him over the hump in his rookie season. "I was really struggling at the start of the season," he says. "Tommy Holmes was our manager at the time. We came into Philadelphia for a series with the Phillies, and Holmes took me aside. 'Eddie,' he said, 'you have to get with the program or you're not going to be here too long.' Ken Heintzelman, a crafty lefthander, was pitching that day for the Phillies, and I hit a home run off him. That kind of broke the ice for me, and I felt much better after that."

Charlie Grimm replaced Holmes as manager after 35 games that season, but the Braves went on to a seventh-place finish. That winter, they moved to Milwaukee.

"At that time, I was so young, it didn't really make any difference to me," Mathews recalls. "We didn't draw well in Boston, and we had a lousy team. So we were very excited about moving to Milwaukee, and we had a tremendous reception when we got there. To me, the move to Atlanta was more disturbing. I was married and we had three children and a house. We were settled in. The move really uprooted us."

Mathews celebrated the Braves' move to Milwaukee with one of his finest seasons. He led the league in home runs with a career high 47, collected 135 RBI, scored 110 runs, and hit .302. No Braves player—not even Hank Aaron—ever hit more than 47 homers in one season. Thirty of Mathews' homers were hit on the road—a National League record at the time. "That had to be my most satisfying season, from a personal standpoint," says Mathews. "Everything seemed to come together. As a young kid, it really meant a lot to me."

Mathews was surrounded on the '53 Braves by such big stickmen as Andy Pafko, Joe Adcock, and Sid Gordon. The following season, though, the company got even better. A rookie named Hank Aaron joined the club in 1954, and until they parted company after the 1966 season, Mathews and Aaron formed one of the most devastating one-two power punches in baseball history.

They were certainly the best the National League ever had. While they played together, they combined for 857 home runs—Aaron with 442 and Mathews with 415—the highest total ever compiled by two players on the same team.

"We complemented each other," Mathews says. "Depending on the manager's whim, he'd bat third and I'd bat fourth, or I'd bat third and he'd bat fourth. We were good friends, and we realized that we helped each other. Nobody could ever pitch around us.

"We had a great hitting ball club," Mathews adds. "Remember, we also had Adcock. In fact, those clubs of ours in the '50s I don't think take a back seat to any club. We not only had power, but we had speed, good defense, excellent pitching. I've never seen a better club. We probably should have won the pennants in '56, '57, '58, and '59."

The Braves, of course, did win pennants in 1957 and 1958 and captured the World Series from the New York Yankees in seven games in '57. In Game Four of that Series, Eddie's two-run homer in the 10th inning gave the Braves and Warren Spahn a 7–5 victory. Mathews beat out an infield single and scored the only run of the game in Lew Burdette's 1–0 shutout in the fifth game. He also drove in two runs with a double and a sacrifice fly and made a dazzling, game-ending fielding play to preserve a 5–0 Burdette shutout in the seventh game. Eddie hit .227 in the Series. He hit only .160 the following year when the Braves bowed in seven games to the Yankees in the Series.

While the Braves were in the thick of National League pennant races each year, Mathews was piling up big numbers for himself. For nine straight years, he hit at least 31 home runs, collecting 40 in 1954 and 41 in 1955—years in which he hit .290 and .289. He slammed a league-leading 46 homers in 1959 while driving in 114 and hitting .306. The following year, he hit 39 home runs and drove in 124, and in 1961 he hit .306 with 32 four-baggers.

Along the way, Mathews, whose only two hits in All-Star games were home runs, was leading the league in walks four times. And he and Aaron and company were having some awesome home run displays.

In 1954, Adcock hit four homers in a 15–7 victory over the Brooklyn Dodgers, and Mathews homered twice in the same game. That year, Eddie also had a string of eight consecutive games in which he drove in at least one run.

Three times, Mathews and Aaron comprised two-thirds of a Braves trio that hit three consecutive homers in one game, teaming with Bobby Thomson in 1956 and with Wes Covington in 1957 and 1958. In 1959 when Eddie led both leagues with 46 home runs, Aaron added 39 to give the Braves the sixth best home run duo in National League history.

Probably the Braves' greatest hitting assault occurred in 1961, when they laced four consecutive home runs, only one of three times it had ever been done in the big leagues. Mathews led off the barrage and was followed by belts by Aaron, Adcock, and Frank Thomas. That year, three Braves wound up collecting more than 30 homers, including 35 by Adcock, 34 by Aaron, and 32 by Mathews.

Mathews was not just a heavy hitter, though. He was also a fine defensive player, twice leading National League third basemen in putouts and three times leading them in assists. He led the league in fielding percentage in 1963.

"Learning to field took a lot of hard work," Mathews recalls. "I always played third base—even as a kid. Don't ask me why. The coach just said, 'You play third.' But I wasn't a very good fielder originally. When I first joined the Braves, they brought in a special instructor for me. It took two or three years until I got to the point where I felt confident. But at least I had a strong chest.

"Hitting, on the other hand, came naturally to me. I could always hit, and I always had power. That's just the way it was. I never tried to hit home runs. They just came.

"That's not to say it was easy," he continues. "Some pitchers used to give me a lot of trouble. Juan Marichal was the toughest for me. And Cincinnati had an old reliever named Bill Henry. He was tough. I used to say, I kept him in the league for an extra four or five years. He had a very unorthodox delivery with a high kick. He threw his pitches at two or three different angles, and he had good control. Guys like him and Stu Miller gave me more trouble than guys like [Sandy] Koufax.

"I batted against Satchel Paige once," Mathews adds. "It was in the All-Star Game in 1953. I didn't realize he was as fast as he was. Boy, he could throw, even then.

"The pitchers were always very careful with me," Mathews says. "That's why I got so many walks. I wasn't about to go after bad pitches. To me, a walk was the same as getting a base hit."

His favorite parks, he claims, were Crosley Field in Cincinnati and Forbes Field in Pittsburgh. "I always hit well in those two places," he says.

Mathews, who hit two or more home runs in one game 49 times in his career (only five other players have performed that feat more often), moved with the Braves to Atlanta in 1966. By then, his career was winding down, and that year he hit under 20 homers for the first time in his 15 years in the majors. After the season, the Braves traded Mathews to Houston.

In 1967, he played in 101 games for Houston, but the Astros swapped him to Detroit late in the season. As a reserve, Mathews stayed with the Tigers long enough to go to the 1968 World Series with them. While the Tigers were winning the Series in seven games, Eddie played in two games and got one hit in three at-bats. He retired as a player after the Series.

"I was very satisfied with my career," he says. "I was very happy I played in the era in which I did. I got to touch shoes with some of the great older players—players such as Rogers Hornsby, Ty Cobb. I got a couple of nice letters from Cobb when I was playing in the minors in Atlanta."

After his playing days ended, Mathews went back to the Braves in 1971 as a coach. He was named manager of the team in August the following year.

After replacing Lum Harris, Eddie brought the Braves from fifth to fourth place in 50 games in 1972. Then the next season, he went the distance and finished fifth with a 76–85 record. He had the club in fourth with a 50–49 mark in 1974 when he was replaced by Clyde King.

Mathews returned to the West Coast, where he worked both as a minor league batting instructor for the Oakland A's and as a scout for the Milwaukee Brewers. He rejoined the Braves in 1986 as a special assignment scout, remaining with the club until 1990, when he retired from the game.

If the young prospects he scouted had gotten hold of a Braves' media guide, they would have found that Eddie ranks second to Aaron in virtually every Braves' all-time hitting category. He is second in at-bats, runs, hits, total bases, doubles, home runs, extra base hits, and RBI and third in slugging percentage (Wally Berger sneaked into second in that category).

Mathews held several National League records for third basemen, including most games played (2,154), until Schmidt came along. A number of his hitting records were also broken by Schmidt, including most home runs by a third baseman.

"I don't mind Schmidt breaking all my records," Mathews says. "I think that's the way it should be. I'm very happy for him. He's my kind of guy. Records are made to be broken. Schmidt did everything better than I did except run."

The seventh player to hit 500 career homers, Mathews saw his 512 career total passed by Schmidt, Aaron, and a handful of others after his playing days ended. But he is still proud of the fact that he is a member of one of baseball's most elite groups.

"To hit 500 home runs, you have to be very fortunate," he says. "You have to stay away from injuries, and you have to be consistent over a long period of time. I'm proud that I was able to do that."

Mathews' proudest moment occurred in 1978 when he was inducted into the Hall of Fame. Yet, it was a bittersweet experience for him.

"It was very exciting," he recalls. "Being elected to the Hall of Fame is the ultimate honor. But I was a little disappointed that I didn't get in sooner. I have almost an identical record with Ernie Banks, and he was elected in his first year of eligibility. I had to wait five years. But that's not going to worry me now. It was a big thrill going in and being able to associate with other Hall of Famers."

Actually, Mathews allows, his whole career was a big thrill. "I had so many thrills, they'd be hard to count," he says. "Just playing every day was a thrill. Then being in three World Series and winning two of them, winning two home run titles. It all was a very exciting career.

"I think I played the game the way it was supposed to be played," Mathews adds. "I'm very comfortable with my accomplishments. I feel I'm up in that elite group of all-time third basemen, and I feel very good about that."

So he should. At a position where good hitters are in abundance, Eddie Mathews is at the top of the list.

Pee Wee Reese

Captain and Sparkplug of the Dodgers

OUTSTANDING SHORTSTOPS have graced big league diamonds since the days when the game began developing into the fine art of baseball. Some could hit, some could field, some could run, and some could throw. And some could do all of the above. Harold (Pee Wee) Reese was one of those who could do all of the above.

He was without a challenge the finest all-around shortstop of his day, a solid player who performed all of the functions of his job—including the often unnoticed subtleties—with exceptional skill.

Reese was, however, more than just a fine player who was eventually inducted into the Hall of Fame. He had many other qualities that transcended his playing ability.

He was the heart and soul of the great Brooklyn Dodgers teams of the 1940s and 1950s—the conscience, the sparkplug, the captain who held together a diverse band of supremely talented players and led them to seven National League pennants.

And if that wasn't enough, Reese played a key role—a larger role than any other Dodger—in the transition of Jackie Robinson from pioneer to player in the major leagues.

With all of his attributes, it is easy to see why Reese was one of the most popular players ever to perform at Ebbets Field. In a city that showered its Dodgers with affection, no one was more representative of the Dodgers' spirit than the battling, durable shortstop.

Reese's numbers enhanced that popularity. In 16 seasons with the Dodgers—including one in Los Angeles—he led the team to pennants in 1941, 1947, 1949, 1952–53, and 1955–56. He was also a member of nine National League All-Star teams.

More than 40 years after his last game, Reese is still the Dodgers' all-time leader in runs scored with 1,338 and walks (1,210). He ranks second in hits (2,170) and at-bats (8,058), third in games (2,166), fourth in doubles (330), fifth in total bases (3,038), sixth in runs batted in (885), and seventh in triples (80), stolen bases (232), and extra base hits (536).

The 5-10, 178-pound native of Ekron, Kentucky, compiled a career batting average of .269 with 126 home runs. He led the league in walks in 1947, in runs in 1949, and in stolen bases in 1952.

One of the outstanding hit-and-run men of his day, an excellent bunter and a fast and clever base-runner, Reese was also an accomplished fielder who had a great knack for playing hitters in just the right spots. He had extremely quick reactions and an accurate and strong arm, and he was especially adept at going back on pop flies. He led the league in putouts four times, in doubleplays twice, and in assists and errors once.

Nicknamed "The Little Colonel" by announcer Red Barber because of his Kentucky heritage, Reese died in 1999 after dividing his time between homes in Louisville and Venice, Florida.

The pinnacle of Reese's post-playing career was reached in 1984 when he was inducted into the Hall of Fame. It was a process that many felt was long overdue.

Prior to his election by the Veterans Committee, Reese's omission from the Hall had been the subject of a considerable amount of controversy. Pee Wee's supporters lobbied long and loud for his candidacy, but—unlike some noted self-promoters—he refused to let himself get drawn into the campaign.

"I was never at a point where I was disappointed that I didn't get in," he said. "It's the epitome of your career to get elected to the Hall of Fame. But I hadn't been that unhappy about not having gotten in.

"I always felt that I was very fortunate. I played in seven World Series. I was just happy to be with the kind of ball club I was with. Everybody said, 'You've got to be unhappy about not being in the Hall of Fame.' But I wasn't.

"I really appreciated it when guys like [Duke] Snider and Campy [Roy Campanella] got elected and said, 'I feel a little guilty about being in the Hall of Fame without Pee Wee.' That's a helluva thing to say. But Duke and those guys went in, and I had no feelings about it in terms of my being there because I played my butt off before they ever got there.

"I'm not being humble. I'm being very sincere. I was tickled to death for them, and it was nice to know the way they felt. But I wasn't going to spend the rest of my life being unhappy if I didn't get in.

"I wasn't ashamed of the way I played," Reese added. "I drove in almost 900 runs while batting first or second. Defensively, I kicked a few around, but I did pretty well there, too.

"And I was durable. To last as long as I did and to play in over 140 games [13 years in a row] every year was pretty good. I played hurt a lot. We were brought up that way. You didn't get out if you had a pulled muscle. You had to shoot novocaine in it or wrap it, and then go ahead and play.

"Burt Shotton was the manager once, and I said, 'Burt, I got a leg that's not too good.' He said, 'Pee Wee, I'd rather have you out there on one leg than I would somebody else on two.' Now, how can you refuse that?

"It's a cliché," Reese continued, "but I was a team player. We had a lot of great players. At the time, I was playing, though, I didn't think about the great players. They were all friends of mine. I had a lot of respect for them. We were all very close."

That closeness had been developed over a number of years, nurtured by the gradual buildup of a collection of players who when finally together formed one of the greatest teams in baseball history.

Reese was the first to arrive on the scene, landing in Brooklyn in 1940 as a nervous kid with just two years of minor league experience. At that point, Reese hadn't even been a shortstop for long.

"I had started out in right field as a kid," he recalled. "When I got a little bigger, I went to second base. It really didn't make a whole lot of difference to me. As long as I could play, I didn't care where it was."

Nonetheless, Reese signed a pro contract at the age of 19, and immediately jumped into pro ball at the Triple-A level with the Louisville Colonels of the American Association. At the time, Louisville was a Boston Red Sox farm club. Reese spent two years there, but his path to Boston was blocked by the presence of Joe Cronin, then the Red Sox shortstop as well as their manager.

Meanwhile, the Dodgers, badly in need of a shortstop to replace their own aging playing-manager, Leo Durocher, eyed Reese enviously. Eventually, the Dodgers bought the Louisville team, essentially so that they could get Reese.

Pee Wee, who got that nickname as a pint-sized marbles whiz when he was about 12 years old, reported to Brooklyn in 1940. Although he missed part of the season after getting beaned, he hit .272 in 84 games as a rookie. But he struggled in the field and often drew the wrath of fans as well as Durocher. It got worse the following year when he committed 47 errors to lead the league. The grandstand wolves screamed for his benching.

"It wasn't hard replacing Durocher at shortstop," Reese said. "He wanted out anyway. But he was very tough on me, especially when I first came up. He defended me a lot of times, too. My being a shortstop, he watched every move I made. He criticized me, but when I look back, it was the best thing that ever happened to me."

With spirited youngsters Reese and Pete Reiser, aptly named the Gold Dust Twins, sparking a team of veterans, the 1941 Dodgers won the National League pennant, giving Brooklyn its first flag since 1920 (the Dodgers lost in five games in the '41 World Series to the New York Yankees). But that Dodgers team was vastly different from the ones that Reese would later captain.

"I really played on two different ball clubs," Pee Wee said. "There was the team before the war and the team after the war. The one before the war was made up of a bunch of fellows who came from other ball clubs. Dolph Camilli and Kirby Higbe came from the Phillies. Cookie Lavagetto was from the Pirates. Mickey Owen, Pete Reiser, and Joe Medwick came from the Cardinals. Billy Herman was from the Cubs. Dixie Walker was from the Tigers.

"Most of the fellows after the war came up through the farm system. Of course, we had a lot of black players who came out of the Negro Leagues."

One was named Jackie Robinson. The first black player in the major leagues in the 20th century, Robinson was welcomed with anything but open arms by the Brooklyn players, some of whom exceeded their abusive treatment of him by staging a short-lived rebellion.

Although he was a southerner, Reese was the one Dodger who went out of his way to befriend Robinson and to help him feel comfortable. "Being from the South, I was brought up where you didn't mix with blacks," Reese said. "You didn't go to school with them. But I had been overseas in World War II, and I had been with black soldiers. When I came back, I just wanted to play ball. I wasn't trying to be the Great White Father. I just wanted to play ball because I hadn't done it for three years.

"Jackie was a very intelligent, very articulate man, and he had the guts of a burglar. He understood what was happening. But if there was ever a chance that I could help him or put my arm around him, I was glad to do it.

"I wouldn't say that all the other players weren't supportive. A lot of them were. I just seemed to get more credit for it. Of course, Jackie played second base, so naturally as a shortstop, I was a lot closer to him.

"He was a super guy. He didn't have the greatest arm in the world. But he had guts. He'd stay right over that bag. You could not move him. He weighed 200 and some-odd pounds, and he was about six feet tall. He was a big man, and he had no fear of anything."

One year before Robinson's arrival, the Dodgers had ended the regular season in a tie for first place. Although they lost to the St. Louis Cardinals in a three-game playoff that year, Brooklyn had begun a streak in which it won six pennants and finished second three times [losing twice in playoffs and once on the last day of the season] over a 10-year period.

"Do you realize how many memorable things happened over that period?" Reese asked. "Al Gionfriddo's catch and Floyd Bevens' near no-hitter in the '47 World Series. Dick Sisler's homer on the last day of the season in 1950 and Bobby Thomson's homer in '51. Don Larsen's perfect game in '56. Something was always happening.

"The most memorable," Reese continued, "which is kind of a sad memory, was the final game of the 1951 playoffs when Thomson hit the home run. Another one like that was the last game of '50. They always blamed Cal Abrams for going home in that game [when he was thrown out at the plate by 15 feet by Richie Ashburn with the potential winning run in the bottom of the ninth], but, hell, somebody sent him home. He didn't go on his own. The guy at third [Milt Stock] sent him in. He should've held him up. There was nobody out.

"Another memorable thing was when Lavagetto broke up Bevens' no-hitter with two outs in the ninth inning. I'll never forget that. I was the next hitter. I didn't exactly want to go up and hit, so I was really relieved when Cookie hit that ball off the scoreboard [not only breaking up the no-hitter, but winning the game for the Dodgers, 3–2]."

While Brooklyn seemed to be staging an event per season that would make baseball history, Reese was at the apex of his game. Between 1946 and 1955, Pee Wee hit below .271 only once, and seven times he cracked double figures in home runs.

In 1947, Reese had his second straight .284 year while driving in 73 runs. Two years later, he tied for the league lead in runs scored with 132 while hitting .279 with a career high 16 home runs.

After hitting in 22 straight games and batting .286 with a career high 84 RBI in 1951, Reese had his only .300 season in 1954 when he batted .309.

"To me, hitting .300 didn't mean that much," Pee Wee said. "I think I had better all-around years. Don't get me wrong. I always wanted to hit .300. But if I hadn't, I wouldn't have been broken up about it."

Reese had many memorable games along the way. In 1949, he scored five runs in one game. Three years later, he set a major league record with a real oddity. He reached first base three times in one inning—twice on walks and once on a single.

Reese played in eight All-Star games. He saved his best for last when in 1953, as his team's leadoff hitter, he hit a single and double and drove in two runs to help the National League to a 5–1 victory at Cincinnati's Crosley Field.

In the seven World Series in which he played, Reese hit .272, getting 46 hits in 163 at-bats. His best Series was in 1952 when he socked 10 hits and batted .345. In the 1955 Series, Reese scored the final run in the seventh game when the Dodgers captured a 2–0 victory for their only Series win in Brooklyn.

In those days, playing in Brooklyn was something special to the players. "I was a very lucky individual," Reese said. "So many great things happened to me in Brooklyn. A lot of people made fun of Brooklyn, but it was a helluva town. People made jokes about it, but it was a very special place. And it was a good place to live.

"Brooklyn had such great fans, too," Reese continued. "They treated you so well. You really had fun at the ballpark."

One place that was not fun—it was more like a war zone—was the Polo Grounds. The Dodgers and New York Giants had one of the great rivalries of baseball in the first half of the 20th century, and whenever one team would go to the other's home park, it was always a sobering experience.

"I don't think there will ever be anything to rival those games between us and the Giants," Reese said. "It was as though every game was a World Series. There was tension in every game. You always had butterflies. I don't care how long you played.

"You'd go into the Polo Grounds, and you'd walk out of those center field bleachers [where the clubhouses were located] and they'd start booing you as soon as you appeared. You didn't mind it, though, You thought, 'Well, they're entitled to do that.' You just didn't like to be booed in Brooklyn."

Reese said the best Brooklyn team he played on was the early 1950s version, which featured four future Hall of Famers (Robinson, Snider, Campanella, and Reese) in the starting lineup, plus four other outstanding regulars.

"It's really hard to rate them because they were all so good," he said. "But I guess you'd have to say the early 1950s teams were the best. You would have to say, though, that the 1955 season was our most successful because that was the only year we won the World Series."

Reese claimed that the best pitcher he faced was the Reds' Ewell Blackwell. "He was the toughest pitcher I ever hit against," Pee Wee said. "He was one tough son of a gun. And he was nasty, too. I bunted on him a few times, and he'd walk in off the mound and say, 'Pee Wee, I don't like people to bunt on me.' He was 6-6, and he got your attention.

"Sam Jones was mighty tough, too. So was [Sal] Maglie. I hit Maglie fairly well, but I never was too crazy about hitting against him."

As his career started to wind down in the late 1950s, two things happened to Reese: The Dodgers shifted him to third base, and shifted themselves to Los Angeles.

"I didn't play that much at third base," Reese said. "It was a much easier position to play than shortstop. By the time we went to L.A., I was 40 years old and had no business playing any more. But they wanted me to go out there because we had lost Robinson and Newcombe and Campanella. The ball club had gotten to the point where they needed someone to go out there.

"I didn't want to move to L.A. I'd spent all those years in Brooklyn. But the L.A. fans were great to me. I can truthfully say that."

Reese's last season as a player was the Dodgers' first in Los Angeles. He retired after the 1958 campaign and became a Dodgers coach.

In 1959, Reese collected one more World Series check when the Dodgers went up against and defeated the Chicago White Sox. It was the only time in his seven World Series that the Dodgers didn't play the Yankees.

One year later, Pee Wee moved from the dugout to the broadcast booth, joining Dizzy Dean as Buddy Blattner's replacement on CBS's nationally televised games. Dean and Reese worked together at CBS through 1965. The following year, when NBC began the Game of the Week, Reese—but not Dean—was hired, and Pee Wee joined Curt Gowdy, working until 1969 when he was replaced by Tony Kubek.

Pee Wee then went to work for the company that makes Louisville sluggers, serving as a goodwill ambassador. He retired from that job in 1984.

Reese looked back at his accomplishments in baseball and concluded that there's only one thing he would do differently.

"If I had the career to do over again, I'd say there's one thing I wouldn't do," Reese stated. "I got something like 1,300 walks [1,210 actually] during my career. I can flat guarantee you that none of them were given to me, as in, 'Hey, put Reese on and pitch to Snider' or somebody like that.

"Consequently, when you take that many pitches, you get yourself in a spot because you can get behind and the pitcher gets you 0 and 2. That's not a situation you want to be in. If I had it to do over, I don't think I'd take as many pitches. Forget about the base on balls. Go ahead and swing the bat."

That's something Reese could always do with proficiency anyway, especially with men on base or the game on the line. He was one of the game's finest clutch hitters.

He was also one of the game's finest shortstops. And one of the game's finest human beings.

Red Schoendienst

A True Pro in Whatever He Did

TO SOME PEOPLE, the game of baseball has given them the high points of their lives. To others, it has been a temporary haven from reality. And to still others, baseball has merely been the means to an end.

To Albert (Red) Schoendienst, the game of baseball has had a much greater meaning. To put it one way, baseball has been his life. More than 57 years after he drew his first paycheck from the sport, Schoendienst is still connected with it. In his entire working life, he has never been employed in any other field.

Schoendienst has served as player, manager, and coach and in the front office, performing with distinction in each capacity. His name has given typesetters fits over the years, but it has been synonymous with outstanding accomplishments.

As a player, Schoendienst was unquestionably one of the game's finest second basemen. He was elected to the Hall of Fame by the Veterans Committee in 1989. An excellent hitter and fielder, he was as good as any second baseman of his era, as his selection to 10 National League All-Star teams, his career batting average of .289, and his lifetime fielding average of .982 attest.

As a manager, Schoendienst won two National League pennants and one World Series while piloting the Cardinals for more than 12 years—the longest anyone ever led the Redbirds. He had a career record of 1,041–955 for a .522 percentage while also finishing second three times and third once.

The switch-hitting Schoendienst spent most of his playing career with the Cardinals, suiting up for them from 1945 to 1956 and again from 1961 to 1963. In between, he played for the New York Giants and Milwaukee Braves, helping the latter to two National League pennants.

He managed the Cardinals from 1965 to 1976 and again briefly as an interim pilot in 1980 and 1990. Except for the 1977–78 seasons when he was a coach with the Oakland A's, he continued as a coach with the Cards from 1979 until the mid-1990s, when he became a special assistant to the general manager.

"It's funny," says Schoendienst, "I didn't live that far from St. Louis as a kid, but I didn't grow up rooting for the Cardinals. I never really rooted for anybody. And I didn't have any idols. I just liked baseball.

"Of course, when I was growing up, the Cardinals and Browns were both in St. Louis. There were mostly Cardinals rooters in the town [Germantown, Illinois] where I lived, but we never went to St. Louis to see a game. We didn't have radios, either, so we could never listen to games. We just played all the time. We played everywhere—in pastures or anyplace else we could find. I learned to take some pretty bad hops from playing on those fields."

Schoendienst played so well that after he graduated from high school, he and some friends decided that they were good enough to attend a Cardinals tryout camp in St. Louis.

"The Cardinals had advertised the camp, so four or five of us decided to go to it," he recalls. "We hitchhiked to St. Louis. Kids came from all over. In fact, there were so many kids they had to send half of them home.

"They kept me there for three days. Then they took me out for lunch and signed me. You might say, my bonus was a glass of milk and a ham sandwich. But I didn't care. I was just grateful to get the chance to play."

Schoendienst was assigned to the low minors, and in the summer of 1942, he made his professional debut. "I gave myself three years to make it," he says. "If I didn't, I told myself I would try something else."

Even then, Schoendienst was a switch-hitter, a practice he began as a youngster. He was also a shortstop. "I was primarily a shortstop throughout the minors," Red says. "But when I reached the Cardinals, they had Marty Marion at shortstop and Emil Verban at second. So they switched me to left field, and that's where I played through most of my first year in St. Louis. The following year, Lou Klein was our second baseman, but he wasn't hitting well, and they moved me to second base. I stayed there the rest of my career."

Schoendienst reached the Cardinals in 1945 after tearing up minor league pitching during parts of three previous seasons. He had led the International League in hitting with a .337 average at Rochester in 1943 and was hitting .373 with the Red Wings the following year before being called into military service after 25 games.

Excused from duty for health reasons in time for the 1945 season, Schoendienst reported to the Cardinals, a freckle-faced, skinny redhead who sportswriters immediately claimed looked like a modern-day Huck Finn.

That year, Schoendienst hit .278 and led the league in stolen bases with 26, a robust total for those days. And a 19-year big league career was launched.

In the ensuing years, Schoendienst became captain of the Cardinals and hit over .300 seven times. He won an All-Star game with a dramatic 14thinning home run. He set fielding records. And he became one of the finest switch-hitters ever to play the game.

Usually batting either first or second in the lineup, the 6-0, 170-pounder produced 2,449 hits, including 427 doubles and 84 home runs. He drove in 773 runs and scored 1,223. His .303 career pinch-hitting average was one of the best in league history.

As a fielder, he was virtually in a league of his own. Sure-handed and smooth, Red would glide effortlessly after ground balls and gobble them up with the certainty of a man flicking on a light switch. He was far-ranging, and he was flawless. He led National League second basemen in fielding percentage six times, and at one point he held NL records for most consecutive chances without an error (320) and highest fielding percentage (.993) in one season for a second baseman.

Schoendienst's career had many thrilling episodes, but few rivaled his first full season as a second baseman in 1946. While Red was hitting .281, the Cardinals had a brilliant season, tying the Brooklyn Dodgers for first place at the end of the year, then beating the Bums in a best-of-three playoff—the first in major league history—for the National League pennant. The Cards then won the World Series in seven games as Enos Slaughter's famous dash from first to home on Harry Walker's long single to left-center provided the winning run in the final game against the Boston Red Sox.

"He just never stopped running," Schoendienst recalls of Slaughter's sprint around the bases. "If the throw [a relay from Boston shortstop Johnny Pesky] had been on the mark, Slaughter would've been out. But nobody told Pesky to throw. Of course, nobody knew Slaughter would be running, either.

"That '46 team of ours," Schoendienst adds, "was a great ball club. I was just very fortunate to have played on it. We beat a helluva club to win the World Series. We were underdogs, but we had outstanding pitching, particularly in [Harry] Brecheen and [Murry] Dickson. Even though I wound up playing mostly at second that year, I also played some at third in the beginning of the season when Whitey Kurowski was holding out, and some at short when Marion got hurt.

"That season gave me the biggest thrill of my career. It was a big thing just coming to the big leagues, but going to the World Series and then winning it was just tremendous. I'll never forget how that last game ended. Brecheen threw a screwball to Tom McBride for the third out in the ninth.

The ball was hit to me, and it was spinning. I caught it with my bare hand and flipped it to Marion at second for the force out."

Other thrills would follow. In 1948, Schoendienst hit eight doubles in three consecutive games. At one point during that streak, he hit five doubles and a home run in a doubleheader to become one of only five National Leaguers who have had six extra base hits in a twin bill. On that same day, Schoendienst's homer came in the same inning in which four-baggers were also hit by Erv Dusak, Slaughter, and Nippy Jones.

In 1950, en route to leading the league in doubles and at-bats while hitting .276, Schoendienst's name blazed across newspaper headlines throughout the country when his 14th-inning home run gave the National League a thrilling 4–3 victory in the All-Star Game at Chicago's Comiskey Park. The homer snapped a four-game NL losing streak.

"Johnny Wyrostek, Walker Cooper, Dick Sisler, and I were standing around kidding," Schoendienst remembers. "I didn't think I'd get into the game. We were going back and forth, kidding about whether or not we would play. They all got in before me. Finally, I got in, I think in the ninth inning.

"Then I wound up hitting the home run that won. I remember it clearly. Ted Gray was pitching, and he threw a slider. On the pitch before that, I thought I had ball four.

"It was a tremendous thrill to hit that homer. It's a big thrill anytime you make an All-Star team, but that one was really special."

Although he never hit another home run quite as dramatic as that one, great moments continued to occur for Schoendienst. In 1951, he became one of only 12 National Leaguers to hit home runs from each side of the plate in the same game. The following season, he embarked on three straight .300 seasons, hitting .303 in 1952, followed by .342 and .315.

His .342, which placed just two points behind league-leader Carl Furillo, was not only a career high, but his 15 homers, 79 RBI, and 107 runs scored that year were also single-season records for Red. He later equaled both the home run and RBI marks.

Schoendienst had another banner year in 1954, at one point hitting in 28 straight games. That year, he participated in 137 doubleplays, an accomplishment that at the time matched the fifth highest total for a second baseman in National League history.

Two years later, after slumping to .268 in 1955, Red was cruising along with a .314 batting average in mid-June when the Cardinals abruptly traded him to the New York Giants in a stunning nine-player deal that brought Al Dark and Whitey Lockman, among others, to St. Louis.

"I was very disappointed," Red remembers. "But I realized that you're going to get traded once in a while. So I tried not to let it bother me."

Schoendienst wound up hitting .296 in a Giants uniform and .302 for the season. He thought he would become a fixture in New York, especially after he got off to a fast start the following year when he was hitting .307.

But the trade winds were blowing again. Exactly one year and one day after he had been swapped to the Giants, Red was sent to the Milwaukee Braves. The Braves, in desperate need of a second baseman, sent three players to the Giants, including 1951 pennant-winning hero Bobby Thomson.

Schoendienst was just what the Braves needed. As one of the final pieces in the puzzle that the Braves had carefully been fitting together, Red provided the spark that drove Milwaukee to the pennant in 1957 and then to a stunning victory over the New York Yankees in the World Series.

Red hit .309 while leading the league in hits with 200. Although he would eventually be connected with nine pennant winners, including another one in Milwaukee the following year, Schoendienst says that the 1957 Braves club was the strongest one with which he was involved.

"The 1957 Milwaukee team was the best team I've ever been on," he says. "It was just an outstanding ball club. Anytime you have guys like [Hank] Aaron, [Eddie] Mathews, [Bill] Bruton, [Warren] Spahn, and [Lew] Burdette on a team, it's got to be a tremendous club. It had everything—hitting, pitching, defense. It was far and away the best ball club."

Schoendienst slipped to .262 in his second season with the Braves, although they again won the pennant before losing in the Series to the Yankees. But by then, it had become increasingly apparent that something was wrong with Red's health, even though he hit .300 in the Series.

The lithe second sacker had always experienced some health problems, wearing down as the season progressed. Year after year he would finish the campaign weakly, his stamina drained. The condition dated back to his days in the military service when he was released early because of his less-than-robust condition.

"I'd always hit .300 up to July," he says. "Then something would start to drag me down. The problem was never diagnosed. I just played with it all those years."

Early in the 1959 season, Schoendienst's condition was finally diagnosed as tuberculosis. He was hospitalized and spent the rest of the season out of baseball.

Although his career as a regular was over, Schoendienst came back to play in 1960. At the end of the season, though, at the age of 36, he was handed his release.

Red was offered a job as the regular second baseman with the new, expansion Los Angeles Angels, but he declined, instead returning to the Cardinals as a playing-coach. He played a little at second but was used mostly as a pinch-hitter, a role in which he excelled.

Schoendienst put together years of .300 and .301 for the Cards—in the later year leading the league in pinch-hits with 22, which at the time tied as the third highest one-season total in National League history.

The switch-hitting redhead retired as a player during the 1963 season. He remained on the Cards' coaching lines until summoned to manage the team in 1965.

After finishing seventh and sixth in his first two seasons, Schoendienst piloted St. Louis to the NL pennant in 1967. The Cards won 101 games during the regular season, then downed the Red Sox four games to three in the World Series with Bob Gibson winning three games, as had Brecheen in 1946 and Burdette in 1957.

St. Louis won the flag again in 1968 but this time lost in the Series to the Detroit Tigers in seven games as Mickey Lolich posted three wins for the victors.

The Cardinals won no more pennants under Schoendienst, but he managed through the 1976 season before being let go. He spent the next two years as a coach with the A's, then came back to the Redbirds in 1979 as a coach under Ken Boyer.

In 1980, Red became the fourth Cardinals manager of the season when he replaced Whitey Herzog, who went briefly upstairs to serve as general manager. When Herzog returned to the field in 1981, Schoendienst went back to his coaching duties.

He replaced Herzog again toward the end of the 1990 season as interim manager but was back coaching in 1991. He continued to coach with the Cardinals until moving into the front office, where he serves as an advisor. Schoendienst also serves as a director of a bank in the St. Louis suburb where he lives, and he is part owner of and helps to operate a retirement home. In 1999, some 57 years after entering the pro ranks, he still held the position as an advisor and also helped instruct young Cardinals infielders in spring training.

If it hadn't been for the presence of Jackie Robinson, Red would have been the premier second baseman in the National League from the mid-1940s to the late 1950s. Along with Robinson and the American League's best—Bobby Doerr—there was no finer trio of second basemen in that era.

"I played all over the field," Schoendienst says. "I hit from different spots in the lineup. It didn't make any difference. I think I had a pretty good career. I'd like to have been a little stronger, a little healthier at times. But I played hurt. It made no difference. A lot of times, I played, but I wasn't up to par. But you had to keep playing because the Cardinals had so many minor league clubs and there was always somebody ready to take your position.

"I played in an era," he continues, "when it was just a great time. I played with and against some of the game's greatest players. It was a thrill watching guys like Joe DiMaggio and Charley Keller, Willie Mays, Ted Williams, and Bobby Doerr. I roomed with Stan Musial for 11 years. That was a great experience. We were together all the time. It was a good relationship."

Schoendienst says that he would like to stay in baseball as long as he can. At this point, few people have stayed in the game as long as he has. "I just love the game," he says. "I like to see guys do well, even when they're on the other team. I enjoy watching good plays, no matter who makes them."

Nobody, though, made good plays more frequently than Schoendienst himself. He was a master of the good play, and one of the great second baseman of his or any other era.

Warren Spahn

The Finest Lefthanded Pitcher

THE HALL OF FAME is filled with the names of great pitchers. But Warren Spahn is in a class by himself. Purely and simply, he is the greatest left-handed pitcher in the history of baseball.

Names such as Lefty Grove, Eddie Plank, Carl Hubbell, and Steve Carlton may be considered among the five best lefthanders of all time. But none ranks as high as the hawk-nosed southpaw who toiled for 20 of his 21 big league seasons with the Boston and Milwaukee Braves.

Spahn's record indisputably states the case. He won more games (363) than any other portsider in baseball history and ranks fifth on the all-time list of winners, trailing only Cy Young, Walter Johnson, Christy Mathewson, and Grover Cleveland Alexander.

He pitched more complete games (382) and more shutouts (63) than any other lefthander in National League history. He led his league in games won (eight) and in complete games (nine) more times than any other pitcher in major league annals, and he won 20 or more games in one season more often (13) than any other lefthander ever to throw a baseball.

No other National League pitcher ever started more games (665), pitched more innings (5,246), or worked more years (21) than Spahn, who ranks eighth on the all-time list in innings pitched, sixth in shutouts, and 16th in strikeouts.

He pitched two no-hitters, was named to 14 All-Star teams, and pitched in three World Series, winning four games. He was baseball's second Cy Young Award winner (in 1957, when one award was given for both leagues). And when he won 23 games at the age of 42, he was the oldest pitcher ever to post a 20-win season.

It was not just as a pitcher that Spahn excelled. He was an outstanding hitter and was often used by the Braves as a pinch-hitter. Spahn slammed more career home runs (35) than any other pitcher in National League history, and his 363 hits rank 12th on the major league's all-time list for pitchers. When Warren won 22 and hit .333 in 1958, he became one of only 14 pitchers in the senior circuit ever to win 20 games and hit .300 in the same season.

Elected to the Hall of Fame in 1973 in his first year of eligibility, Spahn, whose number 21 was retired by the Braves, was as stylish as he was successful. Starting with a big, high kick, he had a classic, smooth windup that culminated with a perfectly balanced follow-through. It was a pure, textbook delivery if there ever was one.

For most of his career, Spahn was the ace of the Braves' staff, teaming first with Johnny Sain and later with Lew Burdette to give his team a fearsome one-two punch that was the bane of most National League hitters.

Between 1947 and 1963, Spahn failed to win 20 games in a season only four times. Twice he posted 23–7 records. Only Cy Young had more and Christy Mathewson as many 20-win seasons.

The mere mention of his name in the same sentence with such immortals is something that Spahn has thought about many times. To this day, it still affects him. "Sometimes I have to pinch myself," says the affable, fun-loving former hurler. "I'll say to myself, 'Was I the guy who did that?' It's an awesome feeling, and it's very comforting and delightful."

As he's always been, Spahn is an analytical person with a finely developed philosophy and the ability to express himself passionately and eloquently.

"If I had to describe myself," he says, "it might be a complex picture because it changed from year to year. I was never satisfied with what I did the year before. I always wanted to improve. I think that is why I experimented with a screwball and why I worked on a slider. I'd go to spring training with something in mind to accomplish every year. It was dedication, concentration. I think you have to be selfish. You have to feast on the other players. I wanted to be one step ahead of the hitters.

"Hitters are usually egotists," Spahn adds, "and anytime you defeat an egotist, I think it's a compliment. When you see a pitcher facing a hitter, you know the monkey's on somebody's back. The personalities of the people involved dictate where that monkey is.

"I often felt like, 'Okay, Mr. Kiner or whoever it was. You can hit 50 home runs off anybody else, but you're not going to hit them off me.' Pretty soon, that respect becomes mutual. I wanted to be the guy who, if you did hit a home run or got a base hit off, you earned it.

"And if you could minimize your mistakes, they would have to earn it even more. After all, hitters feast on mediocre guys, and they have to scramble for base hits off good pitchers. There is combat between every pitcher and every hitter who walks to the plate. But too many times the pitcher defeats himself by not doing the best job he can, especially against the average hitter. I always strived to do the best job I could, using every tactic I knew to hold the upper hand.

"I also think," Spahn continues, "that the people pitching in the major leagues have always been divided into two categories—pitchers and throwers. The throwers are the guys who don't last very long. The pitchers are the perennial winners.

"Even today, when everybody's talking about the lively ball, the good pitchers are still winning. Good pitchers always come to the front. And maybe there are a lot of pitchers today who are making the ball lively.

"Pitching is nothing more than unadulterated hard work," Spahn insists. "That goes for every phase of pitching. For instance, I think I had a pretty good move to first base, but it's because I worked on it. I think I was a pretty good hitter because I worked on it. When I was allowed, I would take extra batting practice. Eddie Stanky and I used to hit and run together. Nobody had ever done that as a pitcher before. I was also a pretty good base-runner, and I wouldn't hesitate to run. But that was all part of baseball. I loved it."

Spahn's love for baseball began to develop at an early age. Growing up in Buffalo, New York, he began playing as a six-year-old in grade school. Later, he played in local sandlot leagues, mostly as a first baseman or outfielder.

"When I went to high school, the kid who was playing first was on the city all-star team. Now, I'm not going to compete with him, but they needed some pitching. That's when I started to pitch."

As a youth Spahn listened to Mel Allen doing Yankees games on the radio. His idol was Lou Gehrig.

Even when he was a kid, Spahn had that big, fluid motion that later virtually became his trademark. "It came pretty naturally to me," Spahn recalls. "My father instilled the idea of having a delivery in which you used your whole body to throw. He was 5-7, 130 pounds. We played on the same team at one point. He always emphasized that if you use your body and be smooth, you're not going to hurt your arm.

"I was a pretty big guy, and I tried to get all the momentum I could in going to the plate. Hitters used to complain about the ball coming out of my uniform because I threw over the top. I guess I released the ball late.

"The high kick and the fact that I threw my glove way up and the ball came out from behind my glove were all plusses for me. They were not for show. They just came normally and were part of my success. And when the hitters would tell me that they had trouble with my delivery, I worked even harder on it."

As a teenage pitcher, Spahn attracted the attention of a Boston Braves scout. "Nobody else had shown any interest in me," Spahn remembers, "so

I signed [for $80 a month] with the Braves. I thought I had a chance to play in the big leagues quicker, which turned out to be true. But after I signed, I had about 10 offers. I had an offer from the Yankees and one from the Phillies. But I'd already signed, so it didn't make any difference.

"I had a scholarship offer to Cornell, but my parents couldn't afford to send me there. They didn't have full scholarships in those days. Besides, I don't know if I could have made it through college."

So, joining the Braves' system as a 19-year-old in 1940, Spahn was sent to Class D ball at Bradford (Pa.) in the Pony League. After posting a 5–4 record, he was promoted the following season to Class B Evansville (Ind.) of the Three-I League, where he went 19–6. A record of 17–12 the next year at Class A Hartford of the Eastern League earned Warren a trip to the Braves at the end of the 1942 season.

"I pitched in four games in relief that season," Spahn recalls. "In one of those games, I was pitching to the Mad Russian, Lou Novikoff of the Cubs. I was always taught that if you get two strikes on a hitter, you waste a pitch. I threw two fastballs that Novikoff missed. On the next pitch, I wanted to get the ball up and in, but I got it out over the plate. Novikoff hit a line drive between my legs. I said to myself, 'Holy Cow, if they hit like this in the big leagues, I don't belong here.' What I didn't realize was that Novikoff [a notorious bad-ball hitter] couldn't hit a strike.

"Then I pitched in a game in the Polo Grounds. This was during World War II when kids got into the ballpark if they brought a certain number of pounds of scrap iron. At first, all these kids were in the upper deck. Then in the seventh inning, they came down to the lower deck. Then they came out on the field. They announced over the loudspeaker that the kids had to get off the field or they'd forfeit the game. There must have been 20,000 people on that field. They forfeited the game, and the Braves won, 9–0. All the records counted except the pitcher's records. I was the pitcher of record, which would've given me my first victory, had it not been for the forfeit."

After the 1942 season, Spahn entered the Army. Trained as a combat engineer, he was slightly wounded while working on the Ludendorf Bridge during heavy fighting along the Rhine. Staff Sergeant Spahn was given a battlefield commission as a second lieutenant, the only major leaguer ever to win such an honor. It would not be until 1946, when he was 25 years old, that he saw another big league diamond.

Warren shook off the rust of three years of baseball inactivity and established himself as one of the league's top rookies as he registered an 8–5 record with a 2.94 ERA.

"I remember my first complete game," Spahn says. "It came in Pittsburgh. I had a shutout going into the ninth inning. Frankie Gustine hit a home run off me, but we won, I think, by a 7–1 score."

Although he flashed signs of brilliance, Spahn had no inkling of what was to come. "You have dreams," he says, "but I don't think anyone could've written the script to make it come out as it did with me. In the beginning, I didn't know how good I was. I idolized those guys I pitched against.

"Probably my time in the service helped me because I grew up and began to realize that those guys put their pants on the same way I did. I was pitching against the Cubs with all those great guys—Phil Cavarretta, Billy Herman, all those people—and they were legends in my eyes. Pretty soon, I found out that they popped up and they struck out. They had weaknesses.

"I think I built confidence as I went along. Whether I started to believe in myself first or whether I found out that they were human beings first is a question. But pretty soon, I was an adult playing an adult game."

Spahn's conversion from a rookie with enormous potential to an established star was swift. In 1947, he became a 20-game winner, posting a 21–10 mark while leading the league in ERA (2.33), shutouts (seven), and innings pitched (289.2).

"What happened between 1946 and 1947 was that I got a chance to go out there every fourth day," Spahn explains. "In '46, I came back and had an opportunity to start because Billy Southworth, our manager, had seen me before I went in the service. I felt, I can't blow this because I might not get another chance. But I wasn't used in the regular rotation until '47. Then the pieces started to fall into place.

"Everything is trial and error. I guess I learned about moving the ball around the strike zone, pitching in, pitching out, changing speeds and so forth. Eventually, you get the feeling of, 'By Golly, I belong.'

"In 1946, I had won my first five starts. But I was going through a transition period. I had waited a lot of years to get married, and I finally did that season. But I didn't have a penny. I hadn't made any money while I was playing before the war, and certainly people in the military didn't make any money, so this was my first opportunity to make a decent salary. I think I got

$500 a month in '46. Then I won 21 in '47, so I made $21,000 the following year."

The Braves won the pennant in 1948. Although Spahn's record slipped to 15–12, he and Sain—a 24-game winner—gave Boston a strong one-two punch that, because the club had little else in the way of starting pitching (with the exception of Vern Bickford), led to what would become the familiar refrain, "Spahn and Sain and pray for rain."

"The '48 club was a conglomeration of Peck's bad boys," Spahn chuckles. "We had Bob Elliott, who came from Pittsburgh. They had gotten rid of him because he wanted to unionize the Pirates. Then we had a catcher named Bill Salkeld. We had the big guy [Jeff Heath] from the Cleveland Indians, who had trouble with Bill Veeck, and we had a bunch of ex-Cardinals. They called us the Back Bay Cardinals because Southworth had brought a lot of them over after they had become passé in St. Louis.

"We had a lot of people who didn't get along at various places they had played. Nelson Potter was a pitcher who did a great job for us in relief. He was a castoff from the St. Louis Browns and Philadelphia A's.

"We also had a nucleus of young people, guys like Al Dark, Earl Torgeson, myself, to go along with veterans like Eddie Stanky, Tommy Holmes, and Phil Masi. It was a sprinkling of young people juicing up the old people. Of course, that ball club disintegrated in 1949 and 1950 when we started a youth movement."

After winning the 1948 pennant by six and one-half games over the second-place Cardinals, the Braves bowed to the Indians in a thrilling World Series, four games to three. Spahn pitched in three games, losing the second game, 4–1, winning the fifth game with five and two-thirds innings of sparkling, one-hit, seven-strikeout relief, 11–5, and coming in from the bullpen and getting no decision in the final game.

Spahn won 64 games over the next three years, but the winds of change were blowing in Boston. A group of outstanding young players was joining the team, but a move for the team was becoming imminent. In 1953, the Braves became the first major league franchise to switch cities since the early part of the century, moving to Milwaukee.

"Personally, I was sorry to move because I had just opened a diner in Boston," Spahn says. "That franchise had been in Boston since the 1800s, and there wasn't any good reason it had to move. The whole move was premature.

"But there was a great friendship between Fred Miller of Miller Brewing Co. and Lou Perini, owner of the Braves. Miller underwrote the move to Milwaukee and guaranteed Perini 850,000 people, whereas we had drawn just 280,000 the last year in Boston.

"Miller wanted Perini to bring the Braves to Milwaukee because Bill Veeck was trying to move the St. Louis Browns there, and he didn't want that. The Braves had territorial rights because Milwaukee was our Triple-A club. I think that Miller would've been the owner of the Braves if he hadn't gotten killed in a plane crash."

With the Braves drawing 1.8 million, Spahn had probably his best all-around season in their first year in Milwaukee. He won the club's home opener, beating the Cardinals, 3–2. That year, he went 23–7 and led the league with a 2.10 ERA. In the nine seasons from 1953 through 1961, he won 20 or more games eight times.

The Braves won the pennant in 1957 and 1958. They faced the New York Yankees both times in the World Series, winning the first time in seven games and losing the following season after jumping to a three-games-to-one advantage.

While Burdette won three games in the 1957 Series, Cy Young winner Spahn was 1–1, losing the opener, 3–1, before going the distance to win the fourth game in 10 innings, 7–5. In 1958, he won the opening game, 4–3, pitched a two-hitter for a 3–0 victory in the fourth game, and lost the sixth game by a 4–3 margin.

"The '57 club was by far the best of the three Braves pennant winners I played on," says Spahn, who won 21 games in 1957 and 22 in 1958. "Not only was it a great ball club talent-wise, but those teams of ours back then had real charisma. And there was a pride and a confidence.

"We had a bunch of hell-raising guys in the clubhouse, but when the ball club went on the field, it was all business. If one guy got into a fight, everybody fought. There was that kind of camaraderie.

"We had guys who came from other ball clubs, and management never had to get on their butts about hustling. The players got on them. They'd say, 'Hey, look, you might have done it that way where you played before, but this is the way we do it here.' We demanded from each other.

"We also had a quiet confidence that we were going to beat anyone we went up against. And with guys like Hank Aaron, Eddie Mathews, Joe

Adcock, Johnny Logan, Red Schoendienst, Billy Bruton, and Del Crandall, we usually beat them, too."

The Braves never won another pennant, but Spahn kept rolling along. One thing still eluded him, though—a no-hitter. But, finally, in 1960, Warren pitched his first no-hitter, blanking the Phillies, 4–0. He struck out 15, including six straight, while walking two.

One year later, Spahn got another no-hitter, this time beating San Francisco, 1–0. He fanned nine and walked two. At age 40, Spahn was at the time the second-oldest player in baseball history to throw a no-hitter (Cy Young performed the feat at the age of 41, and Nolan Ryan did it in 1991 at age 44).

"That was the one I cherished most," Spahn says. "San Francisco had a great-hitting club with Willie Mays, Willie McCovey, and Orlando Cepeda. I had great stuff: excellent control and a good fastball and good screwball. It was one of those games when everything went easily. Sad Sam Jones was the opposing pitcher, and we scored the only run of the game on an unearned run in the first inning."

Long before he pitched his no-hitters, Spahn had made a major adjustment in his technique. He had changed from being a power pitcher to being an off-speed hurler, a move that helped prolong his career.

"When I came up, I was a fastball pitcher with a curve and a change-up," he recalls. "In the beginning, the fastball was always the barometer for every game I pitched. The hitter tells you the story. When you're throwing well, you're literally throwing the ball by the hitter. When they can't pull your fastball, you're throwing pretty well. But when they start hitting line drives, you know the ball's not moving. That was when I started playing around with the screwball.

"I particularly wanted the screwball to combat righthanded hitters. I found that it complemented the fastball and vice versa. On given days, I could throw the fastball as well as I ever did, but I didn't have to rely on it. I had weapons for both lefthanders and righthanders."

Spahn used these weapons to continue pitching well into his 40s. In 1963, at age 42, he rang up a 23–7 record with a 2.60 ERA and led the league in complete games with 22. It was the seventh straight year (and the 10th of 15 years) he had led the league in complete games.

The 6–0, 180-pound lefty, who during his career pitched 10 complete-game, 1–0 victories, hurled one more season with the Braves. He then was sold to the New York Mets. He wound up dividing the 1965 season between the Mets and Giants, then left the majors at the end of the year, having pitched past his 44th birthday and having won more games each year after turning 37 than any other pitcher at the same age level.

"The year 1965 wasn't a fun year," Spahn remembers. "But I still felt I could pitch. When I was with the Mets, we couldn't beat anybody. But I was bound and determined that I was going to show 'em.

"Success is built on failure. To be a good winner, you have to be a loser. I didn't say a good loser. I'm saying you have to suffer defeat, and that makes you stronger.

"When you stop and think about it, you notice that baseball is a game of failure. Ted Williams hit .406 one year, but that means he failed 59 percent of the time. The one who survives in baseball or who does it better than the other guy is the one who comes out on top.

"I always felt that some people mature older than others. I was one of those people. Because of the time I spent in the service, I had a better perspective of what this game was all about.

"So your vision becomes stronger when you're in jeopardy, and you find out that the human animal is pretty strong and determined. It's like the animal that is hunted in the wild. It's survival. I felt like that during my baseball career. And no writer was going to write my epitaph. I was a different breed.

"But I guess it did become harder. I suffered a couple of leg injuries, and maybe I pitched too long. But if I hadn't pitched until I was at least 40, I wouldn't have accomplished a lot of the things I did."

Spahn's biggest accomplishment came eight years after his major league career ended. In 1973, he was inducted into the Hall of Fame. "That was one of those great moments because your career is over, your credentials are out there for your peers. And then they vote that you are one of those very rare people who played baseball and made it to the top.

"A lump gets you right here," he says, gesturing toward his throat. "There have been many thousands of people who have played in the big leagues, and less than 300 have been elected to the Hall of Fame. And you're one of them. Wow! It's a fantastic feeling.

"I go back every year to the inductions. I feel like I owe something to baseball. I go to see the guys get inducted. Plus, I love that golf course."

After his retirement as a player (he pitched briefly in 1966 in Mexico and in 1967 in Tulsa), Spahn spent a number of years still involved in baseball. He managed the Cardinals' Triple-A farm team at Tulsa for five years, winning a league championship and finishing second twice. He then served as pitching coach for the Cleveland Indians for two seasons, was a minor league pitching instructor for the California Angels, and spent five years in Japan as a spring training pitching instructor.

"In 1981, I got tired of riding funny little airplanes and got out of baseball," Spahn says. Eventually, he wound up doing public relations and fundraising work for a number of major organizations and companies.

In recent years, Spahn has spent much of his time running his 2,800-acre ranch in Oklahoma, where 500 head of cattle graze. Spahn bought it in 1948 after deciding that he had had enough of the cold winters in Buffalo.

"I worked on the ranch in the off-season throughout my playing career," he says. "I went to spring training in good shape. I was never overweight. I was able to get in pitching shape in two weeks, while it took everybody else six weeks.

"I always wanted to pitch nine innings before we left spring training because I figured if I could go nine innings in Florida, I sure as hell could go nine innings in Boston.

"That was the kind of tenacity that I think you have to have. And you have to have a love for the game. I think Lou Brock put it best. He said, 'You have to have a love affair with the game.' That doesn't mean a big contract. It doesn't mean anything other than a kid with a taped bat and a taped baseball playing because he likes to play.

"I think that was true in my case. I wanted to get my contract signed and get that out of the way so I could go to work. I honestly felt that I didn't want the season to end. I always wanted it to go on forever."

It was this kind of love for the game, coupled with an abundance of talent and a fierce dedication to excel, that made Spahn a pitcher whose place in baseball history has been assured forever.

Unquestionably, he is in a class with the game's greatest legends.

Billy Williams

Sweet-Swinger Was a Hit in Chicago

BILLY WILLIAMS LIKES to tell the story about the time Hall of Famer Rogers Hornsby, in his capacity as the Chicago Cubs' hitting instructor, toured the country watching the team's minor league batters. At the time, Williams was a wide-eyed, young prospect in the Cubs' farm system. Hornsby, of course, had been one of the greatest hitters ever to hoist a bat.

"He was a guy who really spoke his mind," recalls Williams. "This particular season, he went around to see all the minor league teams, and then he came back to Chicago and said to John Holland, at the time the Cubs' general manager, 'You have two players in your system, Billy Williams and Ron Santo, who can hit big league pitching. You could release everybody else and bring the two of them up right now.'"

While that pronouncement didn't say much for the Cubs' farm system, it spoke volumes for the judgment of the astute Hornsby, as keen a student of the art of hitting as ever lived.

For his part, Williams went on to a spectacular career, toiling 18 seasons in the major leagues and gaining a reputation as one of the finest hitters of his era.

Rookie of the Year in 1961, a six-time National League All-Star and batting champion in 1972, the sweet-swinging Williams hit not only for average, he hit for power during a career spent mostly with the Cubs except for his final two seasons, which were with the Oakland A's.

It was a career that was culminated in 1987 when Billy was inducted into the Hall of Fame at Cooperstown, an event that gave the former outfielder the happiest moment of a life filled with happy moments.

"When they call your name, and you walk out to the podium, cold chills go through you like you wouldn't believe," says Williams. "And you get a lump in your throat. It's just so exciting that words can't describe it.

"Once you make the Hall of Fame, you become part of a group of some of the best players in the country," Williams adds. "You're in a special class. It makes you feel good. You get more calls on the telephone. You get more autograph requests. When you play in an old-timers game, even the other players want your autograph."

Williams had been a strong candidate for the baseball shrine for several years before his election took place. When the news came that he had finally made it, the Williams' household in suburban Chicago became the scene of a rollicking celebration that lasted well into the night.

"I got the call at about 9 P.M.," Williams remembers. "I had expected to get called, so there were a lot of people at the house, and there was a lot of excitement. It was a real good feeling.

"Actually, I wasn't surprised," Billy says about his election. "The only surprise to me was that I didn't go in the year before. I had wanted to go in with Willie McCovey in 1986. It would have been nice for two guys from Mobile, Alabama, to go in at the same time. But that didn't happen, so I was looking forward to going in the following year. When the call came, I was really happy.

"It really doesn't sink in, though, until you get to Cooperstown for the induction ceremony. When the van comes to the airport to take you to the hotel, then you get there and there's all that excitement, that's when you know it's really happened. There are all the people, and then they take you to the Museum, and all of a sudden it hits you and you say to yourself, 'Hey, I'm in a very special place.' It just gives you cold chills."

Cold chills were also what Williams gave opposing pitchers. In a career that stretched from 1959 to 1976 and included appearances in 2,488 games, Williams socked 426 home runs (24th on the all-time list) and batted .290. He laced 2,711 hits, including 434 doubles, drove in 1,475 runs, and scored 1,410 times.

Despite a lean, willowy physique, the 6-1, 175-pound lefthanded hitter could get plenty of muscle on the ball, as his 16 straight years of hitting home runs in double figures suggest. Billy had a career high 42 homers in 1970, and four other times he clouted more than 30 home runs in a season. He also hit two or more home runs in a game 31 times.

Williams had 200 or more hits in one season three times, leading the National League in 1970 with 205 safeties. He is only one of six National League players to have 200 hits and 40 home runs in one season. (The others are Hornsby twice, Chuck Klein twice, and Hank Aaron.)

Billy hit over .300 five times and only once as a regular hit below .270. He drove in more than 100 runs three times and scored more than 100 on five occasions.

Williams was known for his quick wrists, smooth swing, and calm demeanor at the plate. In confrontations with enemy hurlers he never panicked, and with a bat that moved like lightning he usually had the upper hand in the classic match-up of pitcher and batter.

"I had quickness of bat when I signed," Williams recalls. "When I was in the minors, Hornsby worked hours and hours with me. I can see him standing there with a bat in his hands. He emphasized knowing the strike zone.

"After I got to the big leagues, I got stronger. With a quick bat, I was able to read a pitch before I committed to it. I had time to learn what the pitch was before I had to swing the bat."

Williams was not only a splendid hitter, he was also a durable player who at one time held the National League record for playing in 1,117 straight games. Although the record was later broken by Steve Garvey, Williams' mark is still the fifth best in big league history, ranking behind Cal Ripken, Lou Gehrig, Everett Scott, and Garvey.

Billy was the first National League player to appear in 1,000 games in a row when he reached that plateau in 1970. Over a 10-year period between 1962 and 1971, he played in 1,614 games, missing just 10.

"Having the ability to be in the lineup was a key factor in playing all those games," says Williams, who played in more than 160 games eight years in a row. "Plus I had the strength and I was able to stay healthy. But it was tough playing in all that heat at Wrigley Field.

"When I first came to the Cubs, Bob Scheffing was the manager. He put me in the lineup, and I played about three weeks. Then one night at Connie Mack Stadium in Philadelphia, I went 0-for-4. I sat on the bench after the game trying to analyze what I was doing wrong. The next night, I was out of the lineup. I stayed on the bench for three weeks. I promised myself if I ever got back in the lineup, they would have to tear the uniform off me to get me out of there again.

"That kept me going. Once I got back in the lineup, I stayed. I just kept going as long as I could. In 1971, I finally took myself out of the lineup. I thought I could be a little more consistent if I took a rest once in a while."

When he was a youngster, growing up in Mobile with McCovey and the Aaron brothers, Williams had no idea his life would follow such a path. "I didn't ever think I'd make it to the major leagues," he says. "I used to see guys on TV, but I never thought one of them would someday be me. I never dreamed I'd become a major league player, much less a member of the Hall of Fame.

"My early idol," Williams continues, "was Duke Snider. As a kid, I used to listen to Brooklyn Dodgers games. When I was about 10 or 11 years old, I would go out and watch Hank Aaron play. Later, he and McCovey and I would work out together each winter to get ready for the next season."

Williams was originally signed in 1956 as a third baseman by Cubs scout Ivy Griffin, who spotted him playing semi-pro ball for the Mobile Black Bears. "One day we were playing, and a policeman came up to me and said, 'We've got a scout in the stands from the Chicago Cubs.' I thought he was there to look at Tommie Aaron. Luckily, I did something that day, and for the next two weeks he followed us all around.

"Finally, he approached my father, and asked if I wanted to play professional baseball. He asked my dad because I was still a kid. He was the first scout to approach me. When he offered me a contract, I didn't care who it was with. I just wanted to play, so I took it."

In midsummer at the age of 18, Williams was sent to Ponca City of the Class D Sooner State League. Installed in the outfield, he played in 13 games that season, then returned in 1957 and hit .310 with 17 home runs while leading the league in games and doubles.

Williams divided the 1958 season between Pueblo (Col.) of the Western League and Burlington (Iowa) of the Three-I League, hitting .304 with the latter. In 1959, he moved up to San Antonio of the Texas League, where he hit .318 and played some first base. Later in the season, he was promoted to Fort Worth of the American Association, then joined the Cubs, appearing in 18 September games.

"Going to Chicago, I was really scared," Williams recalls. "Here I was just 21 years old. I knew that if you weren't a good player, you didn't stay. I don't remember who we were playing, but I struck out my first time up."

After hitting .152 for the Cubs, Billy spent the 1960 season in Triple-A with Houston, hitting .323 with 26 home runs. At the end of the season, he rejoined the Cubs, this time to stay.

Williams had appeared in just 12 games in 1960 with the Cubs, hitting .277. He was still considered a rookie when he opened the 1961 season in left field under the Cubs' brief but radical system of rotating managers in which for two years eight different coaches took turns managing the team.

"The Cubs didn't have a left fielder at the time," says Williams. "But the people in Chicago believed in my talent, so I went to left field and wound up staying there the rest of my career."

Billy hit .278 with 25 home runs and 86 RBI. No Cubs rookie had ever hit as many home runs or driven in as many runs. At the end of the season, he was chosen the league's Rookie of the Year, the first Cub ever given the award.

The following season, Williams hit .298. He cracked the .300 barrier in 1964 with a .312 mark while hitting 33 home runs. In 1965, he hit .315 with 34 homers.

Williams had his best season up to that point in 1970 when he led the league with 205 hits and 137 runs while hitting .322 with career highs in home runs (42) and RBI (129).

Two years later, he led the league in hitting with a .333 mark and in slugging with a mark of .606 while blasting 37 homers and collecting 122 RBI. That year, *The Sporting News* named him the Major League Player of the Year.

Along the way, Williams had many other memorable achievements. There was the home run in the 1964 All-Star Game. He hit for the cycle in 1966. In 1968, he hit three home runs in one game against the New York Mets and five homers in two consecutive games to earn a share of a modern major league record.

In 1969, Williams hit four doubles in one game, and he drilled two doubles and two home runs—his team's only hits—in a 9–2 loss to the Pittsburgh Pirates. He scored five runs in one game in 1970. And in 1972, he had eight straight hits in a doubleheader with the Houston Astros.

"Overall the biggest thrill for me was just the consistency of play," Williams says. "It was a thrill to go out there day in and day out and do something you love.

"Of course, there were a lot of great moments," he adds. "Opening day games were particularly memorable. The ones you won always stand out."

Williams broke up four no-hitters, ones by Warren Spahn, Woodie Fryman, Steve Blass, and Phil Niekro. He tied a major league record for most times (nine) with 600 or more at-bats in a season, and he led the National League in total bases in 1968, 1970, and 1972.

On the Cubs' all-time list, Billy ranks second in extra-base hits, home runs, and total bases and third in RBI, hits, runs, at-bats, and games.

In most of those categories, he trails his illustrious contemporary, fellow Hall of Famer Ernie Banks. As teammates for much of their careers, Williams and Banks formed one of the great one-two power punches in National League history. Their 644 home runs from 1959 to 1971 rank as the fourth highest two-man total in the league.

Although Banks' huge presence often overshadowed the more reserved Williams, Billy has no regrets about the years they shared in Chicago. "We were always real good friends," he says. "Ernie was Ernie. People looked to him as Mr. Cub. They loved him. I had no problem with that. I just wanted to do my share, although I think that Santo, Fergy [Ferguson Jenkins], and myself didn't get the recognition we deserved."

Playing in Chicago had other disadvantages. Williams never played on a pennant-winning team. In fact, except for a six-year period from 1967 to 1972, most of the Cubs' teams on which he played were buried deep in the standings.

"We came close in 1969," Williams says, recalling the year in which the Cubs led much of the way before fading late in the season and finishing in second place, eight games behind the fast-closing Miracle Mets.

"Not going to a World Series has always stuck in my craw. It was a big letdown in 1969. If we had won that year, I think we could've won the pennant the next four or five years because we had a good club, and we just needed that first pennant under our belts. That was a tough year. A lot of guys carried big wounds for a long time after that.

"It was great playing in Wrigley Field, though," Williams adds. "It was a good hitters' park, and I enjoyed playing all day games there. I wasn't a night person. Wrigley is a small park, and the fans are right on top of you. But they know baseball. They're great fans."

When discussing the toughest pitchers he faced, Williams, a resident of Glen Ellyn, Illinois, has an unexpected choice.

"The normal Hall of Fame guys—Juan Marichal, Bob Gibson, and Sandy Koufax—were all tough," he says. "But one of the toughest for me was Ray Sadecki. When he first came to the Cardinals, he threw really well. He threw a lot of junk that always kept me off balance. I wanted guys to come at me hard. I liked to hit the fastball best, but I could read breaking balls pretty well, too."

Williams' career with the Cubs ended after the 1974 season, when he was traded to Oakland for pitchers Darold Knowles and Bob Locker and second baseman Manny Trillo. He stayed two seasons with the A's, hitting .244 for the AL West Division champs in 1975, then dropping to .211 in 1976 in a part-time role as a designated hitter.

Released after the season, Williams took a year off from baseball, then rejoined the Cubs, first as a batting instructor, then as a coach with the parent club. He left Chicago to join the A's as a coach from 1983 to 1985, then came back to the Cubs to spend a couple more years on the coaching lines.

Before returning to coaching with the Cubs for a third time in 1992—a spot he still occupies—the former slugger spent some time in the team's front office as director of the speakers' bureau. He coordinated the appearances of past and present Cubs players, handling as many as 10 to 15 requests each day.

Naturally, one of the most frequent requests his office handled was for a former player named Billy Williams.

Was it any wonder? After all, he was only one of the most popular players in Cubs history. One of the best, too.

2

Especially Noteworthy

Bobby Avila

First Hispanic Batting Champ

SECOND BASE IS often a position where good players come to roost. They are as good with the bat as they are with the glove, and over the years the position has spawned a goodly number of the game's top players.

During the 1950s, the major leagues were crammed with outstanding second basemen, not the least of whom was a flashy Mexican named Roberto Avila. He was not the first native of Mexico to play major league baseball, nor was he the last. But until Fernando Valenzuela came along, he was certainly the most successful.

The 5-10, 175-pound Avila was a smooth-fielding, fast-moving, solid-hitting athlete who played with a somewhat swashbuckling style. He spent most of his career with the Cleveland Indians, winning berths on three All-Star teams, helping the club to an American League pennant, and in 1954 becoming the eighth and last member of the Tribe and the first Hispanic player to win a batting championship.

And if that wasn't enough, Avila went on to an equally successful career in politics after his playing days ended. Bobby served two terms of three years each in Congress in Mexico, then was elected mayor of Veracruz, a resort city of more than one million people, for two terms. Later, he became supervisor of tax collection in Veracruz.

Avila has had a splendid run at life with his dual careers, a big family that includes four children and 10 grandchildren, and recognition as one of his country's leading citizens. "I enjoyed being in politics as much as I did being in baseball," he says. "I'm very happy with the way both careers turned out."

It was no accident that Avila got involved in government after his 11-year big league career had ended. "I always liked politics, and was always involved in politics in school and while playing baseball," Avila says. "I tried to help players. When I retired in 1959, I spent six months just playing golf. Then I was invited by my party [the PRI] to participate. After working for the party for a couple of years, I was invited to run for Congress."

After his political career, Avila and some others put up money to bring a Mexican League baseball team to Veracruz, a city that had had no professional baseball for more than one decade. Bobby was named president of the team and later served as president of the league before returning to the political arena.

"Baseball helped me in a lot of ways with politics," he says. "When you live with people so closely like you do in baseball, you learn how to deal with people. You learn what they're thinking about. You're always learning something."

Avila also learned at an early age that baseball was the sport for him. "I started as a pitcher when I was a little kid," he says. "As a pitcher, you play only every three or four days. I liked to play every day, so I switched to the infield.

"When I was 18, I became a professional player. I had gone to the university for one year—I wanted to be a lawyer. But I wanted to prove my ability as a baseball player. My father told me to forget about playing baseball.

"I told him that I would try it for two years, and if I couldn't make it, I'd go back to the university. I signed with Pueblo—it was in 1943—and I played in the summer in Mexico and in the winter in Cuba and Venezuela. Eventually, I was making such good money I didn't have to come to the U.S. to play."

The Mexican League was considered at that time an outlaw circuit by organized baseball in the United States, and U.S. players were forbidden to play in it. The league was heavily stocked not only with Latin Americans but also with some of the leading players from the Negro League in the United States.

"At that time," says Avila, "the Mexican League was real strong. So was the league in Cuba. The Cubans had a very good league, and Josh Gibson, Satchel Paige, Monte Irvin—players like that—played in that league during the off-season. Eventually [in 1946 when a handful of major leaguers from the U.S. jumped to the Mexican League], we had some pretty good players in Mexico, too. I played on the same team with Sal Maglie."

While he was playing in Cuba, Avila attracted the attention of U.S. scouts. Bobby was sought by a number of big league teams, each of which saw the lithe infielder as a youngster with exceptional promise, especially after he had led several different leagues in hitting.

"A lot of scouts tried to sign me, but I never agreed," Avila recalls. "I wanted a bonus, which is something players seldom got in those days. First, the [Boston] Braves, then the [Brooklyn] Dodgers, then the [Washington] Senators tried to sign me. Four or five clubs wanted me, but I wouldn't sign. Finally, Cleveland came along and offered me a $20,000, tax-free bonus. I signed."

Avila, then nearly 24 years old—although he was thought to be just under 22—spent his first year (1948) with Baltimore of the International League, by-passing all of the lower levels of the minors. He hit only .220 in 56 games, but the Indians saw enough to bring him to the big leagues the following year. In his first game, Avila remembers getting a pinch-hit single off Billy Pierce of the Chicago White Sox. More significantly, though, he had become only the fourth Mexican native to play in the big leagues (following the debuts of Mel Almada in 1933, Chile Gomez in 1935, and Jesse Flores in 1942).

Avila's ascent to the big leagues launched a career that would run through 1959, when Bobby retired after spending that season with three teams—the Baltimore Orioles, Boston Red Sox, and Milwaukee Braves.

Over those years, Avila established himself as an excellent big league second baseman. He led American League second sackers in fielding percentage in 1953 and twice led his peers in assists as well as in errors. With Cleveland, he had a .978 lifetime fielding percentage.

Avila was also a fine hitter, who finished with a lifetime batting average of .281. In exactly 1,300 games, he had 1,296 hits, including 185 doubles, 35 triples, and 80 home runs. He drove in 465 and scored 725.

"Hitting was real important, and I loved to hit," Avila says. "But a lot of other things in baseball are important, too. You see a guy go 4-for-4 and sometimes that doesn't mean a thing. A lot has to do with what else he can do and what kind of guy he is.

"I loved the game. And I was real honest on my job. I gave 100 percent. Nobody could ever say they saw Bobby Avila drunk or playing around. I was honest about my career, and I gave it everything I had."

When Avila arrived in Cleveland in 1949, power-hitting Joe Gordon was the club's regular second baseman. Bobby had to wait until Gordon stepped aside, which came during the later part of the 1950 season.

Avila had appeared in just 31 games and hit a meager .214 in his rookie year. In 1950, however, he got into 80 games and hit .299. "Gordon got hurt during the season, and I went in," Avila recalls. "He was a great second baseman. There was a lot of pressure on me in the beginning."

Roberto became the Indians' full-time second baseman in 1951. Over the next three years leading up to his batting title, he hit .304, .300, and .286.

In 1951, he had his greatest day with the bat, slugging a single, a double, and three home runs in an Indians 14–8 pasting of the Red Sox. "The game was at Fenway Park," Avila remembers. "I got the hits off five different pitchers."

One year later, he scored 102 runs and led the league in triples with 11. That season, he also tied an American League record when he registered 13 assists in one (19-inning) game. "I was hoping everybody would hit the ball to me that day," Avila recalls. "I had three or four hard plays.

"The Indians back then had a real good team," Avila adds. "When I first came up, they had some great ballplayers—Mickey Vernon was a real good hitter; Jim Hegan was one of the best catchers in baseball. Lou Boudreau was the manager. He was pretty smart, but he didn't get along well with the players. He didn't talk too much to the players because he was busy playing himself.

"Then Al Lopez took over, and he was a real good manager. I loved playing for him. He was very smart, and he didn't play every game like it was the World Series, like a lot of managers do. He played like you have 154 games to play.

"The competition was about as good as it ever was," Avila adds. "There was real good pitching. Whitey Ford was the toughest for me to hit. I just couldn't hit him. He threw me high curveballs. I didn't really have trouble with too many other pitchers."

The year 1954 was special not only for Avila but for the whole Indians team. It was the last time that Cleveland won a pennant until 1995.

Bobby ran away with the batting title, hitting a glittering .341 to finish ahead of second-place Minnie Minoso of the White Sox by 21 points. Avila was third in the league in hits with 189, 12 behind co-leaders, Nellie Fox and Harvey Kuenn. Bobby also had a career-high 15 home runs, 112 runs scored, and 67 RBI.

"I was a slow starter every year, but that year I had a pretty good start," says Avila. "In June, though, Hank Bauer slid into second and broke my thumb. I was hitting .396 at the time. I stopped playing for three days, then Lopez came to me and said, 'Bobby, you've got to play.' I returned to the lineup, and my batting average dropped to .307. I couldn't swing a bat. But my thumb finally healed, and my average went back up.

"It was just one of those seasons that's hard to explain. I started to hit well early, and once you're hitting well, you build confidence. I felt like I could hit anybody.

"I was a pull hitter, and I liked the ball inside. I liked to hit the breaking ball. I always found the hardest pitch to hit was a fastball. But that season, everything just seemed to go right."

At the end of the season, *The Sporting News* named Avila the Outstanding Player in the American League and the major league All-Star second baseman.

To sweeten the pot even more, the Indians ran away with the American League pennant, winning a league record III games while finishing eight games ahead of the second-place New York Yankees, winners of 103 games. The Tribe's record stood until the Yanks broke it in 1998.

"Usually, the Yankees were a little better than us, mostly because they had a real great bench," Avila says. "But that year, we had the best team I ever saw. We had good hitting, good pitching. We must have averaged four or five runs per game. We had two pitchers [Bob Lemon and Early Wynn] who won 23 games and one [Mike Garcia] who won 19. It was just a great ball club."

As often happens, however, great ball clubs have a way of fading in the World Series. The Indians certainly did, losing in four straight to the New York Giants in a shocking upset.

"It was just one of those things where everything they did went right, and everything we did went wrong," Avila remembers. "In a short series, anyone can win. I think we had a little letdown after the regular season. And [Willie] Mays made that great catch [on a 460-foot drive to deep center by Vic Wertz with two men on base and the score tied, 2–2, in the eighth inning of the first game]. That changed the whole Series around."

Also figuring into the outcome, of course, were the batting heroics of Dusty Rhodes. The Giants' pinch-hitter slugged two home runs and drove in seven while delivering key hits in the first three games.

The Indians could do no more than to finish second in each of the next two seasons, and Avila's career had hit its peak in 1954, too. He slipped to .272 in 1955, although he was named to his third American League All-Star team. He had also been named to the squad in 1952 and 1954, a year in which he went 3-for-3 and drove in two runs in the American League's 11–9 victory at Cleveland's Municipal Stadium. "Playing in the All-Star games was always very special," says Avila. "It was an important game for me.

"Every game was important to me, though," adds Avila, a scrappy player who often tried to kick the ball out of opposing fielders' gloves while sliding into second base—a trick that frequently inspired opponents to slide hard into Bobby when he was covering the bag.

"I always played hard. Sometimes, I got in a little trouble because I played hard. But before I played baseball, I played soccer, and that taught me to play hard. Sometimes, because I did play hard, guys would try to slide into me at second. But I accepted that as part of the game."

Avila, also an adept bunter, slumped to .224 in 1956. But he bounced back to .268 and .253 over the next two years. On December 2, 1958, however, the Indians traded him to Baltimore for pitcher Russ Heman and $30,000.

"I would have liked to have stayed in Cleveland, but I'm a professional. I would have played in China if they'd paid me," Avila says. "So I went to Baltimore, and got a raise."

Bobby played in just 20 games in Baltimore before getting sold to the Red Sox. He appeared in 22 games in Boston, then was sold to Milwaukee where he finished the season, playing in 51 games. Overall, Avila hit .227 for the season.

"The Braves needed a second baseman because Red Schoendienst had come down with tuberculosis," Avila recalls. "The Braves owner, Lou Perini, knew the Red Sox owner, Tom Yawkey, so they made a deal for me. I'll never forget that season. We tied with the Dodgers for the pennant, then lost in a special [best-of-three] playoff. We lost both games, including the second one, 6–5, after leading in the ninth, 5–2."

Avila was set to return the following season to Milwaukee, but it didn't happen as planned. "Two weeks before the '59 season ended, the general manager, John Quinn, called me into the office and offered me a $10,000 raise for the next year," Avila says. "I told him I would wait to sign until the winter. That winter, he sent me a contract with a $10,000 cut. I told him he was crazy. I didn't want to play for that kind of money, so I asked for my release. They wouldn't give it to me, so I retired. I was 35. I could have played another four or five years."

Instead, Avila returned to Mexico, and soon plunged into a new career. Mexico's most prominent baseball player became one of the country's most prominent politicians.

For a while, though, especially during a 10-year detour through Cleveland, he was also one of the most prominent second basemen in the United States.

Lou Brissie

War Hero Came Back to Pitch

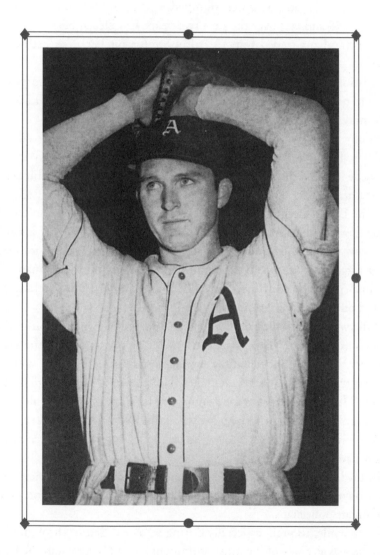

BASEBALL HISTORY IS filled with examples of men who overcame huge obstacles to play the national pastime.

Some were required to surmount serious injuries or illnesses, others had to hurdle the effects of accidents, and still others needed to prevail over some form of personal tragedy.

Names such as Monte Stratton, Art Houtteman, Eddie Waitkus, Herb Score, Jimmy Piersall, Ron LeFlore, and Jim Abbott come quickly to mind. All had serious roadblocks tossed in their paths. And all, to varying degrees, overcame them. To that list most definitely belongs the name of Lou Brissie.

A lefthanded pitcher who did his best work with the Philadelphia A's during a seven-year career that wound up with the Cleveland Indians, Brissie made the major leagues despite a shattered leg that had nearly been blown off during World War II.

Brissie, whose real first name is Leland, not only survived that injury, which required 23 operations and earned for him two Purple Hearts and a Bronze Star, he came back to win 30 games over a two-year period in the big leagues and at one point was considered one of the top southpaws in the American League.

The 6-4½, 210-pound native of Anderson, South Carolina, enjoyed an even more productive career since retiring from baseball after the 1953 season. He was the national director of the American Legion baseball program, a lobbyist in Washington, D.C., and in recent years one of the driving forces behind the movement to get Shoeless Joe Jackson reinstated in baseball and placed in the Hall of Fame.

Brissie can certainly empathize with a case as long on odds as Jackson's. Lou was a huge underdog himself after his promising pitching career was nearly dashed on a battlefield in the Appennine Mountains near Florence, Italy, while he was serving with the 351st Infantry.

"I had enlisted in December 1942," the soft-spoken ex-pitcher relates. "In December 1944, I was hit with shell fire. Our unit had been on the line, but they pulled us off one night and took us back to get a hot shower and breakfast. On the way back to the front, German artillery shells started landing a couple of hundred yards out. We had to get everybody out of the truck. I yelled to the guys to jump back, and as I did, a shell landed nearby. If I had been six feet back, it would have killed me."

As it was, the shell broke Brissie's feet and shattered his left leg, which was split open from the ankle to the knee. Also hit in the right shoulder with mortar fragments, he had to crawl for cover through the mud and in the process bacteria lodged in the wound.

Rushed to a field hospital, Brissie was given emergency treatment. What followed was an odyssey that would take him to scores of hospitals in Europe and the United States. It took 23 operations to piece his leg back together.

"A Major Brubaker saved my leg," Brissie says. "I'll never be able to thank him enough. He wired some bone fragments back into my leg. There were some empty spots in my leg, and he just let the bones grow back together. Basically, what he did was reconstruct my leg with wire.

"After he told me I was going to be okay, I felt it was just a matter of time before I got back on my feet. But I wound up going to hospitals all over. I was the first guy in the Mediterranean Theater who was put on penicillin therapy. I even smelled like penicillin, I had so much of it."

After returning to the United States, Brissie finally got out of the hospital in August 1945 and visited Philadelphia in September to check in with the team that had originally signed him in 1942.

"I told Mr. [Connie] Mack that I felt I'd be ready for spring training in 1947," Brissie says. "I just wanted to let him know I was okay." That, of course, was a big concern of the A's. In 1942, they had gone to great lengths to sign the strapping lefthander, sweetening the pot to get him.

"Chick Galloway, an old shortstop [primarily in the 1920s with the A's], had brought me to Philadelphia in 1941, the day I finished high school," Brissie remembers. "I met Mr. Mack, and agreed to sign with him. At that time, I played first base as much as I pitched, and I signed as both.

"I wanted to go to college, so Mr. Mack gave me three options. I could go to Duke where his old pitcher, Jack Coombs, was the coach. I could go to Holy Cross where his old shortstop, Jack Barry, was the coach. Or I could go to Presbyterian College where Galloway was the coach. I chose Presbyterian, and Mr. Mack sent me there for two years."

By then, Lou had become one of the most talked-about players in South Carolina. He had cut his teeth on the sandlots of Greenville, which were filled with outstanding local players. "In my time, they had textile leagues down south," Brissie recalls. "I started playing textile ball when I was 13.

"We didn't have big league idols. Our heroes were guys who played textile ball, although I was a great Detroit Tigers fan when I was growing up.

I remember their 1935 team that won the World Series. I don't know why I liked them. It just seemed like my kind of club."

Philadelphia, though, was where Brissie was headed, and he was scheduled to report to the A's for spring training in 1943. The war intervened, and Lou didn't get to his first spring training until 1947.

"On the way north after spring training ended that year," Brissie recalls, "the A's dropped me off in Savannah where they had a farm club. I wound up spending my first year in pro ball there."

It was some year. Lou posted a 23–5 record with a 1.19 ERA. He struck out 278 in 254 innings and gave up just 167 hits. Brissie led the South Atlantic League in wins, ERA, and strikeouts.

Osteomyelitis had settled into Brissie's leg, however, and it would give him trouble the rest of his career. "It's a bacterial infection of the bone marrow," Brissie explains. "If it gets into the blood, it can kill you. But I was always able to control it with antibiotics.

"Savannah," he adds, "was a very profitable year. I had something there that I never had in baseball, and I think it made a big difference. They told me I was going to pitch every fourth day, and sometimes I was used in relief on the third day. That way, I stayed in shape. I couldn't run well because of my leg, but pitching that much I didn't need to run."

The A's brought up Brissie at the end of the 1947 season. He started the only game in which he pitched. "It was in Yankee Stadium on the first Babe Ruth Day," Lou recalls. "Honus Wagner, Ty Cobb, Tris Speaker—all the great players I had read about—were there. You talk about a guy not being in the real world. I thought I'd died and gone to heaven. I lost the game, 5–2, but it was a great occasion."

The following spring, Brissie was back in training camp with the A's. This time, he not only made the club, he was a starter on opening day.

"We were in Boston," Lou remembers. "They opened the season with a Patriots Day doubleheader, playing both a morning and an afternoon game. Phil Marchildon pitched the first game. I was told to come to the park at 12:30 because the first game started at 10 A.M. I couldn't wait to get there, so I went to the park early. They wouldn't let me in the pass gate. I had to get somebody to let me in. As I walked in, I heard the fans cheering. The Red Sox had hit three straight home runs. That didn't do a whole lot for my self-assuredness, but it was a banner day."

Brissie pitched a sparkling four-hitter to beat the mighty Red Sox, 4–2, even though in the seventh inning Ted Williams lined a drive off Lou's bad leg, sending him crashing heavily to the ground. As he lay in agony on the field, surrounded by worried players and coaches, Brissie looked up and saw a distraught Williams—himself a war hero—anxiously peering down at him. "For Chrissakes, Williams, pull the damn ball," Brissie barked. Eventually, Lou arose, and after a few tentative warmup pitches, completed not only the inning but the game.

Lou had many other banner days in 1948. While the A's made a solid run at the American League pennant, even holding down first place in mid-August before finally finishing fourth, Brissie had a 14–10 record. Owner of a crackling fastball, a sharp curve, and a deceptive change-up, he was fourth in the league in strikeouts with 127 while working in 39 games.

"I worked awful hard to get to that point," Brissie remembers. "I had a lot of therapy. I did a lot of walking. My leg was wired together, and part of my ankle was gone—even today it bends only 30 percent of what it should.

"The injury changed my pitching style. I couldn't throw as hard or with as much control as I did before. I threw stiff-legged. But I just tried to work around such things. Some days I hurt and some days I didn't. You just have to make the adjustment. It was kind of like going to the office. Some days you don't feel like doing it, but you do it anyway.

"I never thought much about the season," Brissie adds. "I just looked at it day to day. I knew I was realizing a dream that I had for a long time. And I enjoyed every minute of it.

"It was especially enjoyable playing for those A's teams back in the late 1940s," Brissie says. "We had a pretty good pitching staff with Marchildon, Dick Fowler, Joe Coleman, Bill McCahan, Carl Scheib, and later Alex Kellner and Bobby Shantz.

"We were a club that enjoyed playing together. We had a lot of fun and a lot of togetherness. All of us believed we could win. Mr. Mack called it the finest club he ever had from the standpoint of giving effort. If you took us position by position, very few people would pick us. But as a group, we did very well together."

While the 1948 A's finished fourth, 12½ games behind the Cleveland Indians, who won the pennant in a one-game playoff with the Red Sox, the 1949 A's figured to be just as good. Instead, they wound up fifth, this time 16 games behind the front-running Yankees.

Brissie, however, had another splendid season, although he missed most of September when the osteomyelitis flared up in his leg. Not only did he carve out a 16–11 record, he was named to the American League All-Star team. Lou pitched the middle three innings, giving up five hits, including a two-run homer to Ralph Kiner, in his team's 11–7 victory over the National League at Ebbets Field.

"I was like a kid in a candy shop, just sitting on the bench with all those guys like Ted Williams, Lou Boudreau, and Joe DiMaggio," Brissie says. "To pitch in the game was an added thrill."

Pitching against Williams, DiMaggio, and the other great stars of the league was also a special thrill for Brissie, who worked with a protective guard over the lower part of his left leg. "It was always tough pitching to them," he says. "But the big mistake you had to guard against with them was letting guys batting in front of them get on base.

"I seemed to do well against the better hitters," Brissie continues. "But I had trouble with some of the hitters who weren't as renowned. I remember Dave Philley was one of them.

"I didn't know as much about the game as some guys did," Brissie adds. "To me, pitching in the big leagues and against guys like Williams and DiMaggio was an awesome experience. But at the same time, after what I'd lived through and seen, I was just glad to be there. I figured I was the luckiest guy in the ballpark. I wasn't supposed to be there. I had rheumatic fever at the age of 10, and wasn't supposed to live to be 25. I carried two buckets of sand for two years so my arms could open up.

"I guess," he says, "a man who goes to war and sees what he sees learns something about life. I always felt thankful just to be around."

The 1950 A's were starting to show signs of deterioration. Coleman, Fowler, Marchildon, and McCahan were all lost with arm trouble. In Mack's final year as manager, the club finished a distant last, losing 102 games and ending up 46 games out of first place.

Brissie's season did not fare too well either. Although he appeared in more games (46), started more games (31), and had a better ERA (4.02) than he had in his previous two seasons in the majors, Lou's record slipped to 7–19 as the weak-hitting A's gave him little support. Lou led the A's staff in games pitched and innings (246). He also registered eight saves.

After 50 years as A's manager, Mack finally stepped down at the end of the season. The Philadelphia A's would never be the same.

"Mr. Mack was a very quiet person," Brissie says. "His coaches in later years took a lot of the detail work off of him. But he was an ideal modern manager. What do they teach you today? Hands off. Be low key. Develop your players' confidence. He would have been a great modern manager because he did all that."

The following season, Brissie was gone, too. On April 30, after he had appeared in two games with the A's, Lou became part of a mammoth three-team trade with Cleveland and the Chicago White Sox. The A's got outfielders Gus Zernial and Philley and two other players, while the Indians landed Brissie and the White Sox received outfielders Minnie Minoso and Paul Lehner.

"I really didn't want to go," says Brissie, who had become an enormously popular player in Philadelphia. "But the A's needed hitting, and Cleveland was looking for a lefthanded relief pitcher. I still wanted to start because if I was going to stay in shape, I needed to pitch. That's the only way I could stay in shape.

"But they didn't see any place they could use me in the starting rotation. They already had Bob Feller, Bob Lemon, Early Wynn, and Mike Garcia. Hank Greenberg, the general manager, said, 'We'll use you in relief, and you'll start once a week.' But it didn't work out that way."

Brissie wound up starting in just four of 54 games for the Indians, winning four and losing three (he had an overall 4–5 record for the season). In 1952, again in the same situation, Lou posted a 3–2 record while starting just one of 42 games.

With three members of both the '51 and '52 Indians' starting rotation winning 20 games, however, Brissie could at least take solace in the fact that he was a part of one of the greatest pitching staffs of all time.

In 1953, Brissie's playing time was drastically reduced. He appeared in just 16 games, all in relief, and had no decisions. "That fall," Brissie remembers, "the Indians sold me to Indianapolis. But I knew that the Baltimore Orioles had offered to trade for me. Greenberg wouldn't do it. So I said, 'I'm not going to play in Indianapolis. I've paid my dues, and I deserve the opportunity to stay in the big leagues.'" When Greenberg still refused to acquiesce, Brissie decided to pack it in.

"I had my day in the sun, and that was important," he says. "It was a big part of my life. Over the years I had a few good days. Opening day in 1948, the All-Star Game in 1949 were big thrills. I went 14 innings once at Yankee

Stadium and had to face Vic Raschi, Allie Reynolds, and Joe Page. We ended up losing, 2–1, but that was a game to remember.

"I also enjoyed playing at Shibe Park in Philadelphia all those years. I always had a special feeling about that place because it was the first big league park I ever saw. When I came up to visit in 1941, they took me to Shibe Park, and we saw Sugar Ray Robinson fight. We sat in the press box. It was not only the first fight I had ever seen, it was the highest I'd ever been.

"The outfield walls looked so big. They really impressed me. Shibe Park was really a very personal park. Everything was close. But I liked to pitch in it. If I had one complaint about it, it was that the ball carried too well. I liked to pitch in Yankee Stadium, too. If you had a good center fielder there, you could be a very successful pitcher."

After finishing his playing career, Brissie became national director of the American Legion baseball program, working first in Washington, D.C., then—ironically—in Indianapolis. He did that for eight years. Then, after working in industry for 15 years at the management level, he became a lobbyist in Washington, doing legislative work with the regulatory commission on the handling of chemicals.

In recent years Brissie resided in Augusta, Georgia, working for the State Board of Technical Education, an economic development group. He is now retired.

Lou has also been consumed with the effort of a group of South Carolinians to get one of baseball's all-time greatest hitters, Joe Jackson, back in the good graces of the game. Jackson, of course, was banished from baseball after being implicated in the Black Sox scandal of 1919.

"While growing up in Greenville [South Carolina], I was introduced by my uncle to Shoeless Joe when I was a young boy," Brissie says. "I never saw him play, but I used to visit with him all the time. We'd sit on his porch and talk baseball. He talked about his career a little and getting banned from baseball. I think by the time I got to know him, resignation had set in. He just sort of stayed in the background and ran a little liquor store.

"Now," Brissie adds, "I am working with a group to get him reinstated. The more I get into it and the more I see, regardless of what he and I talked about, the more doubts I have that the right thing was done, not only when he was banned, but when commissioner Bart Giamatti refused to reopen the case some years ago. Giamatti should have read more. He would have learned some things he didn't know.

"I have one position myself," adds Brissie. "You hear a lot of things about gambling, and it was prevalent in baseball in those days. But the guy was found innocent by a jury. I think you have to look at that first.

"Some things have never been explored. The age-old excuse is, 'Well, he took the money.' But he didn't take the money. He ran the guy [trying to give it to him] out of the room. The guy left the money on the bed, and Jackson took it to somebody with the club who refused to take it or even to talk to him about it.

"When I see the newspaper accounts of the 1919 World Series, I see what he did [led his team with a .375 batting average and six RBI, while playing errorless defense]. I don't see how you can come to the conclusion that he had any part of throwing the World Series."

Brissie and fellow members of the group conducting a campaign for Jackson aren't about to give up. Lou, of course, knows what it's like to wage an uphill fight.

He did it once himself. Did it quite successfully, too.

Jim Brosnan

Reliever Turned Best-Selling Author

IN THE OFTEN dim-witted world of major league baseball, most players have been content never to exceed the boundaries of their vapid surroundings. Jim Brosnan was different. Brosnan was a guy who took his intellect to a higher level.

It would have been enough that he was an outstanding relief pitcher, who was regarded as one of the premier closers of his day. But Brosnan also gained notoriety on a second front as a writer and best-selling author who pioneered an entirely new concept in baseball literature.

At a time when baseball had barely begun to unburden itself of some of its most primitive traits, Brosnan was the first player to provide a candid, factual representation of life in the big leagues. He did it in *The Long Season*, a lively book that discussed in intimate detail the behind-the-scenes behavior and activities of players and management during the 1959 season.

The notion that a player would write such a revealing book was revolutionary. It became a best-seller and changed forever the way baseball was viewed and written about.

From Brosnan's perspective, it not only changed the size of his bank account and made him a household name all across the country, it had a lasting effect on the way he pitched.

"I became a much better pitcher," he says. "Look at my statistics. They improved. I had to prove that I deserved to be there [as a pitcher]. Larry Jackson [a pitching contemporary] said, 'He's not good enough as a pitcher to write a book like that.' I had to prove that people like that were wrong."

It was not that difficult. Brosnan, who earlier in his career had been nicknamed "Professor" by his teammates because of his glasses, his frequent pipe and beret, and his voracious reading habits, was already a fine pitcher by the time the book came out in 1960. In 1961, he became even finer, realizing the best season of his career with a 10–4 record, 16 saves, and the win that gave his team—the Cincinnati Reds—the National League pennant.

Overall, the 6-4, 210-pound righthander pitched in nine seasons in the big leagues, compiling a career record of 55–47 in 385 games. Brosnan had 67 saves (computed later after the statistic became official) and an earned-run average of 3.54. In 831.1 innings pitched, he gave up 790 hits, struck out 507, and walked 312.

Brosnan played with the Chicago Cubs, St. Louis Cardinals, Reds, and

Chicago White Sox, his career reaching from 1954 to 1963. Although he was a starter throughout his minor league days—which began in 1947—and off and on during his early big league appearances, Brosnan eventually relieved in all but 47 of his major league games.

"Hutch [manager Fred Hutchinson under whom Jim played at St. Louis and Cincinnati] convinced me I should be a reliever," Brosnan says. "I had been starting and doing well, but I was only going seven, sometimes eight innings. I could never get through a whole game.

"Hutch was a guy who believed that you should finish what you start. He remembered me from the Pacific Coast League when he was managing in Seattle and I was pitching in Los Angeles as a seven-inning guy, but a guy who always pitched well the first three innings."

Although Brosnan had started 20 games in 1958 and 10 in 1959, the decision to make him a full-time reliever was made once and for all one night in 1960. The Reds had to finish a game that had previously been halted by a curfew, then play a full game afterward.

"I finished the first game with four pitches," Brosnan recalls. "Then I started the second game, but was knocked out. The next day, Hutch called me up to his room. He had a couple of bottles on the table, and offered me a drink. We talked for a couple of hours." By the time he left the room, Brosnan had become a full-time reliever.

"I was confident that Hutch knew what he was talking about," Brosnan says. "I was perfectly content to take on the role of a closer."

Even being in the big leagues at all was a reality far removed from Brosnan's boyhood intentions. "I had no thoughts as a kid of being a major league ballplayer," he says. "It never occurred to me. As a kid, I spent more time reading books than playing ball."

Even when he did play, Brosnan was mostly a shortstop. His primary success came when he played on an American Legion team in his native Cincinnati.

"I was the shortstop, but in American Legion ball, you usually need three or four pitchers," Brosnan says. "I could throw, so I pitched once in a while. When I pitched, Don Zimmer played shortstop. I had a strong arm. But I was gangly. I had bad hands and I couldn't hit well.

"We went to the American Legion playoffs in Charleston, South Carolina. We didn't win, but I pitched a couple of low-hit games. Tony Lucadello was a scout for the Cubs in Ohio, and he followed me down to Charleston. Afterward, he signed me. I knew hardly anything about pitching. He had to show me how to throw a curveball, and he introduced me to a change."

With some of his bonus money, Brosnan enrolled at Xavier University. After one semester, he left to go to spring training in St. Augustine, Florida, where the Cubs were holding camp for some 250 players, many of whom had recently returned from seeing action in World War II.

Brosnan spent his first pro season in 1947 with Elizabethtown of the Appalachian League and posted a 17–8 record with a 3.04 ERA while leading the league in games pitched (41) and innings (228).

What followed was an odyssey through the minors that over the next seven years included stops at Springfield, Massachusetts, Fayetteville, Macon, Nashville, Des Moines, Decatur, and Beaumont, with several stints at a few of them and two years out for military service.

In 1953, Brosnan's journey nearly came to an end after he went 4–17 in his second stint at Springfield, by then in the International League. "I was going to quit baseball," he says. "I started going to school. I was going to become an accountant."

But a contract arrived in the mail that winter, and Brosnan acquiesced to another baseball season. That spring, he went to training camp with the parent team.

"I saw that I wasn't capable of pitching in the big leagues," Jim says. "But I had a good spring. Actually, the Cubs' pitching staff was so bad they were looking everywhere for arms. I was sent back to the minors, but it turned out to be a good break for me."

After first going to Des Moines of the Western League, Brosnan landed with Beaumont of the Texas League. There, he wound up in the hands of a pair of crafty former major league players, a grizzled old pitcher named Max Lanier, who was still hanging on in pro ball, and catcher-manager Mickey Livingston, who had had a 10-year big league career as a backup catcher with six different teams.

The two gave Brosnan a master course in the subtle art of pitching. Especially significant were Lanier's teaching Jim how to throw a slider and Livingston helping to perfect it from his spot behind the plate.

After he went 7–1 in 13 games at Beaumont, the Cubs summoned Brosnan to Chicago. He pitched in 18 games, won one, and lost none, but he was hammered to the tune of a 9.45 ERA.

It was back to the minors in 1955. Shipped to Los Angeles of the Pacific Coast League, Brosnan had a banner season with a 17–10 record and a 2.38 ERA in 31 games. He came back to the Cubs the following year, and this time he was in the big leagues to stay.

Brosnan came up with a 5–9 log and a 3.79 ERA, starting 10 of the 30 games in which he appeared in 1956. He was 5–5, 3.38 in 41 games (five as a starter) in 1957. "The Cubs had four starters," Jim remembers. "I was the fifth starter, so I didn't get to start too much. I pitched a lot of relief."

Early in the 1958 season, with the Cubs in need of a third baseman, Brosnan was traded to the Cardinals for Alvin Dark. In St. Louis, he first came under the wing of the astute Hutchinson. Brosnan had an 8–4 record in 33 games with the Cardinals, giving him a mark of 11–8 with a 3.35 ERA for the season.

Late in the season, Hutchinson was fired. He was replaced by Stan Hack as an interim manager. The following year, Solly Hemus took over. "Hemus didn't want me on his ball club," Brosnan says.

Near midseason the following year, the Cardinals swapped Jim to the Reds for pitcher Hal Jeffcoat, a converted outfielder, in what St. Louis general manager Bing Devine later confided to Brosnan was the worst trade he ever made.

Brosnan flourished in Cincinnati. He registered an 8–3 mark the rest of the 1959 season (9–6 overall). In 1960, he was 7–2 with 12 saves and a sparkling 2.36 ERA in a career-high 57 games.

By then, he was becoming one of the premier closers in the National League, teaming with southpaw Bill Henry to give Cincinnati one of the league's first left-right bullpen combinations. Brosnan was now also staking a claim in the literary world.

His first published work had been a book review a few years earlier. Then in 1958, he had written two articles during the baseball season for *Sports Illustrated.*

After a third piece for *SI* had failed to materialize, Brosnan was attending a meeting in New York with the magazine's editors when one of them, Bob Boyle, suggested he visit a friend at Harper and Row, a book publisher.

"I went down the street, and 30 minutes later, I came out with a contract for a book," Brosnan relates. "They had seen the two pieces I had written for *Sports Illustrated,* which resulted from diaries I had kept, and they said, 'Could you do this for a whole season?' I said I could try. I kept a diary during spring training and then wrote about 25 pages. They said, 'Great, let's keep going.'"

During the regular season, Brosnan fastidiously recorded his observations and the comings and goings and conversation and activities of his teammates and opponents. Then he wrote about them, candidly and without sparing any details. The result was *The Long Season*.

"I didn't know whether Harper and Row would take it," Jim says. "There were some pretty spicy parts. They brought the lawyers in. We had some battles. Prior to this, baseball books had sold mostly to kids. They thought they would lose that market.

"But I had read all the baseball books and biographies about players from the time I was 10 years old. I didn't believe a word of it. I thought, this isn't the way it was. So, I was pretty frank. A few things got taken out, including the part I led off with that involved a situation in St. Louis."

What was left, though, was a brutally honest book that rocked the baseball world. And Brosnan became the darling of the literary set, not to mention a nationwide celebrity as the book leaped onto the best-seller list.

"I had always wanted a book with my name on it," he says. "When I was a kid, I spent a lot of time in the library. I wanted to see my own book in the library some day."

The Long Season was a courageous effort that had numerous personal repercussions for Brosnan. Many players turned against him. So did most of the baseball establishment, as well as some of the more Neanderthal thinkers among the press and fans.

Jim's pitching, though, just got better. In 1961, his 10–4 record, 16 saves, and glittering 3.04 ERA helped the Hutchinson-managed Reds to their first pennant since 1940. That season, Brosnan hurled the most memorable game of his career.

"We were playing the Cubs at Wrigley Field," he recalls. "I came in in the sixth inning, and got the win. I even drove in a run. That game gave us the pennant.

"Johnny Edwards was the catcher. He said, 'I never saw you throw the ball so hard in your life.' Billy Williams said the same thing later. I had struck out him and George Altman for the final two outs.

"I remember Jerry Lynch won the game with a home run. Before he went up to the plate, he said to me, 'I'm going to hit it out of the park. You hold it [the lead].'

"When we won, goose bumps broke out on my arms. Hutch came out and said to me, 'Why are you shivering?' I couldn't say anything."

The '61 Reds had the misfortune of clashing in the World Series with one of the greatest Yankees teams in New York's history. The Reds were no match for the mighty Yanks. Not only did they have future Hall of Famers Mickey Mantle, Yogi Berra, and Whitey Ford, it was also the year Roger Maris and Mantle waged a torrid home run duel that ended with the former breaking Babe Ruth's record with 61 round-trip clouts. New York won the Series in five games, although Mantle spent most of the time on the bench with an injury.

"That was a pretty darn good team," Brosnan says of the Yanks. "And we weren't playing well. The Yankees oozed confidence. We weren't in the same class." Brosnan pitched in relief in two games. He was tagged for nine hits and five runs in six innings.

The Reds came close to winning the pennant again in 1962, winning 98 games. But they finished three and one-half games out of first and in third place behind the San Francisco Giants and Los Angeles Dodgers, who finished the regular season tied for the lead. Brosnan had a 4–4 record with 13 saves and a 3.34 ERA in 48 games.

The following spring, Jim was traded to the White Sox for pitcher Dom Zanni. Hoyt Wilhelm was the main Chisox reliever, leaving Brosnan to work mostly in a setup role. Brosnan finished the season at 3–8 for the Sox. His overall mark was 3–9 with 14 saves and a 3.13 ERA.

"In the American League, I couldn't use the slider as effectively because the umpires wouldn't give you the low strike," he says.

That winter, Brosnan and the White Sox parted company. It would spell the end of Jim's baseball career.

"Bill DeWitt (Sox general manager) wanted to cut my salary 25 percent," Brosnan says. "And the White Sox said I couldn't write any more. Why? If I could fathom DeWitt's unfathomable mind, he was jealous that I was making money writing."

Brosnan thought he could connect with another National League team, possibly the New York Mets who were desperately in need of pitching. But it never happened. With team owners apparently unwilling to hire a player they perceived to be a rebel, Jim's career as a baseball player came to a sudden end, although he was just 34.

By then, however, Brosnan's writing career was prospering. His second book, *Pennant Race*, which tracked the 1961 season, had been published in 1962. He was also writing other magazine articles.

Eventually, Brosnan got involved in radio and television sportscasting in Chicago. Then, upon the recommendation of Howard Cosell, he became an ABC television correspondent.

Brosnan wrote and broadcast for the better part of the next three decades. He stopped going on the air in the mid-1980s but continued to write until the early 1990s. To date, he has written seven books, including five children's books, and more than 300 magazine articles, many over a 20-year period having appeared in *Boys' Life*. He has published in *Playboy, Life*, and many of the other leading periodicals in the country.

The Long Season is still in print. Since it was first published, it has sold about one-half million copies in hard and soft covers. Five editions have been printed.

In recent years, Brosnan has tapered off on his writing, preferring to spend much of his spare time reading. He's partial to crime books. But despite his literary success, he is still a ballplayer at heart.

How would he like to be thought of? "As a player who wrote," he says. "I think I was as good a pitcher as I could have been. I don't know if I wrote as well as I could have if I'd have had to make a living writing."

Actually, Brosnan probably had the best of both worlds. He was extremely good both as a pitcher and as a writer. And that put him in a class virtually by himself.

Chico Carrasquel

Starting a Trend in Shortstops

FOR 40 YEARS, the Chicago White Sox had a virtually unbroken succession of brilliant shortstops. Luke Appling began the sequence in the early 1930s. Luis Aparicio closed it out in the early 1970s.

In between those Hall of Famers was Chico Carrasquel, a marvelous fielder, an outstanding clutch hitter, and possibly one of the most popular players ever to take the field for the Pale Hose.

His friends in his native Caracas, Venezuela, called Carrasquel "The Big Cat." It was a tribute to the way the lithe shortstop roamed the infield, almost effortlessly pouncing on ground balls as though they were mice in a barn.

Carrasquel was the American League's starting shortstop in three All-Star games and a member of the AL team two other times. In an era in which outstanding shortstops were the rule rather than the exception, Chico topped the list when it came to wielding the leather, leading the league's shortstops in fielding three times. He had remarkably soft hands, the range of a guided missile, and a powerful throwing arm.

"I really loved to field," says Carrasquel. "In those days, every team had a real good shortstop. I had it in my mind that I wanted to be the best. I had to do everything right every day.

"To play shortstop," he adds, "you have to use your head. And you have to give something extra to be a good shortstop. When I started playing in 1946, I'd go to the ballpark at 5:30 every morning and have guys hit the ball to me. I was 16, 17 years old. Then I had to help clean up the ballpark. They called me crazy. But I loved it."

Carrasquel spent from 1950 through 1959 in the big leagues. He played for six of those years with the White Sox, then moved to the Cleveland Indians, and finished his career with the Kansas City A's and Baltimore Orioles.

No slouch at the plate, Chico had a lifetime batting average of .258, which included 1,199 hits in 4,644 trips to the plate. In 1,325 games, he had 55 home runs and 474 RBI, and he scored 568 times.

A 6-0, 170-pounder during his playing days, the still-trim Carrasquel remained very much a part of baseball long after he retired from the field. For most of the 1990s, he broadcast White Sox games on a Spanish-speaking radio station in Chicago. "There are over one million Hispanics living in the Chicago area," he points out.

While maintaining a home in both Chicago and Caracas, Chico spends his winters in Venezuela where he takes a special interest in the youngsters of the city. Every Saturday and Sunday during the off-season, he brings 150 boys 10 to 12 years old to his house where he feeds them lunch and tries to impress on them the need to stay out of trouble.

"They're little leaguers who I want to make sure live a clean life," Carrasquel says. "It's a different group each day. You have to talk to kids these days. I tell them to stay away from drugs. I tell them to be gentlemen. I show them my trophy room. We spend two to three hours each day. I don't get any help from anybody. I just do it myself."

Carrasquel realizes the benefits of strong, adult guidance. He certainly had plenty of it himself, especially from his uncle Alex Carrasquel, a pitcher who spent seven seasons between 1939 and 1945 in the big leagues with the Washington Senators and a brief time in 1949 with the White Sox.

"My uncle was a real big hero in Caracas," says Chico. "He used to tell me stories about Babe Ruth and Lou Gehrig. I decided I wanted to follow him to the big leagues. I asked him a lot of questions when I was a kid. He showed me how to do things. He really helped me a lot.

"I also got a lot of help from Luis Aparicio's father. He was a national hero in Venezuela. They called him 'El Grande.' He was a shortstop and one of the best players Venezuela ever had. He gave me a lot of pointers, and helped me just like I tried to help his son, Luis, when he came along."

The senior Aparicio seemingly started a tradition of fine shortstops in Venezuela that carried on for many years. In addition to Chico and Luis, Jr., Dave Concepcion, Ozzie Guillen, and Omar Vizquel along with a handful of others have also come out of the country to grace big league diamonds.

"From my standpoint, I always wanted to be a ballplayer," says Carrasquel, whose real first name is Alfonso and whose father was a beer salesman in Venezuela. "I had 10 brothers and sisters, and I wanted to make good money to help my family.

"My mother wanted me to go to the university," he adds. "But the first time I got paid playing ball, I gave her the money. She said, 'Where did you get that money?' I said, 'Playing ball.' She said, 'You play baseball every day.'

"I had started out playing in little league in Caracas," Chico says. "I was a pitcher. When I was 14 years old, I played in three games in three days.

Afterward, I couldn't move my arm. I stayed out six months, and when I came back, I started to play shortstop.

"I began playing professionally in 1946 in Caracas. Baseball is the number one sport in Venezuela. Fresco Thompson of the [Brooklyn] Dodgers came down to see me, but he never saw me play because we were having a revolution.

"He said to me, 'If you ever want to play in the U.S., let me know.' I said, 'Okay. I want to play.' He gave me $1,000, which was good money, and I signed with the Dodgers in 1948."

By then 21, Carrasquel spent the 1949 season with the Dodgers' Fort Worth farm club in the Texas League where he not only hit .315 in 128 games but also got the nickname "Chico" from his teammates.

The Dodgers, of course, already had an accomplished shortstop by the name of Pee Wee Reese, and there was little chance for Chico to make it to the big club. That being the case, the Dodgers found it possible to part with him. Frank Lane, who had badgered the club for Chico, was the lucky winner, acquiring the shortstop for the White Sox for $35,000 and two obscure minor leaguers.

Lane, the Chisox general manager, wanted Carrasquel to replace a legend, which is never easy. The long career of Appling, a future Hall of Famer, was winding down. He had been Chicago's regular shortstop since 1931.

"At first, Appling didn't like me," Carrasquel recalls. "I was taking his job. But after a while he started to help me. He turned into a real nice guy, a real gentleman. He talked to me every day in spring training. He taught me how to follow the hitters, how to position myself, all of those things. He helped me a lot.

"I just wanted to be in the big leagues. I was happy to be with the White Sox. When I flew to spring training my first year, I went from Caracas to Miami to Pasadena where we were training. It was a long trip, but all I could think about was, 'I'm going to be in the big leagues.'

"When I got to spring training, I tried so hard. Then I made the starting lineup. I remember my first game. We opened the season in Chicago and played the St. Louis Browns. My second time up, I hit a line drive for a double off Ned Garver. I was so happy. I couldn't believe it."

An outgoing fellow with a sunny disposition whose joy for playing baseball was obvious to all who watched him, Carrasquel soon became extremely popular with the Chicago fans.

"I just loved to play the game," he says. "One year, I played 155 games during the regular season with Chicago, plus spring training, then I went back to Caracas and played winter ball, which included the Caribbean World Series. I played in about 300 games that year because I loved to play baseball."

Chico hit .282 in his rookie year, which turned out to be the highest average of his big league career and third best on the White Sox that season. He had a 24-game hitting streak and was third among shortstops in the league in fielding.

Although Walt Dropo of the Boston Red Sox beat him out for Rookie of the Year honors in the American League, Chico had made an indelible mark in the big leagues, and a bright career was predicted for him.

Carrasquel bounced back from an off-season knee operation in 1951 to hit .264. That year, he beat out the 1950 American League MVP, Phil Rizzuto, for the starting berth in the All-Star Game.

"I was the first Latin American to play in an All-Star Game," Carrasquel says. "I was very proud of that. I was so happy to open the door for Latin players. I'll never forget that day. The game was in Detroit. I got a hit and had no errors [the American League lost, 8–3].

"I was supposed to play in the 1952 All-Star Game, too," Chico adds. "But I broke a finger two days before the game and couldn't play."

He did play, however, in three other games, drawing the starting assignment again in 1953 when the Nationals won a 5–1 decision at Cincinnati and in 1954 when the American League triumphed, 11–9, at Cleveland. Carrasquel also appeared in the 1955 game, getting two hits in what became a 6–5 National League victory at Milwaukee.

In his four All-Star Games, Chico had four hits in 12 at-bats. "Being on the same club and in the same clubhouse with Ted Williams, Yogi Berra, Vern Stephens, and all those guys was quite a thrill," he says. "I'll never forget it."

While he was making the All-Star teams, Carrasquel was performing admirably for the Pale Hose. After a .248 season in 1952, his averages were .279, .255, and .256 over the next three years. In 1954, he had career highs in home runs (12) and RBI (62). That was the year he played in 155 games in the majors.

Along the way, Carrasquel took part in a number of memorable feats. He led American League shortstops in fielding percentage in 1951, 1953, and

1954. In 1951, he tied an American League record (now held by five players) by accepting 18 chances in an extra-inning game (a 19-inning affair). In 1954, he broke Rizzuto's 1949–50 record for most consecutive errorless games (a mark now held by Cal Ripken, Jr.) by accepting 297 chances cleanly. He also led shortstops that year in doubleplays.

"Gene Woodling hit a ball that hit me on the chest," Chico remembers about the end of his errorless streak. "I picked it up and threw to first, but he beat it out and they gave me an error."

Carrasquel scored five runs in one game in 1955 (teammate Minnie Minoso also scored five runs in the same game).

"Another time, I had seven RBI in one game," Carrasquel recalls. "I had a three-run home run, a three-run double, and went 5-for-5. That was when I was with Cleveland. We beat Kansas City, 26–6, in the first game of a doubleheader. We lost the second game, 1–0, to Alex Kellner.

"I remember one day I hit a home run off Early Wynn," he adds. "The next time up, he knocked me down and called me all kinds of names.

"He was a good one. There were a lot of great pitchers in the American League. Everybody had at least a couple of good ones. Camilo Pascual was one of the toughest for me because he had a real good curveball and a good motion. Bob Feller, Virgil Trucks, and Whitey Ford were also tough.

"There were good hitters, too. I think I played with some of the greatest players of all time. Ted Williams, Joe DiMaggio, Bob Feller, Willie Mays, Mickey Mantle, Stan Musial. I played with history makers. Those guys would sure make a lot of money today.

"When I played, though, the money was good enough. I remember one year I hit 12 home runs and was the best shortstop in the league. I told Lane I needed more money the next year. He said, 'Yeah, but you don't steal bases.' So the next year, I went out and stole some bases. That winter when I went in to see him, he said, 'Yeah, but you didn't hit many home runs.'

"But I was making 30 to 35 thousand. That was real good money. Every year, I'd go home and get a new car. The kids would follow me around. All the kids wanted to play shortstop.

"I remember Luis [Aparicio] was the batboy on our club in Caracas in the winter league. He could really play. I told the White Sox about him. They said, 'We heard there's a shortstop down there who is better than you.' I said, 'Yeah, that's right.' They said, 'Sign him up.' You could tell he was going to be good. I worked with him every day. Later, he said, 'Chico helped me learn everything.'"

Another player Carrasquel helped to get established was second baseman Nellie Fox. Fox had just come to the White Sox in 1950, too, after spending the previous season and parts of two others as a reserve with the Philadelphia Athletics. During Chico's years in Chicago, he and Fox formed an outstanding doubleplay combination.

"He was one of the greatest," Carrasquel says of his future Hall of Fame keystone partner. "In the beginning, he couldn't talk Spanish and I couldn't talk English too well. But we gave each other signs. It worked. We worked out every day together. In fact, we were roommates for a while. We got along real well."

Although they were sixth his first year and fourth his second, the White Sox finished third five years in a row while Chico was in Chicago. During that period, he saw the formation of a Chisox club that would eventually win the American League pennant in 1959.

"We had a pretty good ball club," he says. "We had Fox, Minoso, Eddie Robinson, Sherm Lollar. In 1955, we won 14 straight and were in first place most of the year. But we lost out at the end to the Yankees.

"I hated those Yankees. Every year, they won the pennant. I played my best baseball against them, but we could never seem to beat them for the pennant."

After the 1955 season—with Aparicio waiting in the wings to launch what would become a Hall of Fame career—the White Sox could afford to part with Carrasquel. They traded him and outfielder Jim Busby to Cleveland for outfielder Larry Doby. "I was sorry to leave Chicago," Carrasquel says. "I told Aparicio, 'Well, you've got my place now. You better do good.'"

Chico played two full seasons with the Indians, hitting .243 and .276. Then on June 12, 1958, in his third year with the Tribe, Cleveland swapped him to Kansas City for shortstop Billy Hunter.

Carrasquel finished the season with the A's, winding up with a .234 batting average for the year. That winter, he was dealt to the Orioles in a trade for infielder/outfielder Dick Williams.

Chico hit .223 in 114 games with Baltimore. But the 1959 season turned out to be his last one in the big leagues.

Carrasquel returned to Caracas where he became a coach and later manager of the Caracas Lions. He also scouted for first the Kansas City Royals, then the New York Mets.

In 1980, Carrasquel began a new career as a radio and television broadcaster in the Venezuelan Winter League. Ten years later, he joined the White Sox broadcasting team.

"I got paid for doing something I liked," says Chico. "It was really great. I've loved baseball all my life. If I didn't get paid, I'd still have gone to the ballpark anyway.

"In fact," adds Carrasquel, "if I have to be born again, I want to be a ballplayer again. I played 10 years in the big leagues. I'm very happy with that. Baseball gave me everything. I've been all over the world. I've had a chance to meet a lot of people. It's all because of baseball."

It was hardly a one-way street, though. Baseball benefitted as much from Carrasquel as he did from it. He was one of the best of his era at one of the game's most demanding positions.

Jim Maloney

Owner of Three Unusual No-Hitters

FOR A PITCHER, there is nothing quite as special as hurling a no-hitter. It is the ultimate achievement, a feat that every pitcher would like to perform but one so rare that only a few actually do it.

Of those few who do it once, even fewer do it more than once. Since the pitching mound was moved to 60 feet, 6 inches from home plate in 1893, only 21 pitchers have combined skill and luck so successfully that they have hurled at least two no-hitters. Only five of them have tossed more than two no-hitters.

Jim Maloney of the Cincinnati Reds is one of the members of that highly select quintet. Not only did he fire three hitless games, he threw two of them in the same season (although one has been taken away from him because of a recent major league ruling that clarifies what is considered a no-hitter).

That remarkable accomplishment by Maloney was in 1965. At the time, the National League was blessed with an abundance of outstanding hurlers. Mound stars such as Sandy Koufax, Bob Gibson, Juan Marichal, Jim Bunning, and Don Drysdale—all members of the Hall of Fame—were terrorizing enemy batters. Maloney, who also pitched five one-hitters, fit right in with that group.

When he was at his best, nobody was harder to hit than the 6-2, 190-pound righthander from Fresno, California. He threw the ball with all the fury of a raging forest fire. His fastball, which exploded in on batters at nearly 100 miles per hour, was one of the swiftest ever clocked. And his curveball was equally devastating.

"I had a very good curve," Maloney recalls. "Everybody remembers my throwing so hard. But my curve was a good pitch, too.

"For some reason, I could always throw hard," he adds. "As a kid, I had a better arm than anybody else. Pitching just came easily. Then I picked up the curve, and once I learned to throw it, it made the game even easier."

The easiest part for Maloney was blowing the ball past opposing hitters. With his crackling fastball and vicious curve, he ranked nearly every season among the league leaders in strikeouts. During a career that lasted from 1960 through 1971, Jim fanned 1,605 batters. In 302 games, he had a 134–84 record with a 3.19 ERA while allowing 1,518 hits and 810 walks in 1,849.1 innings.

On a list that includes such superb long-term moundsmen as Bucky Walters, Paul Derringer, and Eppa Rixey, Maloney is the Reds' all-time leader in strikeouts, is tied for second in shutouts, and ranks third in walks and fifth in wins. Over his 12-year career, which ended with a final season with the California Angels, Jim struck out 10 or more batters in one game 32 times.

The big flame-thrower, who averaged 7.81 strikeouts per nine-inning game—one of the highest ratios in major league history—had a fastball that was officially clocked at 99.5 mph. Only Nolan Ryan and J. R. Richard were officially timed faster.

Maloney's fastball was never more devastating than on June 14, 1965. On that day, he struck out 18 New York Mets while allowing no hits through 10 innings. In the 11th, he was touched for two hits, including a leadoff home run by Johnny Lewis. Maloney wound up a 1–0 loser. Later, despite old rules that acknowledged no-hitters if they went nine innings, he lost the no-hitter in the record book under a revised definition.

Two months later, on August 8, Maloney pitched another no-hitter. This time, he won by a 1–0 score. The game also went extra innings before Leo Cardenas slammed a 10th inning home run to defeat the Chicago Cubs. Maloney struck out 12 and walked 10, which tied a major league record for most bases on balls in a no-hit game.

With his second no-hitter, Maloney joined Johnny Vander Meer (1938), Allie Reynolds (1951), Virgil Trucks (1952), and Ryan (1973) as the only hurlers who have held the opposition hitless over nine innings twice in one season.

"I had better stuff in the game against the Mets," Maloney recalls. "For 10 innings, they just couldn't do a thing with me. But I was really upset because we lost. When I was pitching the second no-hitter two months later, the regulation game ended, 0–0, and it crossed my mind, 'Can this be another game like the first one?'

"I threw hard in both games," Maloney adds, "but I had a lot more luck in the second game. And I was wild enough. I think I threw more than 200 pitches. The Cubs' hearts weren't in it. They weren't too anxious to go up to the plate."

Although his name was now etched in baseball history, Maloney was far from through. He turned in his third no-hitter on April 30, 1969, with a 13-strikeout, five-walk performance that beat the Houston Astros, 10–0. Ironically, the Astros' Don Wilson came back the next day to hurl a 4–0 no-hitter against the Reds, only the second time opposing teams have staged back-to-back no-hitters on successive days.

Maloney's third no-hitter gave him still another place in baseball history. With it, he joined Ryan (seven), Koufax (four), and Cy Young and Bob Feller (each three) as the only modern pitchers to toss three or more no-hitters. "I might have had my best stuff of the three no-hitters in that game," he says. "At least, with the lead I had, that game had a little less pressure."

Pressure was never anything that Maloney shunned. It was something he had learned to deal with as a schoolboy when his high school team in Fresno won the California state title. "Dick Ellsworth was on that team," he says, "and we had two other pitchers who went professional. Pat Corrales was our catcher."

Back then, Maloney was only a part-time pitcher. "I could hit a little, so I played shortstop," he says. "When I was a senior, there were only 16 teams in the major leagues. Half of them wanted me as a pitcher, and half of them wanted me as a shortstop. Cincinnati offered me a good bonus, so I took it as a pitcher."

Maloney spent two seasons in the minors, compiling a 6–7 record at Topeka and a 14–5 mark at Nashville and combining for 293 strikeouts in 285 innings. He then reported to the Reds late in the 1960 season. "I got my first start in the Los Angeles Coliseum against the Dodgers," Maloney remembers. "Don Drysdale beat me, 2–0.

"I struggled a little my first couple of years," Jim adds. "I probably should have stayed in the minors a little longer."

In 1961, while posting a 6–7 record in 27 games, Maloney got into his only World Series after the Reds won their first pennant since 1940. He pitched two-thirds of an inning in relief and gave up two runs and four hits in a New York Yankees' 13–5 victory in the fifth and final game.

In his first three seasons, Maloney could only account for a total of 17 wins (20 losses). In 1963, however, he suddenly vaulted to a position among the league's pitching leaders. He fashioned a glittering 23–7 record with a 2.77 ERA. And his 265 strikeouts ranked second in the league to Koufax.

In one game that year, Maloney struck out 16 Milwaukee Braves, including eight in a row, which at the time was two short of the league record. After fanning Eddie Mathews to end the first inning, Jim whiffed Norm Larker, Frank Bolling, and Denis Menke in the second and Del Crandall, Bob Hendley, and Mack Jones in the third. He ended the string with a kayo of Lee Maye leading off the fourth. "I don't think I ever had better stuff than that game," Maloney says. "That game was a one-hitter."

Maloney had another memorable game that year when he fanned Stan Musial in the St. Louis Cardinals legend's final game. "I was going for my 24th win," Jim says. "I struck him out, then he got a base hit off me and they took him out. I wound up getting a no-decision."

In the ensuing years, many pitchers found their way to Cincinnati, but only Maloney remained throughout the decade of the 1960s. Hurlers such as Bob Purkey, Jim O'Toole, Joey Jay, Sammy Ellis, and Milt Pappas gave Jim temporary support, but usually they were gone within two or three years.

Maloney, meanwhile, toiled much of the time with a sore arm, a condition that often limited his number of innings pitched and strikeouts. "I had arm problems throughout my career, but I always seemed to get over them," he says.

Maloney won in double figures seven straight years. After his fine season in 1963, he went 15–10, 20–9, 16–8, 15–11, 16–10, and 12–5 while working mostly for Reds teams that were in the middle of the National League standings.

Jim was picked for the National League All-Star team in 1965, his only time on the squad. It was not a successful venture as he gave up five hits and five runs in one and two-thirds innings of a game that the National League went on to win, 6–5.

In 1970, Maloney was coming off a 12–5 season and seemed primed for another good year. But he ruptured an Achilles tendon running out a ground ball in Los Angeles. He pitched in only seven games that year, and for all practical purposes his career was over.

After the season, the Reds traded Jim to the Angels for pitcher Greg Garrett. Maloney worked in 13 games for the Angels, then decided to retire.

Maloney returned to Fresno, where he joined his father in a car dealership. Eventually, his father retired, and Jim first leased, then sold the business. Later, he managed the Class A team in Fresno before returning to auto sales.

In recent years, Maloney worked for a drug and alcohol program in Fresno. "I had problems with alcohol when I got out of baseball," he relates. "So, I'm very interested in this program. I go around to groups and try to help people understand the disease concepts of drug and alcohol abuse. I make a lot of speeches to youth groups, too."

Jim still keeps in touch with baseball. Frequently, he drives to San Francisco to see the Reds when they're in town. When he reflects on his baseball career, he gets a good feeling.

"In the time I spent in the big leagues, my won-lost record was up there with some of the best in the business," he says. "I'm proud of that, and I'm proud of the no-hitters. After all, that's what you try to do every time you go out there. You try not to give up any hits or runs.

"My goals were cut short because of injuries," he adds. "I wanted to win 200 games and play 15 years. But overall, I'm very satisfied with what I did.

"The 1960s were a terrific era. I always had trouble with Willie McCovey. And Willie Stargell, Rusty Staub, and Wes Covington were all rough outs for me, too. I pitched against some great hitters and some great pitchers.

"I played against guys I had read about as a kid. Just thinking about that is very satisfying. I was the last pitcher to pitch against Musial. I faced Hank Aaron and Roberto Clemente. And I pitched against the best in Gibson, Koufax, Marichal, and some of the others."

It was a career in which Maloney had to take a back seat to none of them.

Johnny Podres

Hurled Dodgers to First World Championship

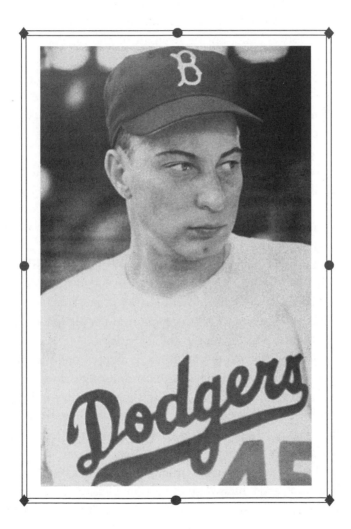

IT IS THE RARE World Series that passes without a special hero.

Since the interleague games began in 1903, there has almost always been some player each year who has risen above the others and, by performing the spectacular, lifted his team to victory.

Some of these players have been obscure hands who surfaced for one brief moment of glory. Others have been players of already existing eminence who merely performed up to their normal capabilities.

In the 1955 World Series, it was a young pitcher named Johnny Podres who stepped forward and, on the strength of his singular brilliance, led the Brooklyn Dodgers to a memorable triumph over the New York Yankees.

He did it by pitching the Dodgers to two victories, the first one coming after the Yankees had opened the World Series with two straight wins, the second clinching the Series for Brooklyn with a sparkling 2–0 shutout victory in the seventh game.

The second win gave the Dodgers their first World Series victory in club history, ending a long drought in which the team had emerged empty-handed after seven pennants. Podres was acclaimed the Most Valuable Player in the Series and won a Corvette from *Sport Magazine* in what was the first year of the award from the publication.

Although the fireballing lefthander went on to a noteworthy career with the Brooklyn and Los Angeles Dodgers that included two All-Star Game appearances, membership on five World Series teams, and a luminous .561 won-lost percentage during a 15-year sojourn in the big leagues, he is best remembered for his performance in the '55 Series.

What made his two victories particularly illuminating was that Podres had entered the Series with just a 9–10 record during the season, his third full campaign in the majors. "At 9–10, I was the club's only losing pitcher," says Podres of the Dodgers' staff that included Don Newcombe, Carl Erskine, Clem Labine, Billy Loes, and rookie Roger Craig (actually, reliever Ed Roebuck had a 5–6 record).

"I started off the season all right, and was 7–2 in June. But then I hurt my arm and my back, and it messed up my season. I was on the disabled list for a month. Then I got hit in the ribs in August by a batting cage while it was being moved, and I was out for three more weeks.

"The Dodgers were very concerned. They were thinking about bringing up Ken Lehman to take my place. I came back in mid-September, and I pitched four good innings in Pittsbugh, so they decided to keep me on the roster. I was just throwing the ball over the plate. I was saying, 'Here it is, pal. I'm throwing good. See if you can hit it.'"

After the Dodgers clinched the pennant, finishing 13 ½ games ahead of the second-place Milwaukee Braves, they entered their fifth World Series in nine years—all against the Yankees. New York won the first two games behind the pitching of Whitey Ford and Tommy Byrne. Brooklyn manager Walter Alston nominated Podres to face 17-game winner Bob Turley in the third game. Not only was the game crucial to the Dodgers' chances of survival, it was Johnny's 23d birthday.

"It was a bit of a surprise," Podres recalls. "I didn't think I'd get to start in the Series. We're down two games, and here's Alston giving me the ball to pitch in the third game."

His injuries behind him, Podres pitched a complete game, a seven-hitter to beat the Yankees, 8–3. Catcher Roy Campanella had a single, double, home run, and three RBI to lead an 11-hit Dodgers attack that knocked out Turley in the second inning.

Brooklyn won the next two games, too, then lost the sixth game as Ford spun a four-hitter. That set the stage for the deciding game October 4 at Yankee Stadium.

Having started a different pitcher in each of the previous six games, Alston chose Podres for the showdown battle. His opponent was Byrne, owner of a 16–5 record during the season.

"There wasn't much pressure on me in the third game," Podres remarks. "Hell, I was just a 9–10 pitcher. But there was really pressure in the seventh game. Everything was riding on that game."

Campanella doubled and scored on a single by Gil Hodges to break a scoreless tie in the fourth inning. Hodges' sacrifice fly with the bases loaded drove in the second Brooklyn run in the sixth.

Meanwhile, Podres was mowing down the Yankees with ease. He ran into a jam, though, in the bottom of the sixth when Billy Martin walked and Gil McDougald beat out a bunt single to lead off the inning.

Entering that inning, Alston had made a defensive change. Second baseman Don Zimmer was pulled, and Jim Gilliam was switched from left field to second with Sandy Amoros taking the field in left. Now, with two men on base and the dangerous Yogi Berra at the plate, the move had an immediate effect.

Berra sliced a fly ball down the left field line. Shaded toward center, Amoros seemed to have little chance to catch the ball, but he sprinted after it and at the last second reached out and caught it right in front of the stands. Then, the fleet Cuban wheeled and made a perfect throw to short-stop Pee Wee Reese, who relayed the ball to Hodges at first to double up McDougald.

Had the ball dropped safely, both Martin and McDougald would have scored and Berra would have been in scoring position in what would have been a 2–2 game. Instead, Amoros' brilliant catch and the subsequent doubleplay pulled Podres and the Dodgers out of deep trouble.

"When Berra hit that ball, I thought at first it was just a fly ball to left," says Podres. "But all of the sudden, I saw the ball slicing. I thought, 'Oh, my God,' and ran over to back up third base. Then I looked up, and saw Amoros running and running—it seemed like forever until he caught the ball. He made a great catch.

"Alston made exactly the right move. He was a genius. He should have been the MVP of the Series. Amoros had a longer reach than Gilliam, and he was lefthanded, which meant he didn't have to backhand the ball. And he had great speed. It was a brilliant move."

Johnny had to escape a two-on, one-out jam in the eighth inning. He entered the ninth, clinging to a 2–0 lead with Bill Skowron, Bob Cerv, and Elston Howard coming to the plate.

Podres got Skowron on a hard bouncer back to the mound for the first out. Then he retired Cerv on a soft fly to Amoros. With Brooklyn fans going berserk, Podres then induced Howard to send a grounder to Reese, who threw to Hodges for the final out.

The Dodgers had their first World Series victory. And Podres, having scattered eight hits, struck out four, and walked two, had his second complete game win of the Series.

That night, driving his newly won Corvette, Podres was the toast of Brooklyn during a massive celebration that lasted far into the night. "I was a young guy, and I had just beaten the Yankees," Johnny recalls. "I was living it up. We had a helluva party. People were all over the streets. I rode all over that night. Those two games made my season."

They also helped to mold Podres' reputation as a clutch pitcher who had a knack of coming through in tight situations.

Podres won two more World Series games after the Dodgers had moved to Los Angeles. He yielded five hits over six innings in a 4–3 victory over the Chicago White Sox in the second game of the 1959 fall classic, which the Dodgers won in six games. And he went 8⅓ innings and gave up six hits to beat the Yankees, 4–1, in the second game of the Dodgers' sweep of the 1963 Series.

"But the last game of the 1955 Series had to be my best game," Johnny says, "although I pitched well in the '63 game. I think I retired 13 or 14 straight hitters [in '63]. Sandy Koufax had struck out 15 batters in the game before that [in a six-hit, 5–2 win]. How'd you like to follow that act?"

It was a tough act to follow, but Podres was used to such things. In the early 1960s he was the dean of a staff that included future Hall of Famers Koufax and Don Drysdale, and he had Newcombe, Preacher Roe, and Erskine as pitching mates early in his career.

Podres had joined the Dodgers' organization in 1951. A native of Witherbee in western New York, he was a hard-throwing youngster who had grown up a Brooklyn fan. "I was always a Dodgers fan," he notes. "Dolph Camilli was my hero.

"I always pitched as a kid," Podres continues. "But I played a little first base and outfield, too."

In high school, Podres had attracted the attention of big league scouts. After graduating, he began getting invitations to tryout sessions.

"I worked out with the Phillies at Shibe Park," he remarks. "But Bob Carpenter thought I was too small. He liked those big pitchers.

"I worked out with the Dodgers at Ebbets Field. My high school principal knew a scout with the Dodgers, and they arranged it so I could go down to Brooklyn and throw. I threw for 15 minutes. George Sisler was there. He was a scout with the Dodgers then. After throwing on the sidelines, they took me up to meet Mr. [Branch] Rickey. I heard him say, 'Don't let that boy get away.'"

They didn't. Podres signed with the Dodgers and was sent first to Newport News where he pitched in seven games in the Piedmont League, then to Hazard, Kentucky, of the Class D Mountain States League. Podres posted a 21–3 record at Hazard while leading the league in strikeouts (228) and earned run average (1.67) in 200 innings.

The following year Podres made the jump all the way to Triple-A, pitching for Montreal in the International League. That season, for the first time, he encountered the back problems that would badger him the rest of his career and spent one month on the disabled list. Johnny had to settle for a 5–5 record while working in just 88 innings.

The back problems eased in 1953, and despite the presence of Erskine, Roe, Loes, Labine, Russ Meyer, and others, Podres made the Brooklyn club, which was without Newcombe, who was in the second year of a two-year Army stint.

"I was in the right place at the right time," Podres says. "The Dodgers had a great pitching staff. Here I was, just a 20-year-old kid. It was kind of awesome."

Being the only lefthander other than the aging Roe, Podres got his big league baptism quickly and under extreme conditions. "My first start was against the Giants and Sal Maglie," he says. "My second start was against the Phillies and Robin Roberts. After that, they sent me down to the bullpen. I got my first win, pitching three or four innings in relief. I think it was against Cincinnati. We had a big inning that gave us the win."

Big innings were not uncommon for the Dodgers of that era. With four future Hall of Famers (Campanella, Reese, Jackie Robinson, and Duke Snider) in the lineup and a starting eight that ranks as one of the great aggregations in baseball history, Brooklyn could put a devastating offense on the field.

"They had some guys who could hit, that's for sure," Podres marvels. "Don't forget, they also had Hodges, Gilliam, and [Carl] Furillo on that team, as well as Billy Cox at third. That was an awesome lineup. All you had to do was pitch like crazy for five innings. If you could hold the other team for that long, you always had a chance to win because you knew we were going to get some runs sooner or later."

Podres featured a blazing fastball, which he threw in the mid-90-mile-per-hour range, a crackling curve, and a dazzling changeup, which he learned to throw as well as any pitcher ever did.

"My second year in spring training, [Chuck] Dressen taught it to me," Podres says. "He taught me how to grip the ball. Al Campanis helped, too. It came to me pretty easily. It was something that was waiting for me to do. Some guys can pick the pitch right up, and others can't. Erskine had a great one.

"It can be a very effective pitch. The whole key is to give the batter a look like you're going to come after him with a fastball. What makes the pitch effective is arm speed."

After going 9–4 in his rookie season, Podres got a chance to pitch in his first World Series. He started the fifth game but lasted just two-thirds of an inning and wound up losing to the Yankees, 11–7. Mickey Mantle's grand slam homer off Russ Meyer in the third inning was the big blow for the Yanks, who went on to capture the Series in six games.

Podres went 11–7 in 1954, again spending one month on the disabled list. Then after the 1955 season, he spent the next year in the Army, thus missing another trip to the World Series in 1956. Johnny returned to the mound in 1957 and, posting a 12–9 record, led the National League in ERA with a 2.66 mark.

Between 1957 and 1963, Podres won in double figures every year, ultimately performing that feat in eight of the 10 seasons in which he was primarily a starter. After winning 14 games in both 1959 and 1960, he fashioned the best season of his career in 1961, posting an 18–5 record and leading the league in winning percentage (.783).

"Every time I went out that year, it seemed like we had a 5–2 lead by the fourth inning," Podres recalls. "It was amazing. I had 18 wins in August. But my back was acting up, and then I lost my dad that year. I only started one game in September and wound up missing seven starts." It turned out to be the closest Podres would come to being a 20-game winner.

By then, the Dodgers had moved from Brooklyn to Los Angeles. It was a move that broke the hearts of Brooklyn fans, as well as those of quite a few of the Dodgers players. "It was a big disappointment to all the guys, except maybe a few like Snider who lived in California," Podres says. "Most of the guys had played in Brooklyn all their lives. Guys like Hodges, Campanella, Furillo . . . they were giants there. It was tough to pick up and go to Los Angeles."

It was especially tough for the pitchers, who were forced to shift from working in the tight confines of Ebbets Field to the off-beat configurations of the Los Angeles Coliseum with its short left field fence and spacious center field.

"The Coliseum was very tough to pitch in because of the short left field, even though I won 11 games there one year. But pitching in Ebbets Field was a nightmare. It was 320 to right-center, 400 to center, 351 to left-center, 297 down the right field line, and 343 down the left field line. That was a tough park to pitch in. Of course, you could give up five runs and still win a game," Podres says.

After his brilliant season in 1961, Podres came back with a 15–13 mark the following year, establishing career highs in games (40), innings (255), and strikeouts (178).

One game that season was particularly noteworthy. In it, Johnny struck out eight consecutive batters, which tied a major league record. On July 2 against the Phillies, Podres fanned Ted Savage to end the fourth inning, then whiffed Roy Sievers, Don Demeter, and Tony Gonzalez in the fifth, Bob Oldis, Bobby Wine, and Jack Hamilton in the sixth, and Mel Roach in the seventh.

"I just missed striking out the ninth straight batter, Johnny Callison, by inches," Podres recalls. "I had a no-hitter going into the seventh inning. It was one of those games where everything was going right. But I ended up not finishing the game. I was completely exhausted after the seventh inning, but we won the game."

Podres had a 14–12 record in 1963, which turned out to be his last big season. In 1964, Johnny was hit in the elbow by a pitch in April and underwent surgery for the removal of bone chips. He pitched in only two games the entire season, as the Dodgers finished sixth.

Johnny came back to work in 27 games and post a 7–6 record in 1965 as the Dodgers won another pennant and the World Series. Then early the following year, the Dodgers sold him to the Detroit Tigers.

Used mostly as a spot starter and a reliever, Podres worked two years for the Tigers, winning seven and losing six in 57 games over that period. At the end of the 1967 season, Detroit released him. Podres did not play in 1968 but came back in 17 games (5–6 record) in 1969 with the San Diego Padres in their first season in the National League.

Johnny retired from the active ranks after that season. He departed with a career record of 148–116. In 440 games, 340 as a starter, he pitched in 2,265.1 innings, allowed 2,239 hits, struck out 1,435, and walked 743. His earned run average over 15 years in the majors was 3.67.

Podres remained with the Padres for the next four seasons as their pitching coach. He then joined the Boston Red Sox, spending five years as a minor league pitching instructor, before joining the parent club as pitching coach in 1980. He held the same position with the Minnesota Twins from 1981 to 1985, after which he served four seasons as a minor league pitching coach in the Dodgers' organization. He then spent five seasons as pitching coach of the Phillies before poor health forced him to retire in 1996. Since then, however, he has continued to work with the club's minor league hurlers on a part-time basis.

During his coaching career, Podres developed a reputation as an expert on the art of throwing the changeup, and he taught it to such pitchers as Frank Viola, Bob Ojeda, John Tudor, and Ramon Martinez, all of whom used it with a considerable degree of success.

A resident of Glens Falls, New York, Podres was connected with baseball for more than 45 years. During that time, he established an impressive set of credentials, both as a player and as a coach.

At the top of that list, though, are his accomplishments when as a young pitcher he took control of a World Series.

Brooklyn fans will never forget it.

Dick Sisler

Dramatic Home Run Won a Pennant

OF THE THOUSANDS of home runs hit in the 117-year history of the Philadelphia Phillies, one stands out above all the others: Dick Sisler's dramatic four-bagger in 1950.

No Phillies homer was ever more memorable. No Phillies homer was ever more important. And no Phillies homer ever produced such joyous results as Sisler's mighty three-run blast on the last day of the 1950 season.

Sisler's home run was to the Phillies on that storied October day what Gabby Harnett's homer was to the Chicago Cubs in 1938, what Bobby Thomson's homer was to the New York Giants in 1951, and what Bill Mazeroski's homer was to the Pittsburgh Pirates in 1960. It rates a special place in baseball history as one of the National League's most celebrated home runs.

The Phillies were locked in a desperate struggle to capture their first National League pennant in 35 years. They had led by as many as nine and one-half games at the end of August. But a devastating September slump had produced panic in Philadelphia and reduced the club's lead to a scant two games entering a two-game series on the final weekend of the season against the surging Brooklyn Dodgers, winners of 12 of their last 15 games.

The Dodgers won the first game (curiously played on a Friday with an off-day on Saturday) to narrow the lead to one game. Another Brooklyn win Sunday would throw the pennant race into a tie. To most fans, that— forcing a best-of-three playoff—would mean almost certain defeat for the fading and worn-out Phillies.

October 1, 1950: Ebbets Field. Robin Roberts and Don Newcombe were the mound opponents in the final game. Each was going for his 20th win.

Roberts, pitching on just two days rest, got a 1–0 lead in the sixth when Sisler scored on Willie Jones' single. But Brooklyn came back with the tying run in the bottom half of the inning as Pee Wee Reese hit a controversial home run that lodged at the base of a wire screen in right-center field.

The tense duel between the two mound titans continued into the ninth inning with the score still tied, 1–1. In the bottom of the inning, however, Cal Abrams opened with a walk and went to second on Reese's single. Then Duke Snider rifled a line drive to center. Playing shallow, Richie Ashburn fielded the ball on one hop, and, with Abrams being unwisely waved home by third base coach Milt Stock—ironically, the Phillies third baseman when the team last won a pennant in 1915—he fired to the plate where catcher Stan Lopata nailed the Dodgers outfielder 15 feet up the line. After an intentional walk to Jackie Robinson, Roberts escaped the jam by retiring Carl Furillo and Gil Hodges with the bases loaded.

The weary Roberts opened the top of the 10th with a single. Eddie Wait-kus followed with another hit. Ashburn tried to sacrifice, but Roberts was thrown out sliding into third.

That brought up Sisler, who already had three singles in the game, as well as a badly sprained wrist. "I remember the situation vividly," Dick said. "Newcombe got two quick strikes on me, then he almost got another on a high, away pitch. I almost swung at it, but I held up at the last moment, and it was called a ball.

"The next pitch was over the plate, high and away. A fastball. Almost the same pitch. I swung hard, just hoping I could make contact. The ball sailed out to left field. I didn't know at the time if it would go out, so I began running. As I rounded first, I saw it was a home run."

The ball cleared the left field wall, and suddenly the Phillies had a 4–1 lead. Roberts set the Dodgers down in order in the 10th, and the Phils danced off the field with only their second pennant in club history.

Pandemonium erupted in the stands where thousands of Phillies fans had come to Brooklyn to cheer their team. Back in Philadelphia, a celebration spilled out into the streets like none the city had ever seen. The 35-year famine since the last pennant was over. After all the miserable teams and long years of frustration, the Phillies were National League champions.

It was to that point the proudest moment in Phillies history. And it would remain the club's finest hour until 1980, when another Phillies team made history by winning the club's first World Series.

For Sisler, who died in 1998, the memories of that heroic moment were never too far away. "As I circled the bases, I thought that would be enough for Roberts because he was tough that day," Dick said. "You talk about competitors. He was dead tired, but he was able to dig down and come up with a little extra in that last inning. Brooklyn had a good ball club, but there wasn't any way they were going to score off Roberts. He just reached back and fired with everything he had.

"I had pretty good luck against Newcombe," added Sisler, who hit .329 that season against Dodger pitching. "When I faced him, he'd usually get me out the first time up because it wasn't quite dark and you couldn't see the ball as well. But after that, I always hit him pretty well. He was a fastball pitcher, and I was a fastball hitter.

"Of course, it's a good thing I hit that home run," Sisler mused. "If I hadn't, I don't think people would have remembered me. I mean I was just another ballplayer, maybe a little bit better than average."

Four decades after he hit his famous home run, Sisler was still getting a lot of mail from admiring fans. "If I hadn't hit it, I don't think people would know what to say to me," Sisler claimed. "But they write, and they were all either there in the park when I hit it, or they heard about it. I sure got a lot of mileage out of that home run. Even though it was a long time ago, people still talk about it."

Contrary to his own assessment, Sisler was no ordinary ballplayer. Over eight years, he had a big league batting average of .276 with 55 home runs and 360 RBI. He had 720 hits in 799 games. He was a major league manager. He earned five World Series rings. And he was the son of a Hall of Famer, George Sisler, one of baseball's greatest hitters and first basemen.

Sisler was not only one of those rare father-son combinations who made the major leagues, he was also one of two brothers to play in the big time. Dick's younger brother Dave spent seven seasons in the majors as a pitcher, most notably with the Boston Red Sox. Another brother, George, is a minor league executive of long standing.

Having a famous father was always tough for Dick. George Sisler had a career batting average of .340 and twice batted over .400. He was one of the early players inducted into the Hall of Fame, selected in the fourth election in 1939.

"It was tough, believe me, it was tough being the son of George Sisler," Dick said. "When I was a kid, I got a lot of this, 'Awww, your dad wouldn't have struck out,' or 'Your dad wouldn't have popped up in that situation.' It got to me then. But later I had a talk with my dad, and he said, 'Dick, you're always going to have that on you, so you might as well get used to it.' I finally did. I wised up. I just figured, I can't change my dad, so I kind of put the whole thing out of my head. I knew I had to make good on my own, and that's what I did."

Sisler remembered seeing his father play many times, but he had no strong recollections of his on-the-field performances. The elder Sisler had broken in with the St. Louis Browns in 1915, five years before Dick was born, and he was with them for 12 seasons, as a player and later as a manager, before finishing his career with the Boston Braves in 1930.

"I was awfully young at the time," Dick recalled. "When he was in Boston, I was eight, nine, 10 years old. I would go to the ballpark every day, and watch him. I remember him hitting a triple one time. I don't know why that sticks out in my mind. Another time, I remember him getting a cheap base hit. I believe the pitcher must have said something to him because he walked over to the mound, and they almost had a fight.

"But at the time, I didn't have any feelings about watching one of baseball's greatest players. You don't realize things like that when you're a kid. I just thought going to the ballpark and watching my dad play was part of life."

Ironically, when Dick hit his home run against the Dodgers, his dad was in the stands. George Sisler was a scout for Brooklyn. "I'm sure he had mixed emotions," said Dick, "because his son hit a home run to beat his ball club. But I know he was awfully happy for me."

Over the years, Dick and his father never spent much time talking about the art of hitting. "We just never talked much about hitting because he was always gone," Sisler explained. "I loved my dad and I respected him in every way, but we just didn't talk baseball much. I guess part of that was my fault. I know that if I would've asked him something, he would've helped me.

"My brother and I used to work out together. We'd pitch to one another. I could always hit. But I wish I had been a little more mature. And I wish I had talked to my dad more.

"Of course, later on, when I was in the big leagues, he was scouting and saw a lot of my games. Then, I would ask him after a game what he thought I was doing right or wrong, and he would help me. But generally, I felt as if I had to do it on my own and not rely on anybody else. Fortunately, I happened to have the God-given talent to be able to hit a baseball."

It was Sisler's hitting—and his famous pedigree—that first attracted scouts in his native St. Louis where he was an outstanding high school player. After taking his talents to Colgate University for one year, he signed in 1939 with the Cardinals.

Sisler spent four years in the minors—his high point coming in 1940 when he hit .322 at Lansing in the Michigan State League. After three years of military duty during World War II, Dick joined the Cardinals in 1946.

Shifting back and forth between the outfield and first base that year, Sisler hit .260, and St. Louis won the National League pennant and the World Series.

"It was a big honor playing in my hometown and where my dad had played all those years," Dick said. "But I had to bear down all the time. There was a lot of pressure on me because of my dad."

With a regular outfield of Enos Slaughter, Terry Moore, and Erv Dusak, backed by reserves Ron Northey and Joe Medwick, and with Stan Musial anchored to first base, Sisler's playing time diminished considerably in 1947. Dick got into only 46 games, and he hit just .203.

"I had done all right my first year," he said. "Then I was injured, and they put Musial on first base, and I never got back. So I played some outfield. But I really didn't realize the seriousness of it all. I was just a big kid trying to do my best.

"After I didn't play much in 1947, I told the Cardinals I wanted to be traded. I told them to trade me anywhere but Philadelphia. So what do they do? They trade me to Philadelphia. As it turned out, it was the biggest break in my life."

The Cardinals shipped Sisler to the Phillies for reserve infielder Ralph LaPointe and $20,000 just before the start of the 1948 season. Dick was immediately installed as the Phillies' starting first baseman.

Playing his first full season as a regular, Sisler hit .274 with 11 home runs and 56 RBI. The following season, though, the Phillies acquired first baseman Eddie Waitkus in a trade with the Chicago Cubs, and Dick was ticketed for reserve duty in the outfield.

In mid-June, however, Waitkus was shot by a crazed, 19-year-old stenographer in a Chicago hotel room, and Sisler was pressed back into service at first base. Dick wound up the season with a .289 average, seven homers, and 50 RBI. Waitkus recovered in time for the 1950 season, and Sisler went to left field. The season would turn into Dick's greatest as a player.

Early in the season, he reeled off eight consecutive hits against the Cardinals. On May 4, he drilled a home run and four singles and drove in five runs. The next day, he spanked three straight singles before being stopped on a ground out, just two hits short of tying the National League record.

Throughout the season, Sisler was a major contributor to the Phillies' offense, and he finished the year with career highs in average (.296), home runs (13), and RBI (83).

Sisler's memorable homer vaulted the Phillies into the World Series, but the hustling Whiz Kids were no match for the haughty New York Yankees.

The Phillies lost in four straight, dropping each of the first three games by one run.

"For us, the World Series was really very anti-climactic," Sisler said. "Our ball club was completely worn out. We enjoyed being in the Series, but we were shot. Our offense was dead, our pitchers were all tired, Andy Seminick was trying to play on a broken ankle, and we didn't even have Curt Simmons, who by then was in the Army.

"We got good pitching in the Series, especially when Jim Konstanty lost the first game, 1–0, and Roberts lost the second, 2–1, in 10 innings. But they had good pitching, too, with [Vic] Raschi, [Allie] Reynolds, [Eddie] Lopat, and [Whitey] Ford. All four were very tough. I doubt if we could've beaten anybody, but especially not the Yankees."

Sisler had just one hit in the Series in 17 at-bats. It drove in the Phillies' first run in a 3–2 loss in the third game.

Dick and the rest of the Phillies went home for the winter to contemplate another run for the pennant. It never happened. The Whiz Kids slipped to fifth place in 1951. Dick hit .287 in what would turn out to be his last year in Philadelphia.

That winter, the Phillies, desperately in need of a second baseman, made a blockbuster trade with the Cincinnati Reds, sending Sisler, his roommate Seminick, reserve infielder Eddie Pellagrini, and pitcher Niles Jordan to the Rhineland for second sacker Connie Ryan, catcher Smoky Burgess, and pitcher Howie Fox.

"The trade really hurt," said Sisler. "I hated to leave Philadelphia, hated to leave the manager [Eddie Sawyer] and the owner [Bob Carpenter], who was always wonderful to me. I was absolutely crushed.

"I had some big hits for Philly, and not just the home run in '50. I hit some other home runs at Shibe Park that were pretty big, too, although I really wasn't a home run hitter. I used to go for line drives, trying to put them all over the field. But I was really sorry to leave the Phillies. In a way, I guess it was really the beginning of the end for me."

Dick was in Cincinnati barely long enough to shake hands. In May, the Reds swapped him and shortstop Virgil Stallcup to the Cardinals for outfielder Wally Westlake and third baseman Eddie Kazak. Dick went back to first base in St. Louis and wound up the season with a .256 average.

Sisler played in 32 games the following year with St. Louis, again hitting .256. But during the season, the Cards shipped him down to the minors, and he spent the rest of the year at Columbus of the International League, where he hit .348 in 39 games.

Dick never returned to the majors as a player. He spent three seasons as a regular with San Diego of the Pacific Coast League—once hitting .318 and once .329—and two seasons with Nashville of the Southern League where he was playing-manager in 1957–58.

After retiring as a player, Sisler managed the Vols again in 1959, then moved to Seattle to skipper the PCL club there. From 1961 to 1964, he was a coach with Cincinnati. The Reds won the National League pennant in 1961.

In midseason in 1964, Sisler was called on to replace Fred Hutchinson after it was discovered that the Reds' manager had lung cancer. Dick piloted the Reds over the final 53 games of the season, finishing in a second-place tie with the Phillies, who had blown a six and one-half game lead that season with 12 games left to play.

Hutchinson died that November, and Sisler was named the regular manager. The Reds finished fourth in 1965, and Sisler was let go. "I managed for one and one-half years in the big leagues, and it was a great honor," said Sisler, "although the way it happened I hated to get that job. Freddy Hutchinson was a good friend of mine. Taking over his club, then watching him die was the toughest thing I ever did. It was a good ball club, and we almost won it for him."

"We had a good club in 1965, too," Sisler added. "But after the season, [general manager] Bill DeWitt wanted somebody else to manage, so I was let go. Nevertheless, it was a great thrill to have managed."

Sisler ended his big league managerial career with a 121–94 record. But he wasn't out of work long. In 1967, he rejoined the Cardinals as a coach, and over the next two years he picked up two more World Series rings to bring his total to five.

Dick was later a hitting coach with the San Diego Padres and New York Mets before moving in 1983 to the Yankees as a minor league batting instructor. In the mid-1980s, he returned to the Cardinals and spent several years as a hitting instructor for the Redbirds' minor league clubs at Johnson City, Tennessee, and Hamilton, Ontario.

"I spent a whole lot more time as a coach than I did anything else," said Sisler. "But I had a whole lot of pleasure from this game. Looking back, I have an awful lot of good memories.

"I am absolutely satisfied with my career. When I see all the guys who would love to be big league ballplayers and all the guys in the minors who I know won't ever make it because they just don't have that little extra, I think how fortunate I've been. I've had a wonderful career, and I thank the good Lord for it."

And Phillies fans still thank Dick Sisler for the home run he hit in 1950. It was a blow that will always rank first in the hearts and minds of Phillies rooters everywhere.

Rick Wise

A No-Hitter Like No Other

WHEN IT COMES to having a career that includes a little bit of everything, Rick Wise would be hard to beat. You name it, and the hard-throwing righthanded pitcher probably did it.

A major leaguer at the age of 18. Owner of a no-hitter. Traded for Steve Carlton once and Dennis Eckersley another time. Winning pitcher in a 1975 World Series game that was one of the most riveting ever played. Ten-time winner in double figures. Pitcher of four one-hitters. Winner of a pennant-clinching game and an All-Star game. And one of baseball's finest hitting pitchers.

These are just some of the accomplishments of Wise during an 18-year career in the major leagues. His career was filled with highlights that made him one of the premier hurlers of his era.

The 6-2, 180-pound native of Jackson, Michigan, did his best work with the Boston Red Sox. He hurled for the Bosox for four years, including the memorable 1975 season. Wise also went to the mound with a substantial measure of success with the Philadelphia Phillies, St. Louis Cardinals, and Cleveland Indians before waging his final campaigns with the San Diego Padres.

His career in the majors began in 1964 when he recorded his first win while pitching the second game of a doubleheader after Jim Bunning had tossed a perfect game in the opener. It ended in 1982 with Wise the owner of a 188–181 lifetime record with a highly commendable 3.69 earned run average.

Altogether, Wise, a resident of Hillsboro, Oregon, appeared in 506 games, 455 as a starter. He worked 3,127 innings, allowing 3,227 hits, striking out 1,647, and walking 804 while registering 138 complete games and 30 shutouts.

Rick won 19 games one season and lost 19 games another season. With a little more luck, he certainly would have had some 20-win seasons and doubtless would have won 200 games in his career.

He didn't pitch often for very good teams, especially in Philadelphia, Cleveland, and San Diego. When he did, his numbers invariably revealed the true measure of the bespectacled hurler's talent.

Unquestionably, Wise's finest season occurred in 1975 when he posted a 19–12 record and was the bellwether of an excellent pitching staff that helped the Red Sox win the American League pennant. He not only led the pitching staff, he also hurled seven strong innings and got the win, 5–3, in the third and deciding game of the League Championship Series in which Boston swept the Oakland A's to win the pennant. Then, after starting and getting no decision in the third game of the World Series against the Cincinnati Reds, he was the winning pitcher with one inning of shutout relief when Carlton Fisk hit his memorable home run in the 12th inning of the sixth game, won by Boston, 7–6. That game has been labeled one of the most dramatic in World Series history.

"It was, absolutely," Wise agrees. "And even though I just pitched the 12th inning, I was thrilled to be part of it. We weren't even supposed to be in the same class as The Big Red Machine, but five games were decided by one run, and we battled them tooth and nail all the way [before losing, 4–3, in the seventh game].

"Carlton Fisk is now immortal for that home run. When he hit it, he was doing that thing with the body English. I was doing the same thing in the dugout. When the ball went out, it was a feeling of total elation. Now, we had a chance to go to the seventh game of the World Series. It was just a tremendous feeling.

"Actually, it was a wonderful year all around," Wise continues. "We had the Rookie of the Year and Most Valuable Player in Fred Lynn. That year, Jim Rice could have done the same thing if he'd been on another team. And then his hand was broken on a pitch by Vern Ruhle with a couple of weeks to go in the season. He never got to compete in postseason play. It was very disappointing for him, and it certainly hurt our chances.

"But it was a wonderful experience, especially for me, because it had been 11 years since I was involved in a pennant race. You never know when you're going to get another chance at postseason play, so 1975 was a very big year for me.

"Obviously, it was one of the highlights of my career. But one of the big things about '75 that was important to me was that I came back from a career-threatening injury the year before. My career could have been over. I had a very bad arm injury. Coming back from that was the thing that really gave me the most gratification."

There were, of course, other times that gratification visited Wise. One was certainly the no-hitter he threw in 1971 for the Phillies against the Reds.

In that game, Rick not only blanked a Cincinnati lineup laden with sluggers such as Johnny Bench, Tony Perez, George Foster, and Pete Rose while striking out three and coming within just one walk (a sixth-inning pass to Dave Concepcion) of a perfect game, he also slammed two home runs. Combined, they drove in three of the runs in the Phillies 4–0 win.

"There have been a couple hundred no-hitters," Wise says. "But that was the only one of its kind in major league history because I also hit two home runs in it. I'm in my own company, and that makes it very special to me.

"It was also special because we won only 67 games that year. It was tough to win with that team. There wasn't much room for error on the pitchers' part. If we got behind, we didn't have the capability of catching up. You had to minimize your mistakes, keep games close, and hope you did well with the bats that day."

Wise came close on several occasions to pitching another no-hitter. In 1975 against the Milwaukee Brewers, he had a perfect game going through six innings and didn't allow a hit until George Scott hit a two-out, two-run homer in the ninth inning. Bobby Darwin followed with another home run, but Wise got the win, 6–3.

Rick also fired four one-hitters during his career, two with Boston in 1976 and two earlier in the National League.

"When I was with the Cardinals, Joe Morgan got a hit off me with one out in the ninth," Rick recalls. "In 1968 when I was with the Phillies, there was a disputed call in Los Angeles against the Dodgers. Jeff Torborg hit a three- or four-hopper up the middle to the left of Bobby Pena, our short-stop. He bobbled the ball. It was clearly an error, but it was ruled a hit, the only hit of the game.

"As soon as the game was over, Bobby went in and called the official scorer, a guy named Phil Collier. He wouldn't reverse the call, and I lost the no-hitter. That hurt. Everyone who played with or against me that day said it was an error.

"Pitching a no-hitter is incredibly tough," Wise adds. "There's no format for it. You have to have at least a couple of good defensive plays behind you. It's a day when the hard-hit balls are right at someone and the pitcher is feeling strong, throwing strikes and is in a rhythm. He can get all his pitches over any time for a strike, and he goes with the flow."

When a no-hitter is in progress, Wise explains, it creates "a feeling that builds like a big wave coming toward the shore. When you have only six outs left, that's when the pitcher really knows he's got a shot at it."

Although the possibility of a no-hitter became an astonishingly frequent part of Wise's pitching regimen, it was someone else's no-hitter that introduced him to the phenomenon. What an introduction it was. On June 21, 1964—Father's Day—Jim Bunning hurled a perfect game for the Phillies against the New York Mets in the first game of a doubleheader at Shea Stadium. The pitcher for the nightcap was none other than the then-18-year-old Wise, making the first start of his major league career.

Somehow, amid the tumult that followed what was the major leagues' first perfect game during the regular season in 42 years, Wise went out and beat the Mets, allowing no hits himself over the first five innings. He wound up pitching six innings, yielding three hits and winning, 8–2.

"What a day," Wise exclaims. "Jim Bunning pitches a perfect game, and then I had to go out and try to do some kind of an encore. Actually, I didn't have time to think about Jim's game. The media was crowding into the clubhouse, and everybody was hooting and hollering. All I was trying to do was find a ball to warm up with, and get ready to pitch.

"But the tension and pre-game jitters were very much with me, as they always were whenever I pitched. As it turned out, I got my first major league win. To me, that was just as big a deal as Jim's perfect game. It was a very thrilling day, to say the least."

Because of a special rule then in effect, Wise had joined the Phillies as a bonus baby and had to be carried on the team's roster despite his youthful age. A pitcher and an occasional shortstop in high school, Wise had signed with the Phillies at the age of 17.

"I signed right out of high school after graduation," he says. "By that time, I was pretty much a full-time pitcher. I enjoyed playing the other position, but as I got toward graduation, I felt my chance to become a professional player was as a pitcher.

"The Phillies sent me to Bakersfield, and I played there in the California League for the rest of the year [posting a 6–3 record in 12 games]. The next year, I was in the big leagues.

"It was awesome. Here you are pitching your high school team to the state championship, and then the next year you're facing Willie Mays, Willie McCovey, and hitters like that. And on top of that, you're in a pennant race."

Phillies manager Gene Mauch carefully picked the spots to start his young hurler. Wise started eight games, relieved in 17 others, and finished the season with a 5–3 record.

The Phillies, meanwhile, spent much of the season in first place and, with 12 games left in the season, commanded a six and one-half game lead. Pennant-starved Phillies fans were about ready to launch their victory celebration when the team went into a nosedive that didn't end until the club had lost 10 straight games and fallen out of the lead, never to return.

"I was really too inexperienced to know what a pennant race was," says Wise. "I didn't start any games down the stretch, although I did relieve in some. In retrospect, I can't second-guess Mauch for not going with an 18-year-old in the thick of a pennant race.

"But I would have been very confident if I had been handed the ball. I did well in the three games I relieved in in September. I didn't worry about it. I didn't try to analyze it. I just tried to prepare myself to be ready when Gene gave me the ball, so that I could do the best I could."

After the disastrous 1964 season, the bonus rule then in existence permitted the Phillies to ship Rick to the minors, which they did. He spent one and one-half years in the Pacific Coast League before returning to the Phils midway through the 1966 season.

At that point, Wise was in the big leagues to stay. Moved into the starting rotation in 1967, Rick posted records of 11–11, 9–15, 15–13, and 13–14 over the next four seasons in Philadelphia. Then, in 1971, he moved into the upper levels of National League pitchers with a 17–14 record, a glittering 2.88 ERA, and his no-hitter.

In addition to the no-hitter, there was another game Wise pitched with the Phillies in 1971 that he regards as his finest. "It was against the Chicago Cubs," he recalls. "I gave up a home run and an unearned run in the first inning and a leadoff home run in the second. I was already down, 3–0. Ray Rippelmeyer, our pitching coach, came out and tried to settle me down a little bit.

"I then retired 32 straight men. I threw over 10 perfect innings, second to Harvey Haddix [who retired 36 in a row in 1959] in big league history. In the ninth inning, I doubled but was stranded. We went three more innings, and finally I drove in the winning run in the bottom of the 12th to win, 4–3. I think that was my all-time best-pitched game. Without a doubt, that was a helluva game, if I may say so.

"In 1971," Wise continues, "I felt that I had finally arrived as a big league pitcher. I led the staff in every major category. I was 17–14 with a team that lost 95 games. I had 37 starts and close to 20 [17] complete games. I pitched a no-hitter. And I had six home runs that year."

Hitting home runs had always been a specialty that was close to Wise's heart. Rick slugged 15 of them during his career, and his six in 1971 were just three shy of Wes Ferrell's all-time major league one-season record for a pitcher. That year, he hit two home runs in one game twice, which tied a major league record.

"I always liked to hit," Wise says. "Without ever having an ounce of hitting instruction, I was just a good, natural hitter. I was a good hitter in Little League, in Babe Ruth, in American Legion ball. I worked at it the best I could, although as pitchers we didn't get that much time to hit. Pitchers got 20 minutes a day for batting practice. We always played little games, like starters against relievers. We'd play for 50 cents a man, and at the end of the year, we'd throw a little party with the money that was accumulated."

Wise's hitting games and his days in Philadelphia, however, were numbered. No sooner had he become established as a bona fide big league star than the Phillies abruptly traded him to St. Louis for Carlton. Phillies fans were livid. Rick had become one of their big favorites, and swapping him for the still somewhat unheralded Carlton made no sense to them.

Wise had been asking the Phillies for a fairly substantial raise and had reached an impasse with the club because general manager John Quinn refused to give in. Simultaneously, Carlton was involved in the same predicament in St. Louis. Quinn, in his last year as Phillies GM, thought he could solve the problem in what would become his final trade.

"I was really surprised," remembers Wise, "particularly after the kind of year I'd just had. At a banquet that winter, Quinn and his wife happened to be seated next to my wife Susan and me. He told Susan, 'We're never going to trade Rick Wise.'

"But nothing's etched in stone in baseball. I didn't have any leeway because we didn't have free agency at that time. So I just accepted it, and went about my business.

"The thing that was weird about it was the politics involved. Neither one of us was very happy with our contracts. I was only making $30,000 after seven years in the big leagues, and I wanted more money. I went to St. Louis and got basically what I had wanted from the Phillies. And Steve came to Philadelphia and got what he had asked St. Louis for. So, it was just a management decision. We had no say in it. We were just professionals trying to do the best we could in a game we loved very much."

The fact that he was swapped for a pitcher who would go on to a Hall of Fame career is not lost on Wise. But he does not regard it as a particular source of satisfaction. "Steve was always a good pitcher," Wise says. "In the years that followed the trade, he was a great pitcher. And he went to the Hall of Fame.

"But the trade doesn't give me any satisfaction because I was traded for a future Hall of Famer. I've been traded for some darn good players over the years. Obviously, my worth in the market was as good as theirs. I think my career speaks for itself. I wouldn't have been traded for them if it hadn't been that way.

"Steve and I were good friends. We lived together during the off-season in St. Louis. We went hunting and fishing together. We never talked about the trade, though."

Wise stayed just two years in St. Louis. He went 16–16, 3.11 for a fourth-place team in 1972, and led the Cardinals' staff with a 16–12, 3.37 mark in 1973. That year, the Redbirds went down to the wire before finishing one and one-half games behind the Mets in a wild pennant race in which five of the six teams in the division were separated by five games.

Wise was also named for the second time to the National League All-Star team that year. He didn't pitch in his first game in 1971, but this time he was given the starting assignment in the game at Kansas City. He pitched two innings, allowing two hits and one run, and was awarded the verdict as the winning pitcher after the Nationals triumphed, 7–1.

Wise, with an assortment of effective pitches and excellent control, was extremely tough on hitters. "I was a fastball-control pitcher," Rick declares. "I also threw a curveball, a slider, and a changeup. I spotted my fastball. Although I was a power pitcher, I wasn't a great strikeout pitcher. But I had a two-to-one [strikeouts-to-walks] ratio, which is considered good. I tried to make them hit the ball."

National League hitters rejoiced when shortly after the 1973 season ended, the Cardinals sent Wise and outfielder Bernie Carbo to the Red Sox for outfielder Reggie Smith and pitcher Ken Tatum. But Boston had to wait a year for the real Rick Wise. In 1974, arm trouble limited him to nine games and a 3–4 record.

The following year, though, Wise made up for lost time. Combining with 18-game winner Luis Tiant and 17-game winner Bill Lee, Rick's 19 wins led the Bosox to the pennant and a berth in the World Series.

Pitching at Fenway Park with its storied left field wall didn't bother Wise. "I just pitched. I didn't worry about the wall," he says. "How can you let a wall bother you?

"Some days, you couldn't shoot a ball out of there with a cannon, the wind was blowing so hard. The wall made you concentrate more. It made you pitch better. But you can't let the dimensions of a ballpark dictate how you pitch. You still have to pitch inside [to righthanded batters] at Fenway, even though it's only 315 feet down the line.

"A lot of times balls that might have gone out, hit the top of the wall and bounced back for long singles or maybe doubles. Other times a ground ball into left field that would have scored a runner in a regulation ballpark wouldn't score the runner because left field was so shallow. So, there was a lot of give and take with the wall."

After 1975, Wise pitched two more years in Boston, compiling records of 14–11 and 11–5. During spring training in 1978, the Red Sox stunned the baseball world by trading Wise, catcher Bo Diaz, and two others to Cleveland for two players, including pitcher Dennis Eckersley.

Wise toiled two years with the Indians, going 9–19 in 1978 and leading the American League in losses. He bounced back in 1979 with a 15–10 log. After that season, he joined the free agent market and signed with the Padres. He was 6–8 and 4–8 in two years in San Diego and pitched in one game in 1982 before drawing his release.

Rick was out of baseball until 1985 when he became pitching coach in the Oakland A's farm system. He spent two years there, then the following three years as a minor league pitching coach in the Houston Astros' organization.

In 1990, Wise made a comeback of sorts as a player, spending the winter pitching for the Winter Haven Super Sox in the now-defunct Senior Professional Baseball Association in Florida and in the summer pitching and coaching in New Brunswick, Canada. He was hired by the Red Sox in 1991 and worked as a pitching coach in the minors through most of the 1990s.

"I enjoy coaching very much," Wise says. "It keeps me in baseball, which

I love, and it gives me a chance to work with young people and try to help them realize their dreams to become major league pitchers.

"I just try to help them," he adds. "I don't emphasize my own career. I don't want clones of Rick Wise. I try to take their strengths and work accordingly. You have to take each individual's strength and work with it."

If some of them happen to pitch like Wise, however, so much the better. But that is rather unlikely.

Players who can pitch like he did, who can also hit, and who have had as varied and as successful a career as Rick Wise don't come along very often.

3

Men on
the Mound

Ralph Branca

One Pitch Obscured a Fine Career

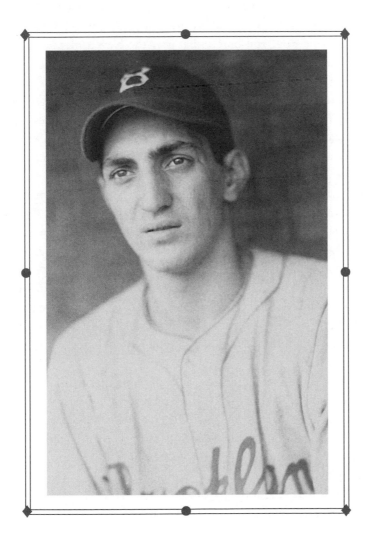

IN A SPORT in which contradictions occur with astonishing regularity, Ralph Branca might represent baseball's greatest paradox.

Branca, of course, was the man who—as any baseball fan should know—threw what could be charitably described as one of the most inopportune pitches ever hurled. It was just one pitch. But it not only fostered one of the most shocking defeats the game has ever witnessed, it would indelibly link Branca's name with misfortune and haunt him for the rest of his life.

And that's too bad. It's too bad because one pitch—which Bobby Thomson blasted for a three-run homer that gave the New York Giants the National League pennant on October 3, 1951—obliterated what was otherwise a fine career for Branca.

Although it was a career cut short by injuries, Branca was an excellent pitcher for the Brooklyn Dodgers. He appeared in the major leagues in 12 different seasons, posting an 88–68 lifetime record with a 3.79 ERA in 322 games. For a time, Branca was considered one of the finest young moundsmen in the game.

In 1947, at the tender age of 21, Branca had a 21–12 record, making him one of the youngest pitchers in baseball history to win 20 games. Only seven other pitchers (Bob Feller, Babe Ruth, Rube Marquard, Joe Wood, Dwight Gooden, Kid Nichols, and Noodles Hahn) have won more games than Branca at the age of 21 or younger.

Branca was well on his way to 20-win seasons three other times but was sidetracked by injuries and other bad luck. The 6-3, 220-pound righthander from Mt. Vernon, New York, had a sizzling fastball and a devastating curve, and when he was healthy, National League batters hated to come to the plate against him.

Yet, Branca is best remembered for the pitch he threw to Thomson. It is a lamentable albatross that the likeable ex-hurler still carries with him.

"The one thing I'm remembered for is throwing a home run pitch," says Branca. "But I could give you trivia questions: who's the youngest guy in history ever to start a playoff game? who's the only guy ever to start a triple play in a playoff game? I started a World Series game at the age of 21. I started an All-Star game at the age of 22. I made the All-Star team at the ages of 21, 22, and 23. Nobody remembers that stuff.

"I'll tell you one thing. They didn't send in the worst pitcher they had [to face Thomson]. They sent in their best pitcher in that spot."

The spot, of course, was the bottom of the ninth inning in the third game of a best-of-three playoff between the Giants and Branca's Dodgers. With a hot streak in which they won 37 of their last 44 regular-season games, the Giants had overcome a 13½-game Dodgers lead to tie for first place, forcing a special playoff to decide the National League pennant-winner.

The teams split the first two games of the series with Thomson's two-run home run beating Branca, 3–1, in the opener and the Dodgers exploding to a 10–0 win in the second game.

In the last game, held at New York's Polo Grounds, the Dodgers led, 4–1, entering the last inning. Don Newcombe had struck out the side in the eighth, but in the bottom of the ninth he gave up singles to Alvin Dark and Don Mueller, then a one-out double to Whitey Lockman. While Mueller, who had broken his ankle sliding into third on Lockman's hit, was being treated, the Dodgers summoned Branca from the bullpen to face the hard-hitting Thomson.

The Scotsman took the first pitch for a strike, then slammed the next offering—a fastball—into the stands in left field, giving the Giants a dramatic 5–4 victory and sending them into the World Series for the first time since 1937. The homer, dubbed "The Shot Heard 'Round the World," made Thomson a national hero.

For Branca, though, the residue was vastly different. While the nation's newspapers were filled the next day with pictures of the jubilant Thomson, stories told of the crestfallen Dodgers hurler sobbing on the steps in the Brooklyn clubhouse. In the moments following the game, Ralph was a tragic figure, but his grief, he says, did not last long.

"As I watched the ball go out, I was devastated," Branca recalls. "I was absolutely shattered. But an hour later, I met my wife-to-be [Ralph and Ann Mulvey were married 17 days later] out in the parking lot—we were going out to dinner with another couple. When we got to the restaurant, a priest who was dean of discipline at Fordham University was there. He made it easy for me. He said, 'God chose you to bear this cross because he knew your faith was strong enough to bear it.' From that point on, I was okay. I thought about it, and said, 'Hey, it's part of the game. He hit a home run and beat me. He was a better man that day.'

"I think the whole thing was tougher on my family," Branca adds, "because they had no retort to people who'd give them the needle about me throwing the home run pitch. But I could always tell people, 'They sent in a guy who was willing and aggressive enough to say, "Give me the ball."'

"People forget," Ralph continues, "that I pitched parts of two innings on Sunday, relieving against the Phillies in a 14-inning game [a game that Brooklyn won on Jackie Robinson's home run to gain a tie for the pennant]. I think I pitched that Saturday, too. Then I pitched eight innings in the first playoff game on Monday. I started and pitched very effectively, only giving up four hits. I kiddingly say, 'I scattered two hits—two in the park and two outside the park.' Thomson beat me with a home run in that one, too. Nobody remembers that.

"They just remember the second one he hit," Branca laments. "But even that one got blown out of proportion. The only reason it got so much publicity was because there were two New York teams playing, and New York's the media capital of the world. Actually, Brooklyn had two famous home runs hit against it in successive years. In 1950, it was almost the same thing. Dick Sisler hit a three-run homer in the last inning to beat Newcombe and win the pennant for the Phillies.

"Bill Mazeroski also hit one in the bottom of the ninth inning to beat the New York Yankees in a World Series. What could be more dramatic than that? You've had dozens of famous home runs. But the one people remember most is the one I gave up. It was just more in the spotlight because it was in New York, and it's been kept alive. Even Russ Hodges' call on the radio helped to keep it alive."

So does the media, says Branca, even though the event took place nearly 50 years ago. "The media has to talk about it. I accept that," Branca says. "I know I'm going to hear about it until the day they put me in the grave. It didn't bother me for about 25 years. Then it bothered me because I got tired of it. I wanted people to remember me because I was a good, young pitcher. The last few years, it's eased off. I can talk about it again."

He even talks to Thomson about it. Because fate threw the two together, they have become good friends over the years. The two even have a routine they do together at sports banquets, singing an amended version of the one-time hit song *It Had to Be You*.

"Bobby's a good guy," Ralph says. "He's a very humble guy. He's a gentleman; a class act. He has a wonderful wife. We all get along very well. We go out together. In fact, we took a cruise together."

If only, though, he hadn't thrown him that fastball.

"It's funny because some years ago, I was at a dinner and Sal Maglie was there," Branca recalls. "He had been my roommate in Brooklyn when he came over in 1956 and in 1957. I was telling him, if I had to do it over again, I would try to waste a fastball because I wanted him to hit the curveball.

"Maglie said, 'Hey, if you wanted him to hit the curveball, why the hell didn't you throw him the curveball?' That made sense because here we were at the most crucial part of the whole season, and I was still being a pitcher. In that situation, you don't pitch. You have nothing to set him up for. You just go ahead and make him hit your pitch."

Over the years, Branca did make a huge assortment of batters hit his pitch. He always had a good hit-to-innings pitched ratio. During his entire career, he allowed 1,372 hits while working in 1,484 innings. He struck out 829 and walked 663.

"The fastball was my best pitch," he recalls, "but I had a curveball, slider, and changeup. The curveball was one of those big overhand downers. I threw it too hard and never really mastered it. If I could've shortened it and got control of it, I could've been more effective. But we had no pitching coach in those days, and I didn't know how to do it. I only knew one way to throw it.

"Basically," Branca continues, "I pitched the ball inside. But there were inside hitters like Puddinhead Jones and Eddie Waitkus of the Phillies and Nippy Jones of the Cardinals. They hit me for a while until I started pitching them away.

"Stan Musial was the toughest guy I faced," Ralph adds. "But he was tough on everybody. I didn't pitch against Ted Williams enough, but I could see what little I pitched against him that he was a very, very tough hitter.

"In the National League, you went in spurts. Some guys hit me for a while, then I'd find out how to pitch to them. Ralph Kiner hit me good for one year. Monte Irvin hit me good for one year. Whitey Kurowski did, too. But nobody could call me 'cousin.'"

Quite the contrary: Before injuries started to take a toll, Branca was as tough to hit as any pitcher in the league. Batters especially disliked going up against his heavy fastball, a pitch that came in at 93–94 miles per hour and made their bats feel like they were made out of lead when the ball and bat made contact.

Ironically, Branca hadn't always been a pitcher. "When I started out, I was a second baseman," he recalls. "Then the Cooper brothers [pitcher

Mort and catcher Walker] were in vogue. So I became a catcher for my older brother John, who was a pitcher. But he got too old for the league, so I became the pitcher. I remember it was in a 12-and-under league.

"I was a Giants fan as a kid," Branca adds. "That's ironic, isn't it? My hometown of Mt. Vernon was mostly Yankees fans, about 70 to 30 Yankees over the Giants, I'd say. There was no measurable number of Dodgers fans. I only knew one kid when I was growing up who was a Dodgers fan."

When he became old enough to begin thinking of a professional career, Branca at first gave no consideration to signing with the Dodgers. He was anxious to become a Giant.

"In those days, they had tryout camps," he remembers. "I went to one at the Polo Grounds. They had a tremendous throng there, but we got rained out and I never got to throw the ball. My brother was the star pitcher in high school, so he got to throw. But I was only 16, and I didn't get a chance.

"Then we went to Yankee Stadium and worked out there. They said I was too young, and that they'd get in touch with me next year, which they never did.

"Then we went to Brooklyn. They had a tryout camp way out at Sheepshead Bay. I threw there and they liked me. They had me come back and throw batting practice for them. Afterward, they kept tabs on me. I signed the next year when I was 17."

Branca spent his first season with Olean, New York, of the Pony League, racking up a 5–5 record in 14 games. The following spring he jumped all the way to the Dodgers, but after working in 21 games (0–2 record) he was shipped out to Montreal of the International League, where he went 4–5 the rest of the season.

Ralph began the 1945 campaign with St. Paul of the American Association. After going 6–5, he was called up to Brooklyn where he was 5–6 in 16 games. More important, Branca was in the big leagues to stay.

"I first got to the big leagues at the age of 18," says Branca, who attended New York University in the off-season during his first two years as a pro. "I probably would've made the big leagues early in my career, anyway. But I got there at 18 because it was during the war, and if you were in the big leagues you were either too old or too young to join the service.

"I was too young to be drafted, so they put me on the team. They had a lot of old guys on the club. In fact, in my first big league win, Babe Herman got a pinch-hit in the eighth inning to win the game for me. He was 42 and I was 19. We beat the Boston Braves, 3–2."

In 1946, the war had ended and players were returning in droves to the majors from the military. "There was a real backup of talent right after the war," Branca recalls. "There were guys who had been in the service and guys who had been in the minor leagues and matured. The teams all had 30-man rosters for a while to accommodate all the extra players."

Nevertheless, Branca managed to withstand the huge influx of talent and win a job with the Dodgers, although he was still a raw 20-year-old with little experience. He pitched in only 24 games, starting 10 of them. His record was 3–1 for the season.

"I guess the game that really made me was the one I'd call the best game of my career," Branca says. "I had made the starting rotation, but then I got hit in the arm in Boston and never got back in the rotation. Now, it was mid-September. We were playing the Cardinals and fighting for the pennant. They were one-half game behind us.

"Leo Durocher wanted me to pitch to the first batter, then bring in [Vic] Lombardi, a little lefthander. The Cards had a predominantly good lefthanded-batting club.

"Well, my fuse was short then. I was warming up, saying, 'Sacrificial lamb, my butt.' I ended up getting them out on five pitches in the first inning, and Durocher never brought in Lombardi. The end result was I pitched a three-hit shutout and beat them, 5–0.

"The next start, I also pitched a shutout. I beat the Pirates. But that start against the Cardinals at the age of 20 was a game I'll never forget. I'll always consider it my best game. I struck out nine and didn't walk a batter."

Although the Dodgers would tie for the pennant, then lose in a best-of-three playoff to the Cardinals, those back-to-back shutouts served as a clear indication of what was to follow for Branca.

In 1947, Ralph became the big man of the Brooklyn pitching staff, hurling the Dodgers to the National League pennant with a glittering 21–12 record. Branca led the league with 36 starts and was third in earned run average with a 2.67 and second in both innings pitched (280) and strikeouts (148).

It was a great year for National League pitchers as Branca was joined as a 20-game winner by Cincinnati's Ewell Blackwell (22–8), New York's

Larry Jansen (21–5), and Boston's Warren Spahn (21–10) and Johnny Sain (21–12).

"I knew I belonged in that group," Branca says. "I was just 21 years old, and I really didn't realize how tough it was to win. I could blow the ball by guys, and I had a big curveball. For a guy that young, I got the ball over the plate. I walked guys, but I was always around the plate. I wasn't really a wild man. I just went out and pitched every four days."

The workhorse of the Dodger staff, Branca registered 15 complete games and four shutouts. And not only did he get named to the NL All-Star team (although he didn't play), he was chosen to the Major League All-Star team at the end of the season by *The Sporting News*.

Branca was the starting pitcher for Brooklyn in the World Series opener against New York. After retiring the first 12 batters, he was knocked out in the fifth inning when the Yankees scored five runs en route to a 5–3 victory.

Ralph relieved in the third game, a 9–8 Dodger victory. He relieved again in the sixth game and received credit for the win in an 8–6 Brooklyn triumph in the game made famous by Al Gionfriddo's catch of Joe DiMaggio's 415-foot drive to the left-center field fence off of Joe Hatten.

In 1948, Branca picked up where he had left off the previous year. By mid-season, he had a 12–5 record and was named the National League's starting pitcher in the All-Star Game in St. Louis. Ralph worked the first three innings but was not involved in the decision in a 5–2 American League victory. He won only two more games the rest of the season, finishing with a 14–9 record.

"I had gotten hit in the leg by a teammate who was fooling around and let a bat go," Branca explains. "It hit me in the shins. In those days, they didn't know enough to put ice on an injury. I just went out in the field and did some running. The trainer never treated the leg at all. Two months later, my leg got infected. I tried to favor it when I pitched, and that led to a sore arm. My arm was really hurting. I ended up going into the hospital for two weeks and taking a huge amount of penicillin to get the infection out of my leg."

Misfortune struck again in 1949. Ralph had a 10–1 record in July, but more arm trouble put him on the sidelines and he settled for a 13–5 record for the year. With Brooklyn back in the World Series, he took the loss in the third game when the Yankees beat him, 4–3.

Over the next two years, Branca divided his time between the starting rotation and the bullpen, posting a 7–9 record in 1950 and a 13–12 mark in 1951.

"I was going both ways in 1951," Branca recalls. "I started the season as a reliever. I was the stopper in the bullpen. By July, they needed another starter, so I got the call against the Phillies in a game against Robin Roberts. I think we went six innings in the rain. In the seventh, I went into the clubhouse, took a shower, changed my shirt, got a rubdown, and went back out and pitched the last three innings. We won the game, 6–2.

"Dick Young was a great writer from New York. His lead on the story the next day was, 'Ralph Branca relieves Ralph Branca.'

"After that, I won, 2–1 and 3–1. The next game, I was losing 1–0 after seven innings, but we won, 2–1, when Gil Hodges hit a home run in the ninth. Then I won another game, 4–2. I straightened out the pitching staff. In the span of five games, I pitched 43 innings out of a possible 45."

Starting 27 games and relieving in 13 in 1951, Branca teamed with 20-game winners Newcombe (20–9) and Preacher Roe (22–3) and with Carl Erskine (16–12) to drive the Dodgers to a big midseason lead and then to the meetings with the red-hot Giants in that fateful playoff series at the end of the season.

There have been suggestions that the number 13 that Branca wore on his back did nothing to embellish his luck in that series. Why did he wear that number?

"I wore number 13 because I'm a contrary guy," Ralph says. "I would've worn it anyway, but the clubhouse guy, when he was giving out uniforms, said to me, 'Are you superstitious?' I said, 'No.' So he gave it to me. I loved it. Probably, if I had to do it all over, I'd take number 77, though. Maybe that would've changed my luck."

After the 1951 season, Branca had more physical trouble, and slipped to a 4–2 record the next year in just 16 games. "My one regret," he says, "is that I hurt my back in 1952 in spring training. I know I would've had a good year. My arm was strong again. I knew how to pitch. I was only 26. I had enough maturity that I would've had a good year, and the onus of that home run pitch would've been far less. If I'd have had another good year in the big leagues, won 15 or 20, it might have eased some of the heartache.

"Instead, I hurt my back so severely that I couldn't really throw effectively after that. I could throw, but not like I had before. I struggled after that for five years, then I just gave it up."

Branca worked in seven games for the Dodgers in 1953 (0–0 record) before they sold him at midseason to the Detroit Tigers. Ralph went 4–7 for Detroit in 1953, then was 4–3 for the Tigers and Yankees in 1954.

He did not pitch in the big leagues in 1955 but rejoined the Dodgers the following year in a comeback attempt. Branca worked just two innings of one game and then decided to retire. He did so, safe in the knowledge that he had played in the best of times.

"I played for a real good ball club," he says. "The Cardinals were always a good ball club in that era, too. And the Braves were tough, especially in 1948. Then the Phillies came on in 1949 and 1950 and the Giants in 1951.

"I would say that the era from 1946 to 1957 was probably the golden era of baseball as far as talent goes. There were 12,000–15,000 minor leaguers and only 400 big leaguers and 16 ball clubs. When they started to expand and television started killing the minors, the talent got diluted. Now, there are 750 big leaguers and only 3,000 minor leaguers. Other sports have taken away athletes. They're playing football, basketball, golf, tennis, even soccer."

Branca is still connected with baseball, although it involves players at the opposite end of the spectrum from today's millionaire performers. Ralph is executive director of Baseball Alumni Team (BAT), an organization of former major league players who have joined forces primarily to raise funds for needy ex-players.

Formed in 1986, BAT, which operates out of the commissioner's office, raises funds mostly through old-timers games and private donations. To date, more than 100 former players have been helped. Not all of them are old. Some of them are 40 years of age or less.

BAT has given money to players too poor to pay their medical bills. It has provided burial expenses. It has helped ex-players meet mortgages and other obligations that they were unable to pay on their own. And it has come up with funds for numerous other needs of the former players or their widows. BAT also helps ex-players find jobs, assists them in getting legal help and other services, and generally offers to pitch in whenever necessary.

"Baseball is a microcosm of society," Branca says. "You have guys who make a million and lose a million. They make big bucks in baseball, then suddenly the money stops. They come out into the real world, and have no training of any kind. A lot of them can't cope with that."

Branca got involved not only because he cares about such things but because he has a corporate background that allows him to navigate smoothly in the tricky waters of high finance and big business. "I'm really a life insurance agent who got into pensions and corporate benefit plans," he says. "I've been doing that since I got out of baseball. I work for a pension consulting firm in New York."

Ralph served a three-year term as BAT president. "Realistically, it takes a lot out of my life," he says. "Somebody asked me if I mind. Do I resent it? I said, 'Not at all.' The reward is much greater than the time I spend. When you know you're helping some guy and he's in a bind and you can make his life easier, you have to feel good about it."

It's the same kind of good feeling Branca has about his own years as a baseball player. Today, he can look back on his playing days and realize that one pitch was hardly enough to erase the memory of an otherwise fine career.

Elroy Face

The Epitome of a Real Reliever

BACK IN THE DAYS when Elroy Face pitched, a relief pitcher was a real relief pitcher.

There was none of this coming in from the bullpen and facing one batter stuff. No one was a one-inning specialist who ran out of gas if he worked a second inning. There were no labels such as middle-inning workers, set-up men, or closers and no lefthanders who just pitched to lefthanders or right-handers who only faced righthanders. And no one ever heard of that bogus statistic known as a save . . . you know, the one where a guy comes into a game in the ninth with a three-run lead, gives up two runs, then pats himself on the back for "saving" the win.

No, indeed. When Elroy Face took the mound, it was different. Relief pitchers were guys who might get into a game in the third inning and pitch the rest of the way. They'd face everybody—both lefthanded and right-handed batters. If they had to pitch two or three days in a row, they would.

"Relief pitching sure was different when I pitched," says Face. "You might go four or five or six innings. And you'd come back the next day if they needed you. Now, they pitch to one or two batters. One year," he adds, "I either got in the game or warmed up 110 different games. The next year, it was 112."

Pitching long and often never bothered the slightly built righthander, who—despite his 5-8, 155-pound stature—could throw about as hard as anybody and who never had a sore arm in his 16 years in the big leagues.

For nine straight years and 11 of 12 seasons, he never appeared in less than 54 games. Twice, he led the National League with 68 appearances, and five times he marched in from the bullpen more than 60 times in one season.

Only 16 pitchers in big league history have appeared in more games than Face's total of 848. Roy also has the sixth-highest total of career wins in relief (96). And, although no one counted saves when he pitched, when the sta-tistic was instituted in 1969, research showed that he had 193 saves, which placed him in the top 25 among big league relievers—virtually all of them from recent times when saves had become as common as leaves on a tree.

Face has some other noteworthy numbers. His 18–1 record in 1959 is not only the highest winning percentage (.947) in major league history, his 18 relief wins in one season constitute a big league record.

Face pitched in nine straight games during one point in the 1956 season. He won 22 straight games in relief in 1959–60. And in the magic year of 1960, when the Pittsburgh Pirates won the National League pennant and the World Series, Roy was the ironman of the Bucs' staff, credited with 10 wins and 24 saves during the season and three saves in four appearances in the Series.

At the height of his career, Face pitched in 92 straight games without a loss. He pitched in three All-Star games and was voted Fireman of the Year in 1962.

For his career, Face had a 104–95 record and a 3.48 earned run average. In 1,375 innings, he allowed 1,347 hits, struck out 877, and walked 362.

One might easily surmise that Roy's figures are of Hall of Fame caliber. If the point is raised with Face, he is not reluctant to state his case, at times expressing anger that he has not been elected.

"Hell, yes, I think I should be in the Hall of Fame," he fumes. "I think I deserve to be there. Ask any of the guys I played with, and they say the same thing. There are certainly guys in there now who I should be ahead of. But it's all politics and the fact that the sportswriters are the ones who vote. Most of them never saw me play.

"I think I should be considered one of the premier relief pitchers in baseball, but it's sort of a letdown that I'm not in the Hall of Fame."

Although it's now up to the Veterans Committee—and not the sportswriters—to determine whether Roy becomes a member of the Hall of Fame, his not being selected is one of the few letdowns that he has faced. While pitching from 1953 to 1969 in the big leagues, he was about as tough a relief pitcher as there was. When Roy came striding in from the bullpen, hitters knew they were in for a rugged battle.

"I enjoyed relief pitching," he says. "I got to pitch a lot more often than I would have as a starter. And I enjoyed the competition between me and the hitter.

"There was never any pressure on me. The batter was the one who had the pressure. He was the guy who had to hit the ball. I had eight guys behind me. If you throw strikes and make them hit the ball, you have a chance to get them out.

"I threw hard," Face adds. "I had a knack for getting a strikeout the first guy I faced. I could throw the ball by guys. Hank Foiles was my catcher during that 18–1 year, and he said that day in and day out I threw consistently as hard as [Bob] Friend and [Vernon] Law.

"I also threw a curve, a slider, and a forkball. When it was going good, I threw the forkball 60 to 70 percent of the time. My forkball was an off-speed pitch for me. It usually sank, and it made my other pitches better."

Face's pitches were never better than in the 1959 and 1960 seasons when he won 22 straight and went 92 games without a loss. In 1959, when he posted the 18–1 record, he had a 2.70 ERA in 57 games and was later credited with 10 saves. In 1960, he went 10–8 in 68 games with a 2.90 ERA and 24 saves.

"There were six or eight games I could have lost during that streak," Face recalls. "Some of those games we came back to win in the ninth. It was a combination of luck and good defense. I really think I had a better year in 1960. I think I was more effective that year."

That year, the Pirates won the National League pennant by seven games over the Milwaukee Braves, then participated with the New York Yankees in what would become one of the most memorable World Series in history.

The Pirates won the first game, 6–4, with Face pitching two innings and getting a save. They lost the next two games by scores of 16–3 and 10–0 but won the fourth game, 3–2, with Face again getting a save and retiring eight Yankees in a row.

Face notched his third save (remember, saves were not recorded at the time but were attributed later) in Game Five, a 5–2 Pittsburgh win in which Elroy hurled another two and two-thirds scoreless innings.

The little reliever next appeared in Game Seven after the Yankees had evened the Series with a 12–0 win in the sixth game. He pitched three innings, giving up six hits and four runs. He departed in the bottom of the eighth for pinch-hitter Gino Cimoli, who singled during a wild five-run inning in which the Pirates came back from a 7–4 deficit to take a 9–7 lead into the ninth.

In the bottom of the ninth, after the Yanks had gained a 9–9 tie, Bill Mazeroski hit what many consider the greatest clutch home run in baseball history to give Pittsburgh a 10–9 victory and the World Championship.

"I didn't see the home run because I was already out of the game and in the clubhouse," Face remembers. "But it was a great feeling.

"Probably my most memorable game was the one in Yankee Stadium (Game Four) when I came in with a couple of guys on base and retired eight batters in a row. I had three saves in the Series, and I would've won the last game if I hadn't been taken out. The Most Valuable Player award was between me and Bobby Richardson [who had 11 hits and drove in a record 12 runs]. Richardson won it, and it was the first time they'd ever given the award to a player on the losing team.

"It was a great Series, though. One of the greatest of all time. After we won, they had what was probably the biggest celebration ever held in Pittsburgh. Everybody had a good time. It wasn't like the one in 1979 [after another Pirates' Series triumph] when people went on a crime spree, looting and vandalizing everything in sight."

The Pirates team, managed by Danny Murtaugh, was an especially close-knit group, according to Face. "It was just a great ball club. No one was a big hero. Everybody did his job and everybody pulled for the other guy. We had good hitting, good pitching, and good defense. And the guys never gave up. They battled to the end. They all got along, too. Guys were always getting together after a game. Sometimes, seven or eight of us would go out for dinner together.

"Murtaugh was a good manager," Face adds. "He left you alone. He only bothered you if you dogged it. Then he would let you know about it. Otherwise, he'd just let you play. He'd let the pitchers pitch their own games."

It was Murtaugh who turned Face into a reliever. Roy had been a starting pitcher throughout the early part of his career.

"Bobby Bragan became manager of the Pirates in 1956," Face says. "I had played for him in 1952 in the minors. He knew I had a good arm and could throw pretty often. He started using me in relief, but I still started. I started one game in 1957. I was supposed to start another, but Bragan was fired that day, so I didn't start. Murtaugh took over, and he turned me into a full-time reliever.

"It was a good move. I never had arm problems. I was just gifted with a good arm. I did carpentry work in the winter, and that helped keep my arm in shape. And I kept my weight down. In 1957 and 1958, I finished the season at 146 pounds."

The smallness of his stature almost conspired with his age to keep Face out of professional baseball. He didn't sign a pro contract until he was 21, and at that point he was still not a full-time pitcher.

"I was an infielder and pitcher in high school," says the native of Stephentown, New York, a tiny town east of Albany. "Mostly, I played shortstop and pitcher, rotating back and forth with another guy. I didn't play at all until I was 16 years old. We had no little league in my hometown. After high school, I went into the Army. When I came out, I pitched in a semipro league. I was signed as an infielder and pitcher."

Face was signed by a scout named Fred Mathews, who saw him play while vacationing in the area. Roy got a contract calling for $140 a month. It was to be the start of a jig-jag journey to the majors.

"I spent the first two years in the Phillies organization," Face says. "They were the ones who signed me originally. I was sent to Bradford [Pa.] of the Pony League. I was 14–2 and 18–5 my first two years, but for some reason, the Phillies didn't protect me, and I was drafted by the Brooklyn Dodgers. They sent me to Pueblo [Colorado] of the Western League, and I was 23–9 for a sixth-place club and led the league in wins."

The following season, Face posted a 14–11 record at Fort Worth of the Texas League. By then, Branch Rickey, who had originally plucked Face out of the Phillies organization for the Dodgers, was working for Pittsburgh. Once again, Rickey drafted Face, this time bringing him to the Pirates. Face made the Pirates roster in 1953, appearing in 41 games, starting 13 of them, and registering a 6–8 record.

"I remember my first game in the big leagues," he says. "I came in against the Dodgers. The Pirates were getting beaten, 11–2. The Dodgers had the bases loaded, and I struck out Gil Hodges, Jackie Robinson, and Roy Campanella to get out of the inning. Just because I struck out the side, though," Roy adds, "didn't make me think it [pitching in the big leagues] was easy. I knew it wasn't easy. It wasn't even easy in the minors."

The minors were where Face wound up in 1954 after it became apparent that he needed to add more pitches to his arsenal. "When I came up, all I had was a fastball and a curve," Face says. "I won throughout the minors on two pitches. So the Pirates sent me to New Orleans in 1954 to work on an off-speed pitch. That's when I developed my forkball.

"I also pitched mostly sidearm then," Roy continues. "Then I changed to more of an overhand pitcher. It felt better, and I was more comfortable throwing that way."

Even when he returned to Pittsburgh in 1955 after fashioning a 12–11 record at New Orleans, Roy was still an occasional starter. In 42 games that year, he drew 10 starting assignments while going 5–7 for the season.

While leading the league with 68 appearances in 1956, he started three games and finished the season at 12–13. Face would start just one more game the rest of his career (in 1957).

As a full-time reliever, Face's annual numbers of games appearances were 68, 59, 57, 57, 68, 62, 63, 56, and 55. A knee injury that required surgery after he damaged a cartilage while chasing a fly ball during batting practice limited his appearances to 16 in 1965. But he bounced back to work in 54, then 61 games the next two years.

All the while, Roy enjoyed a reputation for his toughness and for being as fearless as any pitcher who ever marched to the mound. Hitters dreaded going up against him, but Roy relished the idea of entering a game and squashing an enemy rally.

"There were some pretty tough hitters in the league," Face recalls. "Richie Ashburn was one. So was Walt Moryn. I was giving pitches away, and he knew it. He told me that after he came to the Pirates later on. Dick Groat, Felipe Alou, they were also tough.

"I didn't have much trouble with the big power hitters. Hank Aaron hit one home run off me, and that was the last time I faced him. Musial beat me once or twice, but I didn't have much trouble against him." Musial later named Face as one of the toughest pitchers he ever came up against. His list also included Bob Gibson, Warren Spahn, Sandy Koufax, and Clem Labine.

While traveling in such select company, Face pitched in four All-Star games. He worked in both games in 1959 and the first game in both 1960 and 1961.

During those years, Face was at the height of his career. After his brilliant 18–1 season in 1959 and his 10–8 mark in 1960, he went 6–12, then 8–7 with a sparkling 1.88 ERA and a career-high 28 saves.

Late in the 1968 season, Face was sold to the Detroit Tigers, ending a string of nearly 15 seasons in Pittsburgh.

"I was not disappointed about leaving," he says. "Brown [general manager Joe Brown] and I didn't hit it off well from 1961 on. But I got to Detroit, and they had 13 straight complete games. I pitched in two games, then they released me at the end of the season."

Face wound up signing the following spring with the expansion Montreal Expos where he played under the redoubtable Gene Mauch. "I really enjoyed playing for him," Face says. "He was for his players, regardless of what happened. He stood behind them. And he was smart. He could tell you in the first inning what he would do in certain situations in the seventh inning."

Face spent the 1969 season with the Expos, going 4–2 in 44 games. Released after the season, he played briefly in Hawaii with the Islanders in 1970 before retiring from baseball at the age of 42.

Afterward, Roy returned to the Pittsburgh area and held a variety of jobs before landing one in 1979 as a carpenter at a state hospital near Pittsburgh. One and one-half years later, he became foreman of the carpenters and remained in that post until retiring in 1990.

Face, who lives in North Versailles, a suburb of Pittsburgh, is an active member of the Pirates alumni association. He still follows baseball closely.

"Basically, baseball is the same game it was when I played," he says. "You have to hit the ball, catch it, and run. The game hasn't changed. Only the players have."

Although he appeared in more games (802) than any other pitcher in Pirates history, it galls Face that he is only mentioned with an asterisk on the Bucs list of all-time save leaders in the team's media guides. Without the asterisk—used because saves did not become an official statistic until 1969—Roy would be the club's all-time leader in that category, too.

"That really ticks me off," he says. "It's not right. I have 30 more saves than the guy they list as the all-time leader [Kent Tekulve], but I only get an asterisk at the bottom of the page. I don't know why they do that."

Face does know, though, that his baseball career was a resounding success, and he is extremely proud of his many accomplishments. "I'd do it all over again, too," he says. "I wouldn't change anything. I played professionally for 21 years and with a lot of very good players. It was an enjoyable career."

And during that career, Face established himself as not only one of the premier relief pitchers of his day but one of the top firemen of all time.

Ned Garver

Pride of the St. Louis Browns

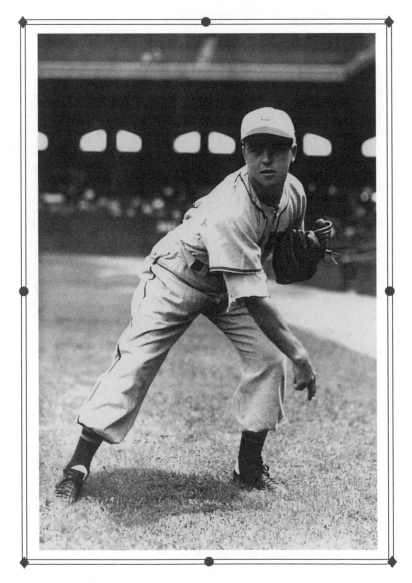

THERE WAS ALWAYS something about Ned Garver that put him in a class by himself.

Garver was a pitcher who through the heart of his career toiled for the lowly St. Louis Browns. That in itself was enough to win Garver a special award for valor. But of even greater significance, Garver was eminently successful, despite his surroundings.

The Browns of the late 1940s and early 1950s were a team that usually fell just short of being atrocious. Either seventh or eighth place in the American League standings was theirs on a regular basis. And good players on the Browns were about as rare as first-division finishes.

This was a team, after all, that once resorted to using a midget as a publicity stunt. It won one pennant in its entire history. And when the barrier finally came down that allowed teams to move to other cities, who do you think was first in line in the American League?

Amid all of this failure, Garver stood out like a cool breeze on an August night in St. Louis. He was a jewel in a pile of rocks; a thoroughbred among nags. No matter how bad the Browns were, Garver never fell into the quagmire with them.

In an era when outstanding pitchers blossomed throughout the major leagues, Ned stood firmly among them. He won 20 games for a team that lost 100. Nobody else in baseball history ever did that.

Garver won 45 games over a three-year period when the Browns won only 163 games altogether (while losing 299). Imagine what he would have done had he been pitching for the Yankees or the Red Sox during that period.

Yet, this bulldog of a pitcher never let things like that or the fact that he never pitched for a first-division team in his 14 years in the big leagues bother him. "I didn't spend any time feeling sorry for myself," says the righthander from Ney, Ohio. "I was just tickled to be there. I could hardly believe that the Good Lord had given me enough ability to play in the big leagues, where, as a kid, I worshipped those people.

"When I was a kid," adds Garver, who played at 5-10, 180 pounds, "I'd go up to Detroit maybe two or three times a year and see [Hank] Greenberg, [Charley] Gehringer, and those fellows play. But to think I'd ever put on a uniform and go on the same field, why that was almost out of the question.

"But here I was doing it. I got to play for a lot of years. And on top of that, I played a lot. The first eight years I was in the big leagues, I pitched 1,760 innings. I got to play that much. If you get to play that much, sitting on the bench would have been a little difficult.

"But I was always allowed to play. Sure, I would have won more games if I'd been with a good club. On the other hand, if I'd have gone with the Yankees or Cleveland or somebody else, I might have been in the minor leagues longer. Also, I might have found it tougher to break in as a starting pitcher. So, I don't dwell on having signed with the Browns."

The Browns, of course, were happy to have a guy like Garver. After all, in his three best years with the club, which ran from 1949 to 1951, no other pitcher even came close to winning in double figures. But Ned won 12 one year, 13 the next, and 20 the third for clubs that twice lost more than 100 games in a season and close to 100 a third time. He led the American League in complete games twice during that period and in 1951 was the starting pitcher for the American League in the All-Star Game.

Garver, who was born on Christmas Day in 1925, pitched in a little less than five seasons in St. Louis. He also pitched for the Detroit Tigers and Kansas City A's before finishing his career in 1961 with the Los Angeles Angels.

Overall, Garver had a 129–157 record with a 3.73 earned run average. He appeared in 402 games, starting 330 and completing 153 of them. In 2,477.1 innings, he gave up 2,471 hits and, ironically, struck out 881 and walked 881.

"I was a good pitcher," he appraises, "and I was a good competitor. I was certainly not an overpowering pitcher. It wasn't often that I tried to strike somebody out.

"I was a sinker-slider pitcher. I had a pretty good sinker, and I had a pretty good slider. Ted Williams will tell you that my slider was a pitch that he had trouble picking up the spin on. And he could pick up the spin on a ball very, very well.

"I would strike out people with it. Satchel Paige used to say, 'Oh boy, if you just had a strikeout pitch.' Well, I didn't strike out a lot of people, but I had good control and I would throw any pitch other than the fastball when I was behind in the count.

"A lot of people back then weren't doing that. They'd get behind in the count, and then they'd come in with the fastball. I didn't do that. I learned to pitch in the minor leagues, and a guy taught me that you deliberately get behind some hitters so you can throw them a change-up or a change-curve and get them out.

"I was a thinker. I pitched smart. Sometimes, you'd outsmart yourself pitching against guys like Yogi [Berra]. Sometimes, you'd guess he was going to do this, and maybe he'd do something else.

"I don't think there was a better hitter than Yogi Berra for one time at bat late in a ball game with the tying run on second. But he'd make a lot of easy outs, too. If the score wasn't close, he didn't bear down like some guys.

"Williams never had a time at bat that he didn't bear down. He was the greatest hitter I ever saw. Joe DiMaggio was a great hitter, too. I didn't see all that much of [Stan] Musial, but he never had any weaknesses that I ever found, so I'd consider him a great hitter. But there weren't many great hitters. A great hitter in my opinion was a guy who didn't have any weaknesses.

"The first time I pitched against Hank Aaron, I told the guys in the dugout, 'That guy's here to stay.' I had a good slider, but he hit my slider. I threw it over the outside part of the plate. I didn't even think he was going to hit it, he waited so long. I thought the catcher was going to catch it. But with those quick wrists, Aaron lashed out at that ball, and hit a line drive to center field that Bill Tuttle caught."

Although he won in double figures eight times during his career, Garver enjoyed his finest season in 1951 when he posted a 20–12 record with a 3.73 ERA for the Browns, who that year finished in last place with a 52–102 record, 45 games behind the first-place Yankees.

Only six other pitchers in the major leagues, including Nolan Ryan and Steve Carlton, won 20 games with a last-place team. The next biggest winner on the St. Louis staff was Duane Pillette, whose record was 6–14.

Ned led the American League that year in complete games with 24. He also made the only appearance of his career in an All-Star Game, working the first three innings and giving up one hit and one run in what eventually became an 8–3 National League victory at Detroit's Briggs Stadium.

"I was lucky to win 20 that year," Garver recalls. "I don't think I was any better that year than I was the year before when I was second in the league in ERA and was never knocked out in the last 19 times I went out there as a starter. I led the league in complete games in 1950, too.

"But we always seemed to score some runs when I was pitching. I think the players thought that if they scored some runs for me, I would probably win. We don't know how much the mental attitude has to do with the game, but I know it had a lot to do with our games on the days I pitched.

"I had 16 wins and a chance to start four more times to win 20," Garver adds. "That meant working about every third day at the end, including the last day of the season.

"I was just barely going to get four starts. I won the first three and then we came down to the last game, and it was the most memorable moment in my baseball career. I was standing on the mound in the ninth inning, and saw the right fielder catch a ball for the final out that made me a 20-game winner. I never had a better feeling."

Always a good man with a bat, Garver also had a banner year at the plate in 1951, hitting a career high .305. Only 16 other pitchers in American League history, including Cy Young, Babe Ruth, and Walter Johnson, hit .300 and won 20 games in the same season.

"I hit seventh in the lineup a lot that year," Garver says. "I could always hit pretty good. In fact, some of the people back home, including some of the coaches I played against, thought I missed the boat by not going into pro ball as a shortstop.

"The first year I played organized ball, I hit .407. Hitting was always easy for me. I could see the ball, and I could hit it. I couldn't hit it terribly far—I hit only seven home runs in the big leagues—but I could hit it often. I think if I'd have played every day, I'd have been a good hitter."

Garver certainly did not lack for strength. Having grown up on a farm in northern Ohio, he built a strong body by doing chores on a daily basis. "We farmed the hard way," he says. "We farmed with horses. There's no question that it was a good way to build strength.

"But I also had two older brothers, and they were good players. That's how you get good—playing against people who are better than you are and not having somebody telling you how good you are all the time.

"I was playing against people who were better than I was, so I was constantly trying to learn and get as good as they were. Some of these kids today, their parents think they're so wonderful, their coaches think they're so wonderful. By the time they're 14 years old, they think they're as good as they need to be, and they quit learning. And they quit getting better. Then, as soon as they start playing against people who are as good as they are, they quit. They find excuses.

"When I scouted for Cincinnati and worked for a while as a minor league pitching coach, every spring we'd bring in all the best kids we'd scouted all over the country. Some of these kids had to play against kids who were as good as they were, and they hadn't done that before. You'd be amazed at how they would come up and tell me, 'Well, I didn't sleep too good last night' or 'I don't feel too good.' They'd have all kinds of alibis. Next thing you know, we'd have to send them home."

For a young Ned Garver, there was no such problem. He was determined to be a pro player. The only question was, at what position?

"I played for Ft. Wayne, Indiana, in the Junior Federation League," Ned remembers. "We went to the national tournament. In that tournament, I played third base, the outfield, and pitcher. When it was over, I had several offers from pro teams. But I had to go into the service first. When I got out, I went to my manager, and said, 'I want to give baseball a try.' I had played several different positions for him. I was really only the third pitcher on that team.

"He said, 'What do you want to go as?' I had pitched all the time in high school and legion ball, and I'd been pretty good at it, so I said, 'Well, I've pitched more than anything else. I think I'll go as a pitcher.' So that was the decision. But it was not cut and dried. Everybody agreed that I could have made it at some other position.

"My manager was a guy named P. L. McCormick. He was a bird-dog scout. He didn't have any real territory, but he recommended people to the Browns. He suggested to me that I stay with him another year and pitch for his club instead of signing. I don't think he should have gotten a whole heckuva lot of credit, but he finally got me a contract for $100 a month with the Browns' Toledo ball club. When I turned out pretty good, he got to be a regular scout with [a territory of] three states.

"He made the announcement that I'd signed after we got eliminated in the national tournament at Youngstown. I didn't even have sense enough to know that four scouts had come to him and offered me a contract to sign. He didn't contact anybody for me or give me their names. He didn't think about which organization would be the best for me. He didn't do anything. And I wasn't smart enough to contact those people myself. But the Browns had sold or traded some of their best players, so I figured I had a good chance with them, and I signed."

Sticking close to home, the 18-year-old Garver spent his first season in pro ball in 1944—the year of the Browns' only pennant—with Newark of the Class D Ohio State League. He was an immediate sensation, garnering a 21–8 record and leading the league in wins, ERA (1.21), innings pitched (245), and strikeouts (221). He also pitched a no-hitter against Marion.

Moved up in 1945, Garver split the season between Elmira (3–1, 2.18) of the Eastern League and Toledo (5–8, 4.64) of the American Association. He spent the 1946 and 1947 seasons with San Antonio of the Texas League, going 8–8 and 17–14, respectively.

Garver joined the Browns in 1948. Pitching in 38 games, he went 7–11. He became the club's top starter the following year, posting a 12–17 mark while leading the league in losses and runs. The Browns lost 101 games that year, and no other St. Louis pitcher won more than eight.

The next year, when the Browns lost only 96, Garver logged a 13–18 mark, placing second in the league to Early Wynn in ERA with a 3.39, tying with Bob Lemon for the lead in complete games with 22, and placing third in innings pitched with 260.

By now, Garver had arrived as one of the premier pitchers in the junior circuit. He was developing a reputation as an outstanding hurler with a terrible team. He was also becoming known as a pitcher who refused to buckle, no matter what odds stood against him.

"I wasn't awed and I wasn't scared pitching in the big leagues," Garver says. "I don't know why I wasn't, but I wasn't. I remember one time I was warming up to start a game at Fenway Park. Boston had Dom DiMaggio, Johnny Pesky, Ted Williams, Vern Stephens, Bobby Doerr, Walt Dropo, Al Zarilla, and Birdie Tebbetts in the lineup. One of the writers was standing there, and I could hear him say to Gerry Priddy, one of our players, 'Well, I'll tell you one thing. He [Garver] won't be scared.' And I wasn't.

"Oh, that was a great era," Garver adds. "The Dodgers and Cardinals had 23 or 24 farm clubs, for heaven's sake. In 1951, the Browns even had 15. And there were only eight teams in each league, so you know there were a lot of people competing for jobs.

"A lot more good people were down in the minors learning how to play. Take a guy like Harvey Haddix. When he got to the big leagues, he won 20 games his first [full] year. He should have been in the big leagues about four years before that, but the competition was just too great."

The competition wasn't too much for Garver in 1951. The baby-faced hurler went to the mound 30 times as a starter, completed 24 games, and won 20. He also got in three relief assignments.

Few pitchers ever put on a better performance, considering not only the fierce competition of the American League at the time but also the lowly state of the Browns. Ned won more games than the combined total of the team's next four highest winners.

The 1951 season was also the year in which Browns president Bill Veeck pulled off some of his most famous publicity stunts. "Bill Veeck was a treat to be around," Garver says. "I never say anything bad about him. I participated in two things that were completely unmatched in the history of baseball. One was the use of the midget [Eddie Gaedel] as a pinch-hitter. The other was when Veeck staged the grandstand manager night [fans dictated strategy by holding up signs that indicated what move the team should make]."

The 1952 season turned out to be Garver's last one in a St. Louis uniform. Ned got off to a slow start. In August, while only 7–10, Veeck traded him and three others to the Tigers in a blockbuster, eight-player deal that brought outfielders Vic Wertz and Don Lenhardt to the Browns. The deal was a stunning one for Garver.

"I always liked any place I played," he says. "Even after I got out of baseball, I always liked the organizations I worked for. But getting traded from the Browns was a disappointment because I was such a part of the organization. I wasn't just there. I was a real part of it."

Garver finished the season at 8–10, then went 11–11, 14–11, and 12–16 over the next three years with Detroit teams that roosted in the American League's second division.

After arm problems reduced his playing time to six games in 1956, Garver was traded by the Tigers to Kansas City in another eight-player swap. The key players in the deal were Garver and pitcher Virgil Trucks, who went to the A's, and first baseman Eddie Robinson and third baseman Jim Finigan, who came to the Tigers.

Between 1957 and 1960, Garver notched 6–13, 12–11, 10–13, and 4–9 records with A's teams that also never escaped the second division. In 1961, Garver was picked up by the expansion Angels and was 0–3 in 12 games before deciding to retire.

Garver lingered in baseball for a little while longer as a scout and minor league coach. Eventually, he went to work for a meat-packing company back in Ohio.

"I grew into a corporate job," he says. "I was the personnel and industrial relations manager. I had told them when I went there that I never really wanted to be tied down to an office job. But I ended up in one.

"After playing 18 years in baseball, I worked there for 18 more years. I figured I was never going to own a company, so I retired in 1980. I gave them one year's notice."

Now, Garver is far removed from the days nearly 50 years ago when he was just about the only good thing the Browns had. But that doesn't mean he has forgotten those times. Garver has many pleasant memories of those days, and he speaks passionately about them.

"I started an All-Star Game," he says. "I won 20 games in the big leagues in one season and 129 games altogether. My goal was to win at least 100 games. I did that, and a lot of other things that I really didn't suppose I'd get done."

But get them done he did. And that put Garver in a special bracket. He was a pitcher who always was a lot more successful than the teams on which he played.

Sid Hudson

An Indelible Link with Washington

NEARLY SIX DECADES after he threw his first pitch as a professional, Sid Hudson was still waging war against enemy hitters.

Hudson spent the better part of his life—not to mention his energy—trying to figure out what a pitcher has to do to get the upper hand on a batter. His calculations have always been pretty good.

Hudson was a successful major league pitcher for 12 seasons. And for much of the time since then, he was a successful pitching coach at both the professional and collegiate levels.

To anyone who followed baseball in the 1940s, the name Sid Hudson is synonymous with the Washington Senators. The hard-throwing right-hander was a key figure on Senators teams from 1940 to 1952. Not only was Hudson one of the club's top hurlers, he was also one of the most popular players in the nation's capital.

After just two years in the minor leagues, Hudson jumped all the way from Class D to the majors. He won 17 games in his rookie year, including two one-hitters. In his first three years with Washington teams that finished seventh each season, Hudson won 40 games and was twice named to the American League All-Star team.

Hudson developed an arm problem while serving in the military during World War II and had to alter his entire pitching style. Yet he continued to pitch, and wound up working in the big leagues through 1954, pitching his last two and one-half seasons with the Boston Red Sox.

Sid was the player representative for the Senators and Red Sox during a crucial time in the development of players' rights and the Players Association. When his days on the field ended, he became a scout with the Red Sox, then a pitching coach with the expansion Washington Senators, then with the Texas Rangers.

In recent years, Hudson was the pitching coach of the varsity baseball team at Baylor University in Waco, Texas. He made such a success of the job that he became a kind of Texas legend. After taking the post in 1986, following his retirement from the Rangers, Hudson produced two first-round draft choices—Pat Combs of the Philadelphia Phillies in 1988 and Scott Ruffcorn of the Chicago White Sox in 1991. Six of his other pitchers from Baylor made it to the minor leagues.

Perhaps some of them will compile records as accomplished as the erect ex-hurler who served as their mentor.

In 380 big league games, Hudson, a member of the Texas Sports Hall of Fame, posted a 104–152 career record while pitching mostly for Washington teams that only twice finished higher than seventh place. The 6-4, 180-pounder had a 4.28 ERA, working in 2,181 innings, allowing 2,384 hits, striking out 734, and walking 835. He completed 123 of the 279 games he started.

"I had a good arm with a good curve and a good fastball," Hudson recalls. "I worked at it. But I think the main thing was somebody gave me the chance, namely Bucky Harris, our manager, and Clark Griffith, the owner. I thought Bucky was the best manager I ever played for.

"Pitching for the Senators was never easy," Hudson adds. "You'd get all enthused at the start of the season, but pretty soon you'd be five or six games out, and you'd begin to wonder.

"But we didn't let up. We always tried to win. After all, we were playing in the big leagues. I don't care if it's with the Washington Senators or who it is, it's still the big leagues."

Playing in Washington, however, did have some benefits, especially on opening day when the Senators traditionally began the baseball season and the president of the United States threw out the first ball.

"Washington was a fun place to play," says Hudson. "Washington fans were very good. They were really with you. There was never a day like opening day in Washington. It was always very exciting. I got to play before three presidents and shake hands with them—Roosevelt, Truman, and Eisenhower. Truman took a real interest in the game. He'd give you a big smile and call you by name. It was a big thrill playing in front of the president of the United States."

One especially big thrill came during Sid's rookie year in 1940 when he narrowly missed catching the opening day ball thrown out by Roosevelt. In those days, presidents tossed the ball into a waiting crowd of players who scrambled for the ball. The lucky winner got the chief executive to sign it.

Actually, the 1940 season was pretty exciting in other ways for Hudson, who had only begun to throw in earnest a mere two seasons earlier. Before then, he had been primarily a first baseman.

"I'm from a big family—12 kids," he says. "My father died rather young. When I was eight, we moved from Coalfield, Tennessee, where I was born, to Chattanooga. I always had baseball on my mind. As a young kid, I played all the time. We didn't have a high school team, but I played American Legion ball. I was a first baseman, and I pitched some, too.

"Joe Engel was the owner of the Chattanooga team. A scout called him and tried to get him to take me to spring training in 1938. Engel said, 'No, we're filled up. Tell him to come back next spring.'

"Then I got a call from a guy in Sanford, Florida. They had a Class D team down there. They wanted to sign me as a first baseman, so I went down and joined them. I did well, but then they fired the manager.

"The new manager's name was Rawmeat Rogers. He brought in his own first baseman, so I was out of a job. But one day, he said to me, 'You've got a good arm. Can you pitch?' I said, 'Yeah. I've pitched a little.' He sent me into a game, and I struck out the side in the eighth and ninth innings. He said, 'From now on, you're a pitcher.'"

And a career was born. Hudson pitched in 27 games that season and finished with an 11–7 record and a 2.02 ERA. The following year, while pitching for the same Florida State League team, Sid went 24–4 with a 1.80 ERA, and he led the league in strikeouts (182), wins, and percentage (.857) while hurling his team to the pennant.

"I took my regular turn each time, and I played some first base, too," Hudson recalls. "I won two more games in the playoffs, then we had a series with the winner of the Georgia-Alabama League. I won two games in that. Overall, I started 27 games during the season, and finished 27 games—one of my losses came in relief—plus I pitched four complete games in the playoffs."

At the end of the season, the Sanford owner came to Hudson with some interesting news. "I've got a chance to sell you to the big leagues," he said. "Two teams are interested in you—the Cleveland Indians and the Washington Senators. You pick which one you'd like to go to."

"I figured the Indians had Bob Feller and Mel Harder and Johnny Allen," Hudson says. "I wouldn't get much chance to pitch with them. So I picked the Senators. It's really strange how things worked out, but I made the right choice."

Hudson made the big club in his first shot, winning a spot in the starting rotation as the number two pitcher behind knuckleballer Dutch Leonard. Sid started the second game of the season against the Red Sox but got knocked out after four innings following a home run by Jimmie Foxx.

"I was pretty nervous to start with, but I'm pretty calm most of the time, and everything just fell into place," he remembers. "I was in awe of the Red Sox, though. I'd read about all those players. They had five future Hall of Famers on that team [Foxx, Ted Williams, Bobby Doerr, Joe Cronin, and Lefty Grove].

"After that game," Hudson continues, "I won two. Then I lost seven in a row. Griffith called me into his office. He said, 'We think you have enough stuff that you can make it. We're going to stick with you.' I went out and won six in a row, including two one-hitters."

In the first one-hitter, Hudson beat the St. Louis Browns, 1–0, yielding the only hit to Rip Radcliffe leading off the ninth inning. "I knew I had a no-hitter going because everybody in the stands was yelling," he recalls. "Radcliffe hit a ball down the right field line that hit chalk and went for a double. Then [George] McQuinn tried to bunt. Our catcher, Jake Early, missed the ball, and Radcliffe went to third. So here I am trying to protect a 1–0 lead with the tying run on third base with nobody out. I finally struck out McQuinn. Then Harlond Clift popped out and [Walt] Judnich flied out to center field."

Hudson's other one-hitter, coming just six weeks later, was far less dramatic. Washington beat the Philadelphia Athletics, 11–0, with the A's only hit coming on a seventh-inning single by Sam Chapman.

Sid was not quite through with sparkling engagements, though. In early September in the first game of a doubleheader, he beat Grove and the Red Sox, 1–0, in 13 innings. "I used to follow all the big leaguers in the paper when I was growing up," Hudson says. "But Grove was always kind of my idol. I didn't try to emulate him or anybody else, but I always liked the way he pitched, so it was quite a thrill to beat him."

Hudson finished his rookie season with a 17–16 record, which would turn out to be a career high in wins for him.

"I began to think I was a pretty good pitcher," he says. "I had a lot of confidence. In 1941, though, I thought I was a better pitcher. I had better control, a better ERA (4.57 to 3.46), and I didn't make as many mistakes. I just tried to learn from other pitchers." That included opposing pitchers, who in those days didn't mind giving a fellow pitcher a helpful tip, even if he played with the enemy.

"A pitcher might have a good fastball. You'd talk to him about how he held it," Hudson says. "Bucky Harris had Ted Lyons come over and show me how to throw a change-up. It was all different then. You wouldn't do something like that with an opposing team's pitcher today."

In 1941, Hudson had a 13–14 record for another seventh-place Senators team. During the season, he was selected for a berth on the American League All-Star team. Sid pitched one inning in his team's stirring 7–5 victory that featured a two-out, three-run home run by Ted Williams in the bottom of the ninth inning.

"I gave up a two-run homer to Arky Vaughan in the seventh, then got lifted for a pinch-hitter [Charley Keller]," Hudson remembers. "Then Edgar Smith came in and gave up another two-run homer to Vaughan in the eighth. Finally, Williams hit the homer to give us the win."

Hudson also pitched in another memorable game that season. In the final regular-season game of the year, he blanked the New York Yankees, 4–0. The Yanks had already clinched the American League pennant and were headed for a date with the Brooklyn Dodgers in the World Series.

"Joe DiMaggio said that there wasn't a pitcher on the Dodgers who showed as much as Sid Hudson," the former hurler says proudly. "And at that time, the Dodgers had guys like Kirby Higbe, Whit Wyatt, and Hugh Casey. They had some pretty good pitchers.

"DiMaggio," he adds, "was the greatest player I ever saw. Williams was the best hitter. If there was a runner in scoring position and you got the ball close to the plate, DiMaggio was going to take a whack at it. Williams would take the pitch in that situation if it wasn't just where he wanted it. I always had pretty good luck against DiMaggio," says Hudson, who yielded just one hit in six at-bats to the Yankee Clipper during his 56-game hitting streak in 1941.

"Bobby Doerr was the guy in Boston who hit me good. Larry Doby hit some long balls off me, and Yogi Berra hit me good, although you could get him out sometimes. For a couple of years, the toughest hitter for me was Vic Wertz. It got to be I didn't know what to throw him."

Hudson was named again in 1942 to the American League All-Star team but didn't make an appearance in the game. That season, he registered a 10–17 record for yet another seventh-place Nats club.

By that time, Hudson was making a whopping sum of $8,000 per year.

He can document that because he has the contract in a frame in his den. He got it from a fan who had fished it out of a trash can when Griffith Stadium was being torn down in the 1960s.

"You had to fight Clark Griffith for a raise every year," says Hudson. "My first year, I signed for $200 a month. Two or three weeks into the season, I got a raise to $400. Then I got another raise, and I ended up making $3,000 my first year. When I got a $3,000 raise for my second season, I was on Cloud Nine."

Before Hudson could begin his fourth big league season, he was drafted for military duty. Like many players who served in World War II, it had a profound effect on his career.

Sid wound up being stationed at Fort Hood, near Waco, Texas, where he was given the duty of getting the troops in condition. Every day for two years he led the squad in calisthenics, doing all the pushups and other exercises he asked his men to do. He also pitched by his own estimate about 250 innings for his Army team.

"I developed a spur on my right shoulder," Hudson says. "After I got out of the service following a stint in Guam, the Senators sent me to a specialist at Johns Hopkins Hospital in Baltimore. He said it was due to excessive strain from all the exercises and pitching I did in the Army. He wanted to operate and take it off, but I wouldn't let him."

With the spur still present, Hudson could no longer use the overhand delivery he employed before the war. Instead, he was forced to become a sidearm pitcher. "The doctor said I'd have to find some other way to throw or I'd probably be through," Hudson says. "I had thrown three-quarter arm, but now I could only throw sidearm. I started throwing that way, and eventually it began to get better. I threw that way for the last nine years of my career."

Although he maintains that he could still throw hard, Hudson's yearly records didn't always measure up to the standards he had achieved before the war. Between 1946 and 1949, he went 8–11, 6–9, 4–16, and 8–17, the Senators being either seventh or eighth in all but one of those years.

Gradually, however, Sid's arm was regaining strength. And along the way, he had more memorable experiences to add to his scrapbook. One in particular was a game in 1947 at Yankee Stadium. It was Babe Ruth Day, and the Yankees had put together a special celebration to honor the former slugger, now dying of cancer. Hudson was the starting pitcher for the Senators.

"I had met Babe Ruth once before, during the 1942 season when a team of all-stars played a team made up of Yankees, Dodgers, and Giants in a war bond game at the Polo Grounds," Hudson remembers. "I came into the clubhouse, and there was Babe sitting at a desk.

"This time, though, he was real thin. It was sad, seeing him. He had great difficulty walking. When he went out to home plate to give his little speech, I was down in the bullpen warming up. There was quite a lot of commotion. Then they told me the game was going to start 15 minutes late. It was a packed house, and the crowd gave Babe a big ovation."

When the game got under way, Hudson and Spud Chandler locked horns in a tense pitching duel. Finally, the Senators prevailed by a 1–0 score. Sid singled and scored the winning run on a hit by Buddy Lewis.

Hudson has vivid recollections of another game in Yankee Stadium. It was the first game of a doubleheader, and the Yanks and Nats entered the ninth inning with the score tied.

"The Yankees had a man on third with Bill Dickey the hitter," Hudson recalls. "He bunted down the third-base line. It was fairly hard and looked like it might roll foul. We had a third baseman named Bobby Estalella. I kept yelling to him, 'Let it go, let it go.' But he picked it up, and by the time his throw reached first Dickey had crossed the bag and the winning run had scored.

"I wasn't too pleased. During the second game, I went up in the stands and sat down. This woman sitting next to me leaned over and said to me, 'What did you say to that third baseman?' The woman was Ethel Merman.

"Baseball in those days was fun," Hudson adds. "We were all one big happy family. We'd ride the train together, play cards together. We had more fun playing ball than they do now. And we had more desire. We had to do a little better each year so we could make more money."

In 1950, with Harris managing the Senators for the third time, Washington jumped to fifth place. Hudson had a 14–14 record, his best mark since his rookie season.

Despite having a team that included the likes of Mickey Vernon, Eddie Yost, Sam Mele, Gil Coan, Cass Michaels, Pete Runnels, and Irv Noren, the Senators tumbled back into seventh in 1951. Sid slumped to a 5–12 record.

After going 3–4 in seven games in 1952, Hudson was traded to Boston for pitchers Walt Masterson and Randy Gumpert. Sid finished the year at 10–13 with the best ERA (3.34) of his career.

Was he disappointed about leaving Washington? "I was thrilled," he says. "I knew the Red Sox had a better club. We were going to New England and getting away from the hot Washington weather. My wife and I were excited about going to Boston."

The dreaded left field wall at Fenway Park didn't bother him, either. "I kind of had the wrong idea about pitching in Boston all those years," Hudson says. "I had always thrown outside to righthanded hitters. But I started throwing inside to them, and it worked."

Hudson pitched two more years in Boston, going 6–9 in 1953 and 3–4 the next year. In 1955, he went to spring training with the Red Sox but was released by general manager Joe Cronin. Sid would soon launch another career. "Cronin offered me a job as a scout," he recalls. "I took it, and scouted for the Red Sox for five years."

Hudson then began a long career as a pitching coach, working first with his old pal Mickey Vernon with the expansion Washington Senators (Sid's original Nats had moved to Minnesota to become the Twins), then for the Rangers after the new Senators moved to Arlington, Texas.

In addition to Vernon, Hudson worked under an array of managers, including Gil Hodges, Jim Lemon, Billy Martin, Ted Williams, Whitey Herzog, Frank Lucchesi, and Billy Hunter. "They were all different," he says. "The toughest to work for was Hodges. When the game started, he took over. He never consulted anybody. Didn't ask for anybody's advice. Williams was great to work for. He didn't have enough patience with youngsters, but he was very good with veteran players."

Hudson's last year as Rangers pitching coach was in 1978. After that, he scouted the Texas–New Mexico area for the club while also serving as a pitching instructor for the team's rookie league club.

One of the players he scouted and recommended to the Rangers was a flame-throwing pitcher from the University of Texas. But the Rangers, like a lot of other teams, didn't like Roger Clemens' lack of consistent velocity and lost interest in him.

Hudson lived during much of his playing career in his wife's hometown of Lubbock, Texas. But in 1955, the Hudsons moved to Waco and were still living there when Sid retired from the Rangers in 1986. Soon after Hudson's retirement, Baylor baseball coach Mickey Sullivan asked him to work with the team's pitchers. Sid agreed, and he became a fixture in the highly successful Baylor baseball program.

Hudson developed a large following throughout the state of Texas. Often, high school pitchers being recruited by Baylor asked if Hudson was going to be there when they arrived. Despite the vast difference in their ages, Hudson was an effective communicator and worked well with the young collegians during a decade at Baylor.

"I was very friendly with them," he says. "I got a lot of respect from them, but I wanted them to like me. Then I could agitate them, get tough with them.

"I always tried to teach them," he adds. "Any time you suggest a change to a pitcher, you have to have a good reason for it because you're going to be questioned about it."

Often, Hudson even provided a live demonstration if necessary, despite being in his 80s. He would suit up and get right in there with the players, throwing the ball as he wanted it to be thrown. "You had to teach them everything," he says. "Most of them didn't even know how to hold the ball."

In his comfortable home on a tree-lined street in Waco, Hudson looks at his long baseball career, and allows that there's precious little he would change about it. "Maybe I would've thrown more during the winter," he says. "Of course, if I knew then what I know now, I would've been a lot better pitcher.

"But baseball has been good to me. I've been very fortunate. I certainly didn't get rich as they do today, but I've had a lot of other benefits."

He's also had a lot of success. One doesn't spend more than six decades in baseball without substantial accomplishments. As a player, scout, and coach, this classy gentleman has certainly done that.

Max Lanier

Converted Lefty Was Stingy with Runs

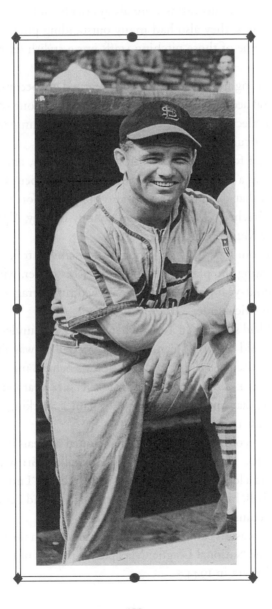

IN THE 1940s the St. Louis Cardinals had some of the finest teams ever to grace a baseball diamond.

There wasn't a year that went by during that decade that the Cards weren't in the race for the National League pennant. They won flags in 1942, 1943, 1944, and 1946 and finished second five other times. Three times they captured the World Series.

While those St. Louis teams were always richly endowed with a collection of fine hitters, they also had many outstanding pitchers. One of the mainstays of some of those pitching staffs was a stylish lefthander named Max Lanier.

Originally a righthander, Lanier had learned to become a southpaw after a boyhood accident and had gone on to become one of the National League's most effective hurlers before an ill-conceived jump to the Mexican League short-circuited his career.

The father of former major league infielder, coach, and manager Hal Lanier, Max was a chunky portsider who was a member of fine St. Louis pitching staffs that during the 1940s also included Mort Cooper, Howie Pollet, Harry Brecheen, Murry Dickson, Johnny Beazley, Alpha Brazle, Ted Wilks, George Munger, and others.

What stood out mostly about Lanier was his ability to keep the opposition from crossing the plate. At the height of his career, when he won 55 games over a four-year period, Max had earned run averages under 3.00 all four years and twice under 2.00.

"Overall, I had six years in a row when my ERA was under 3.00," Lanier says. "I could hold the other team, but it seemed like I was always pitching against a good pitcher. I didn't get a lot of runs behind me."

Lanier's career ERA was just 3.01, spread over a 14-year period from 1938 to 1953. During that time, he pitched in 327 games, working 1,618.1 innings and allowing just 1,490 hits.

His lifetime record was 108–82, which included six years in which he won in double figures. Lanier struck out 821 and walked 611 while hurling 21 shutouts. "I had a lot of different pitches," Max recalls. "I mixed them up—curveball, fastball, high, low. I had a moving fastball, and I could pitch a lot of guys high because my ball took off."

Lanier's best seasons came during World War II when the Cardinals were the terrors of the National League. Max posted records of 13–8 in 1942, 15–7 in 1943, and 17–12 in 1944.

He also won two key World Series games. In 1942, he won Game Four with three shutout innings of relief in a 9–6 victory over the New York Yankees. He also singled home an insurance run in the ninth inning.

Max was the winning pitcher in Game Six of the 1944 Series against the St. Louis Browns, getting the decision in a 3–1 Cards victory in the deciding game. Lanier scattered three hits and one run over five and one-third innings before Wilks retired the last 11 batters in a row to preserve the win.

Lanier was the starting pitcher in the second game of the '44 Series, going seven innings and giving up five hits and two runs. The Cards won that game in the 11th inning, 3–2, with Blix Donnelly getting the decision.

"The 1944 win was a big one for me," says Lanier, "because it gave us the World Series. But I really liked the '42 win the best because it was my first World Series win and because it beat a great team like the Yankees. I thought we really accomplished something by beating them.

"The Yankees had won the first game of the Series," Max recalls. "Then we came back to win four straight. We beat a heckuva ball club. They had [Joe] DiMaggio, [Charley] Keller, [Bill] Dickey, [Phil] Rizzuto, and [Joe] Gordon. But we were better. I think that was the best club I ever played on."

The Cardinals featured a starting lineup that included future Hall of Famers Stan Musial and Enos Slaughter, plus standouts such as Marty Marion, Terry Moore, Whitey Kurowski, Walker Cooper, and Johnny Hopp. In beating the Yankees in five games, St. Louis handed the New York club its first World Series setback since 1926.

Lanier also started two games in the 1943 World Series when the Yankees got revenge and beat the Cardinals in five games. Max got the nod in Game One but dropped a 4–2 decision to Spud Chandler when the Yanks broke a 2–2 tie with a pair of runs in the sixth inning. Lanier started Game Four but was lifted for a pinch-hitter after allowing four hits and one run in seven innings. The Yanks broke a 1–1 tie with a run in the eighth to gain a 2–1 decision.

Overall, Lanier pitched in seven World Series games during that three-year period. He posted a 2–1 record with a sparkling 1.71 ERA. Not bad for a guy who originally wasn't even supposed to be a lefthander. "I was originally a righthander," Lanier states. "When I was a real small kid of about nine years old, I broke my arm cranking a model-T Ford. I couldn't use my right arm, so I became a lefthander."

Born in Denton, North Carolina, Lanier became a fine pitcher in his hometown after learning to hurl as a southpaw. He played no other position.

"I was pitching in a high school game and Frank Rickey [brother of Branch and a Cardinals scout] was there," Lanier recalls. "I happened to pitch a shutout that day.

"He met me at the gate when the game was over," Lanier remembers. "He said, 'How about after you get a shower I drive you home?' I didn't know him and he didn't show me any credentials, but I said, 'OK.' So I went with him, and on the way home he got to talking to me about playing pro ball. I decided I wanted to do it. He pulled out a contract that looked about as big as a dugout."

After a brief stint at Greensboro in the Piedmont League, Lanier's professional career got a big boost in 1937 when he went 10–4 at Columbus, Ohio, of the American Association. Max came up to St. Louis in 1938 and appeared in 18 games (0–3 record) before going back to Columbus where he spent the next year and one-half. After going 10–16 there in 1939, he returned to the Cardinals to stay at the end of the season.

"I remember my first game in 1938," Lanier says. "It was against the Chicago Cubs in St. Louis. I didn't pitch much in 1938, so it was a little frightening because I hadn't had a lot of experience.

"Of course, I had previously pitched a lot of good semipro ball back in the Carolinas against guys who had played in the pros. Some had even been in the major leagues. Once, I pitched against Shoeless Joe Jackson when I was 16 years old. It was down in South Carolina. He was about 50 years old, but he could still hit. He was one of the most natural hitters there's ever been. I heard a lot of guys who played with and against him say that, too."

Lanier says that once he got to the majors he pitched against a slew of other tough hitters. "There were quite a few," he says. "Frank McCormick was one. Paul Waner, Bob Elliott —they could all hit." But most hitters found it wasn't easy hitting the slants of the 5-10, 190-pound lefty.

After going 2–1 at the end of the 1939 season with the Cardinals, Lanier spent all of 1940 with St. Louis and posted a 9–6 record while starting in 11 of his 35 games. He moved up to 10–8 in 1941, again working in 35 games but starting 18 of them. He followed up with a 13–8 log in 1942 in 34 games (20 as a starter).

That year Lanier pitched in what he called his most memorable game. "In 1942 we were 10½ games back of Brooklyn in mid-August," Max remembers. "We got hot, and on our last road trip of the season we went into Brooklyn in mid-September, still two games back. There was a double-header. Mort Cooper pitched the first game and shut out Whit Wyatt, 3–0. The next game I had had a little trouble with my elbow. Billy Southworth, our manager, came in and said, 'I believe I'll pitch [Johnny] Beazley and let you have another day's rest.' I said, 'No, I want to pitch. I beat them four times already this season. I can beat them another time.' He let me pitch, and I beat them, 2–1. That tied us for first place. We went on to win 23 of our last 29 games, and wound up winning the pennant by two games over the Dodgers."

The Cardinals won 106 that season, while the Dodgers won 104 in one of the greatest one-two finishes in baseball history. That began a string of three straight pennants for the Cardinals.

In 1943 Lanier was 15–7 with a 1.90 ERA in what was his finest season. With Cardinal pitchers capturing the first three positions in the National League, he was second to Pollet in the league in ERA, third in winning percentage with .682, and fourth in strikeouts with 123.

Max was second in the league in strikeouts (141) and fourth in ERA (2.65) in 1944 while notching a 17–12 record. He started off 2–2 in four games in 1945 but spent most of the season in military service.

Back to the Cardinals in 1946, Lanier vaulted out to a 6–0 start with a 1.93 ERA. There seemed little doubt that he was headed for his finest season.

But lurking in the shadows was the then-outlawed Mexican League. Under its president, Jorge Pasquel, the league had set out to raid major league baseball of some of its talent by offering large salaries to star players. A number of Cardinals, including Musial, Slaughter, and Lanier, were among the league's targets.

"I'd won 17 ball games and a World Series game in 1944, and they gave me a $500 raise," Lanier recalls. "I signed that contract, but I wasn't satisfied. They said, 'You can take it, or go home.'

"When I came back from the service in '46, I won six in a row, but I had had a little trouble with my elbow in the last game I pitched. I thought, well they're not paying me anything. I had to do something. So I signed with the Mexican League."

Lanier, Sal Maglie, Mickey Owen, and a handful of other players wound up in Mexico with big salaries. But the honeymoon was soon over. "I thought the conditions would be better," Lanier says. "I never dreamed they would be as bad as they were. It just didn't turn out to be what we expected. Then after the first year, he [Pasquel] wanted to cut everybody's salary in half. That's when most of us quit. We played there one season and part of another, and then came home. It almost broke up the league."

It almost broke the careers of those who jumped, too. Commissioner A. B.(Happy) Chandler banned them from organized baseball. "Maglie and I and quite a few others played up in Canada for a while after we came back," recalls Lanier. "We weren't allowed to play in the big leagues, which hurt. Except for that, I guess you could say it was worth it going to Mexico." They were finally reinstated in 1949 in the big leagues. But, like some of the others, the three years away had cost Max some of the primest time of his career.

After shaking off the rust that came from being away, Lanier began to regroup in 1949. He finished the season with a 5–4 record, starting all 15 games in which he pitched.

He was 11–9 in both 1950 and 1951, taking the mound a total of 58 times over that two-year period. At the end of the '51 season, St. Louis traded Lanier to the New York Giants as part of a deal that brought second baseman Eddie Stanky to the Cardinals.

Lanier went 7–12 with the '52 Giants. After three games in 1953, he was sold to the St. Louis Browns. He was 0–1 in 10 games with the Browns, then departed from the majors for good at the end of the season.

After playing a little more in the minors, Max spent the next 20 years managing teams in the minor leagues. Along the way, he also saw his son Hal make it to the professional level and spend 10 years as a big league infielder with the San Francisco Giants and New York Yankees, after which he was a coach with several teams and manager of the Houston Astros.

"I worked with him a lot because he asked for it," says Max. "But I really didn't have too much to do with his development. He'd come home from school and we'd go out and throw. I'd pitch batting practice to him. He was hitting them into people's homes, so we had to quit.

"Hal was originally a pitcher, too," Max adds. "But he played shortstop in high school when he wasn't pitching. His team went to the state championships and he won two games. They wanted him to pitch a third time and

I wouldn't let him. I said, 'There are 32 scouts here. If you hurt your arm, they'll all walk away from you.'"

After his retirement, Max settled near Hal in Dunnellon, Florida, in the west-central part of the state. Max is an avid fisherman. When asked, he also gets a huge amount of pleasure out of reminiscing about those brilliant Cardinal teams of the 1940s.

They were teams on which Max Lanier played a major role.

Ray Narleski

Pioneer Relief Pitcher

IT IS TAKEN for granted these days in baseball that to be effective, a team's bullpen must have a strong left-right combination. The best teams almost always have one. There was a time, however, when no such phenomenon existed. It was simply enough to have one good reliever, and which side of the mound he threw from was irrelevant.

Then, along came Ray Narleski, and—teaming with Don Mossi—the formula for successful bullpens was changed forever. Narleski, the right-hander, and Mossi, the southpaw, formed the first important right-left relief combination in baseball when they broke in together with the Cleveland Indians in 1954.

That also happened to be the year in which the Indians won an American League record for that time of 111 games with what is often labeled as the finest pitching staff ever assembled.

Narleski, a strong, slender, 6-1, 175-pounder, made his contribution to the evolution of baseball bullpens with a blazing fastball that eventually propelled him to a place as the Indians' third-highest all-time save leader. In five years with the Tribe, one of which was spent primarily as a starter, Narleski registered 53 saves, including a league-leading 19 in 1955.

Overall, Narleski had a 43–33 record in six big league seasons, including one with the Detroit Tigers. He had a career 3.60 earned run average and 58 saves while appearing in 266 games, striking out 454, walking 335, and yielding 606 hits in 702 innings.

A two-time American League All-Star who in 1955 led the junior circuit in games with 60, Narleski came close to being a member of the first three-generation family to play in the big leagues (a distinction later achieved by the Boone family—Ray, Bob, and Bret).

Ray's father, Bill, was an infielder with the 1929–30 Boston Red Sox, while his son, Steve, spent eight years as a pitcher in the Indians' farm system. Another son, Jeff, played the infield for one year in the chain of the Chicago White Sox.

The mid-generation Narleski, a resident of Laurel Springs, New Jersey, in the same area in which he grew up, arrived in Cleveland at exactly the same time as Mossi. "I had never seen him before except for a couple of days when we crossed paths in Cleveland in 1953," Ray says. "But we became good friends and roomed together the whole time we were in Cleveland."

Behind every good starting rotation is a good bullpen, and with rookies Narleski and Mossi forming the backbone of the Indians' relief brigade,

Cleveland in 1954 put together a fabled pitching staff, led by future Hall of Famers Bob Feller, Bob Lemon, and Early Wynn. Behind the trio, the club also had Mike Garcia, Hal Newhouser (another future Hall of Famer), Art Houtteman, and Bob Hooper—all excellent pitchers, too. "I don't think you'll ever see another pitching staff like that one," Narleski says. "Where are you going to get a staff like that today?"

Lemon and Wynn each won 23 games in 1954, Garcia won 19 while leading the league in ERA, and Houtteman and Feller won 15 and 13, respectively. None of the five had an earned run average higher than 3.35. Narleski and Mossi were integral parts of the staff, despite their youth.

"Don and I sort of took the pressure off the starters," Narleski says. "Before we came along, they had to relieve each other.

"But it worked out pretty well. There weren't any left-right combinations before us. The Yankees had Joe Page, the Dodgers had Hugh Casey, and the Phillies had Jim Konstanty. But nobody had both a lefthander and a right-hander coming out of the bullpen. "It was Al Lopez's [Cleveland manager] idea," he adds. "He thought it was worth trying. We were the first one to do it.

"When we got to the eighth or ninth inning, it was our time. At first, I was what you'd call today the closer. Then Mossi closed some, too. We both wound up with our share of work."

As might be expected, Narleski was originally reluctant to become a relief pitcher. Ray had been a starter throughout the early part of his career, and the idea of going to the bullpen was alien to him. "Back then," he says, "it could really tear you apart if they said they wanted you to be a reliever. If you didn't go nine innings in those days, you weren't considered much good.

"I was still in the minors when they made me a reliever. I was pitching for Indianapolis and had just pitched 12 innings and gotten beat, 3–2. Birdie Tebbetts, the manager, said to me, 'I'm going to make you a reliever.' I said, 'Bullfeathers.' He said, 'For two or three innings, you can throw the ball past anybody.'

"I didn't want to relieve. I was afraid I'd get lost. A reliever was a guy who wasn't very good, so I argued with Birdie, but I finally became a reliever. The funny thing was, I was wild as a starter, but after I changed to relieving, I wasn't wild any more.

"But I still always wanted to start, even when I was relieving in the big leagues. If you started, you had a chance to win 20 games. And if you won

20 games back then, you had a chance to get a 10 or 20 thousand dollar raise. No reliever could do that. Who wouldn't want to start?"

Narleski had been a starter since his youth in the area around Camden, New Jersey. A schoolboy sensation, he had attracted a considerable amount of attention by the time he reached high school, not only because of his blazing fastball but because he was the son of a well-known local player.

"I was just one, two years old when my father was playing in the big leagues," says Narleski. "But afterward, he played for a long time in the Red Sox and Cardinals systems, and then he played many years of semipro ball both in South Jersey and in Wilmington [Delaware]. He was mostly an infielder, but once in a while he'd pitch. I remember going to his games and always having ballplayers around the house. He was a good, hard-nosed player. He was like all the old-timers you hear about—a tough little player."

The senior Narleski, who hit .265 in 135 games during his two years in Boston, was—his son claims—a big help to the junior Narleski's baseball development. "He always told me to throw hard," Ray says. "He'd say, 'I'll kick your butt if you don't throw hard. Throw hard even when the count is three-and-two. Throw hard and throw over the top.' That's what he always preached."

The father's advice proved to be fruitful, and by the time Ray was ready to leave high school the scouts were beating a steady path to his doorstep.

"I was 9–2 in my last year in high school," Narleski recalls. "I was a strikeout pitcher. Cleveland really stayed on my trail. The Yankees and Red Sox also followed me, and they offered me contracts, but they were for Class C ball and I wouldn't take them. Cleveland offered me a Class A contract, and I took it."

The Indians packed off Narleski in 1948 to their Eastern League team at Wilkes-Barre. In 20 games, Ray had a 2–10 record.

"I was just a kid out of high school," Ray says. "I didn't know anything. I struggled. The whole team struggled. I think we only won about 47 or 48 games that year.

"I was paid $250 a month. The next season, I said I wanted more. They wouldn't give it to me, so I quit. I came home and sat out the whole 1949 season. I played in a pretty good semipro league that had a lot of former major and minor leaguers in it. The Yankees came around, and said they wanted to sign me. Then Cleveland called, and I went back with them."

Narleski spent the 1950 season at Cedar Rapids in the Three-I League, going 9–5. Then in 1951 he moved to Dallas of the Texas League, where he boosted his record to 15–8. In one game that season, he pitched a one-hitter, striking out 13 and walking nine. The only hit was a bloop single over short-stop by Johnny Temple.

Still a starter, Narleski went up to Indianapolis in 1952 and posted an 11–15 log. The following season, he became a reliever, went 6–8, and was about to be called up by the Indians when he broke his jaw in a collision while running in the outfield.

His arrival in Cleveland finally took place in 1954. Ray was then a polished 25-year-old with five years of minor league experience. "I had made up my mind that if I didn't make it in '54, that was it," Narleski remembers. "I was going to go home and look for a job."

Right from the start, though, Narleski made a good impression on the Indians, who liked his scorching fastball and his style of pitching.

"I had a rising fastball that I could throw 95–100 miles per hour," he claims. "The batters would hit underneath it and pop it up. I had a knuckle-curve in the minors, but Bill Norman, one of my managers, said to forget it. I had a slider, too. Mel Harder [the Indians' pitching coach and former hurler] taught me how to throw a curve later on. He also helped me a lot with my motion.

"Back in those days," Ray adds, "we all threw with big motions. Guys now throw with just their arms. I'd probably have a hard time now, anyway, because I pitched inside all the time. They don't do that anymore."

After rookie Narleski made the vaunted Indians pitching staff, it didn't take long for him to establish himself in the bullpen. "In my first game, Lopez brought me in for an inning or so against the White Sox," Ray recalls. "He wanted me to get the feel of things. I got my big chance a little while later in a game against the Yankees.

"We had a 3–2 lead, and Lopez took out Lemon and brought me in with no outs and a man on in the ninth. I was nervous. I knew I had to come through. I got two outs, then Gil McDougald came up. I went 3–0 to him, then struck him out. From then on, I was the club's closer."

There were some critical games that followed. One was against the Detroit Tigers. Narleski entered the game in relief of Feller and struck out three straight Tigers (Frank House, Harvey Kuenn, and Bill Tuttle) on 10 pitches.

"I remember another game when we were playing the White Sox," Narleski says. "Garcia was pitching, and he broke a blood vessel in the second inning. I came in and had a no-hitter going into the ninth. I ran out of gas, and Wynn came in and gave up the only hit of the game—a single to Minnie Minoso. We won, 2–0.

"Another game I remember that year was one against the Yankees. Allie Reynolds was pitching for them, and the Yankees knocked out Wynn in the second inning and had a 7–0 lead. A whole bunch of us relieved, and we didn't give up a hit the rest of the way. Meanwhile, Lopez was razzing Reynolds the whole game. He was really getting on him. We kept chipping away at Reynolds, and finally we won the game, 8–7, in the 10th inning."

With their magnificent starting rotation, which had 77 complete games in 1954, Narleski and Mossi throwing smoke out of the bullpen, and a starting eight that included both the league batting champion (Bobby Avila) and home run and RBI king (Larry Doby), the Indians cruised to the pennant, finishing the season with an 111–43 record, eight games ahead of the Yankees, who won 103.

Narleski ended the year with a 3–3 record, 13 saves, and a 2.22 ERA in 42 games (two of which he started). The Indians had not hesitated to use the rookie in tight situations, and Ray accepted the challenge.

"As a kid, all I ever wanted to do was make the big leagues," he says. "I wasn't awed or scared. It got so that they wanted me to pitch in tight spots against the top teams, and that didn't bother me at all. That's the way I wanted it."

The 1954 World Series was a memorable one, not only because the Indians were stunningly swept by the New York Giants but because of the hitting of unheralded reserve outfielder Dusty Rhodes, who manhandled Tribe pitching while winning three games with his bat, and the sensational over-the-shoulder running catch by Willie Mays of Vic Wertz's long drive to deep center in the first game.

"Mays made one helluva catch," says Narleski. "If he hadn't caught that ball, it might have turned the whole Series around for us. We were sitting in the bullpen in right-center when he made it. We could see the ball was way over his head. The curious thing is that we had two runners on base, and not one of them advanced [after the catch].

"As for Dusty, he was fantastic. He got the hits when it counted. He was hitting us so well that when I struck him out in the third game, I got a standing ovation from the Cleveland fans. I was just so mad at him, I threw three straight balls past him.

"The Giants had good pitching the whole Series," Narleski adds. "That's often overlooked. They pitched great ball. Everybody expected our pitching staff to do it for us, but in those four games, the Giants were better."

The '54 pennant would be the last one flown in Cleveland until 1995. But for Narleski, who had pitched in two games in the Series and allowed one hit in four innings, things would keep getting better.

In 1955, Ray had a sparkling 9–1 record while leading the league with 19 saves and 60 appearances. (At that point in the baseball galaxy, save totals—although the statistic was not accepted until 1969 and figures for Narleski's era were retrospective—were considerably lower than they are today, due largely to the much higher number of complete games.)

"I think what really helped me that season was something Newhouser had told me," Ray says. "He said, 'Just go out there and relax.' In the beginning of the season, I was really getting hit around. My ERA must have been about 99. But then I went 38 innings without allowing a run, and won nine straight games. At one point, I worked in nine games in a row. I didn't lose until I got beat by a bloop hit late in the season."

Narleski had back spasms late in the season and had to sit out the final few weeks. Meanwhile, Cleveland's two-game lead with two weeks to play disappeared, and the Yankees roared past them to win the flag by three games.

The Indians were bridesmaids to the Yankees again in 1956, this time finishing nine games out despite having three 20-game winners in Wynn, Lemon, and Herb Score. Although his back continued to bother him, seriously curtailing his amount of activity, Narleski continued to pitch effectively, posting a glittering 1.52 ERA in 32 games while winning three, losing two, and saving four.

Bullpen life agreed with Ray, even though he still yearned to be a starter. "I always knew where I wanted to throw the ball," he says. "I had Jim Hegan behind the plate, and he knew what I could do. I'd just rear back and throw. I watched the hitters while I was in the bullpen. That way, I got to know what a hitter liked or didn't like to hit.

"I always threw Nellie Fox down and away, but he hit some shots until I starting pitching him inside. Feller and Lemon used to pitch Ted Williams low and inside. I could never throw the ball past him. When he came up, it was no laughing matter.

"Al Kaline was another tough hitter. The toughest, though, was Pete Runnels. I could never find a spot where I could get him out. He didn't have a natural swing. He just sort of served the ball. He was tough, and so was Yogi Berra. He usually hit the pitch wherever it was thrown."

By 1957, the Cleveland pitching staff had deteriorated. Feller had retired, Lemon had slowed to a crawl, Garcia was fading fast, Score was fighting for his life after being hit in the face by a line drive, and only the ageless Wynn was still pitching consistently well. The Indians were forced to move both Narleski and Mossi into the starting rotation.

Ray started 15 of the 46 games in which he appeared, and registered an 11–5 record with a 3.09 ERA. He still managed 16 saves, however, while switching back and forth between starts and relief chores.

Narleski's starts became even more frequent in 1958 when he began 24 of the 44 games in which he appeared. That year, he had a 13–10 record while pitching in a career-high 183.1 innings. He also tossed three and one-third one-hit scoreless innings in the American League's 4–3 victory in the first All-Star Game played in Baltimore.

"I had talked to our manager, Bobby Bragan, early in the season about starting," Narleski says. "If he had a pitching staff, I would have continued to relieve. But he didn't, so he said, 'Fine, you start.' Later, Frank Lane, who had become the general manager, sent me back to the bullpen."

Lane and Narleski were not meant to coexist, and the 1958 season turned out to be Ray's last one in Cleveland. "I had words with him over my contract," Ray remembers. "I said to him, 'Just trade me. Get me out of here.'" Lane complied and, in a major swap, sent not only Narleski but also Mossi and infielder Ozzie Alvarez to the Tigers for pitcher Al Cicotte and second baseman Billy Martin.

Although he had had one operation, Narleski's back problems flared again. He pitched in 42 games in 1959, including 10 as a starter, but his record slipped to 4–12 as his delivery was severely hampered.

Along the way, Detroit had tried to send Narleski to Denver, but he refused to report. Then, in spring training in 1960, the Tigers offered him a minor league contract. He rejected it and came home.

"I made up my mind when I left the minors in 1953 that I was never going to play another year in the minors," Narleski says. "The minors were a nightmare. It was awful playing down there. So when they wanted to send me down, I said, 'Forget it' and walked out."

Returning to his roots, Narleski pitched in local semipro leagues. For several years, he hurled for a team in Wilmington, Delaware, that also included former major leaguers Harry Anderson and Jack Crimian, future Phillies president Ruly Carpenter at third base, and several former minor league players.

"In 1964," Ray says, "Jocko Collins [a noted area scout] wanted to sign me for the Phillies. I went up to Connie Mack Stadium and worked out. Everything was supposed to be all set. But I was still the property of Detroit, and they wouldn't let me go, so I never joined the Phillies. That was the year they lost 10 in a row at the end of the season and blew the pennant after having a big [six-and-one-half-game] lead."

There's no way to tell whether Narleski would have helped the Phils avert that disaster, but—given the weakened condition of the Phils' pitching staff at that point—it's more than likely he would have been a worthwhile acquisition. Some years later, Narleski did get to wear a Phillies uniform, although only as a batting practice pitcher in the late 1970s.

By then, Ray had become active as a coach of youth teams in his area, while spending his days working in a plant in Camden that built truck bodies. He worked there for 28 years until retiring.

For Narleski—who, when he broke in with the Indians, began a process that would forever change the face of major league baseball—the memories of his playing days remain crystal clear.

"It made me feel just great to play in the major leagues," he says. "Playing in the major leagues was the greatest thing there ever was. I enjoyed it. I pitched to some of the best players in the game. It was a great era.

"We didn't have saves back then, so it was hard to measure how good a reliever was. There was no way to count the value of a reliever. But one thing's for sure, after we came along, everybody wanted guys like Mossi and Narleski. Don and I set a standard that everybody tried to copy."

Many may have tried. But in those early days when the specialty of relief pitching was in its infancy, nobody could duplicate the pioneering left-right combination of the Cleveland Indians' tandem.

Dick Radatz

"The Monster"—A Nickname That Fit

THEY CALLED Dick Radatz "The Monster." It was a name that fit perfectly.

At his peak, there was no more terrifying pitcher. Radatz rose to a height of 6-6, weighed 230 pounds, and when he stood on the mound glaring in for the sign, batters' hands shook, their knees knocked, and their stomachs churned. And if the sight of the huge Radatz wasn't enough, the thought of his forthcoming fastball would surely turn all but the most daring hitters to jelly.

For a four-year period in the 1960s, no pitcher ever wreaked more havoc on the psyches—not to mention the batting averages—of big league hitters than the imposing Boston Red Sox reliever. In that span, Radatz worked in 270 games, winning 49 of them and saving 100 more. In 538.1 innings pitched, he struck out 608 batters.

His fastball was delivered to the plate at speeds that used to be reserved for racing cars. It was Dick's only pitch, but it made no difference that the hitters knew it was coming. They couldn't hit it anyway.

Such was the case one day when future Hall of Famer Mickey Mantle barely saw three 95-mile-per-hour Radatz fastballs in a game in which the Red Sox were facing the New York Yankees. "I struck Mickey out with the bases loaded at Yankee Stadium," Radatz recalls. "As he walked back to the dugout, he screamed about four or five four-letter adjectives. Then he called me a monster. A lot of people in the press box heard it, and they started calling me that. The name took off."

The Monster was indeed intimidating. Although he pitched for Red Sox teams annually buried deep in the American League standings and at a time before the term "closer" became fashionable, he was the premier American League reliever of his day. Others may have pitched in more games, but Richard Raymond Radatz was the glamour name in relief pitching at a time when the art was still being developed.

"I think I was probably the first pitcher who was taught how to pitch relief in the minor leagues," Radatz says. "Back in those days, most relievers were guys who had been demoted as starters."

Radatz pitched seven years in the big leagues, appearing in 381 games, all in relief. He compiled a 52–43 record with 122 saves and a 3.13 earned run average. In 693.2 innings, he gave up 532 hits, struck out 745, and walked 296.

While Radatz had his best years with the Red Sox, he also pitched for the Cleveland Indians, Chicago Cubs, Detroit Tigers, and Montreal Expos.

Dick still makes his home in the Boston area where he is involved in numerous activities in and out of baseball. In his regular job, he works as a sales representative in the industrial packaging business. He also has been involved as the host of a radio sports talk show, he is a partner in Red Sox fantasy camps, and he stages clinics throughout the Boston area.

Although he was born in Detroit and grew up in a suburb north of that city, Radatz says he always had a passing interest in the Red Sox. "I sort of grew up idolizing Ted Williams, Bob Feller, and Hal Newhouser," Dick says. "When I was a boy, my dad only took me to see two different teams play the Tigers. We'd either go to see Williams with Boston or Feller with Cleveland. Often we'd see Feller pitch against Newhouser."

Eventually, Radatz became a pitcher himself, and throughout his schoolboy days that was the only position he played. But baseball wasn't Dick's main sport. He fancied himself a basketball player.

"I had a number of basketball and football scholarship offers when I got out of high school," Radatz recalls. "I had very few offers from baseball. Baseball was an afterthought for me. I played it only because my buddies did.

"I wound up going to Michigan State on a basketball scholarship," he adds. "I thought I was the next John Havlicek. As it turned out, I was more like Mrs. Havlicek."

Radatz played basketball in his first year at Michigan State. It was a year in which the Spartans pushed North Carolina to three extra periods before bowing in the NCAA semifinals, 74–70. North Carolina then went on to defeat Kansas and Wilt Chamberlain in the finals, 54–53.

"That was the year Johnny Green [who went on to a long and highly respectable career in the NBA] was the big star at Michigan State," Radatz remembers. "In fact, he put me on the bench. I always thought I could jump pretty well, but when I started going up for rebounds, there was always an arm extended about two feet above mine. I knew then I wasn't in the same league with Jumpin' Johnny, and I figured it was time to look elsewhere."

Elsewhere turned out to be on the baseball field. "I started getting serious about baseball my sophomore year in college," Radatz recalls. "I finally started to realize that I had some talent." So did others. Major league teams began sending scouts out to Big Ten games to watch the giant pitcher with the crackling fastball.

"I had a chance to sign with Baltimore and Detroit," Radatz says. "But a man named Maury Deleau was a scout for the Red Sox. He was very straightforward with me, and I liked his attitude. He approached me my senior year at Michigan State. Back then, I was a starter. There was no thought given to my being a reliever.

"Maury said he thought there was a distinct possibility for me to move rather quickly through the Red Sox organization. He was honest with me, and I appreciated that. So I signed with the Red Sox, and as it turned out, Maury was right."

After getting his degree in education at MSU, Radatz joined Raleigh of the Carolina League. Two and one-half years later, after stops at Minneapolis and Seattle and a career minor league record of 21–16, Dick landed in the majors.

Radatz was still a starting pitcher when he arrived in 1961 in Seattle, then a Pacific Coast League team managed by former Red Sox star Johnny Pesky. "He is the one who converted me into a reliever," Radatz notes. "He said to me, 'Dick, you're a one-pitch pitcher. The great relievers usually have the one outstanding pitch, and we don't feel that you have a big enough assortment to be a starter in the big leagues.'

"I didn't like the idea at first. I thought it was a demotion. I didn't feel like I was part of the ball club. But Pesky taught me some things about being a reliever, and it turned out he was absolutely right about me."

Radatz reached Boston the following season. Although a bit unpolished, Dick had an awesome fastball and the Red Sox realized they had a diamond in the rough.

"I was always able to throw the ball hard," Radatz says. "It was a God-given talent. I could throw it by people, and I always had good control.

"But it wasn't until I got to Boston in 1962 that I really developed my fastball. Sal Maglie was the pitching coach. He taught me how to use my legs, my body and to push off the rubber. I had been a sort of standup pitcher, but when Sal got a hold of me and taught me how to use the rubber, it made me rather successful."

In his rookie season, Radatz led the league in saves (24), games won by a reliever (nine), and games pitched (62). He lost out in the Rookie of the Year voting to the Yankees' Tom Tresh but was named American League Fireman of the Year by *The Sporting News*, an honor he would win again in 1964.

Between 1962 and 1965, Radatz was downright awesome. He strung together won-lost-save records of 9–6–24, 15–6–25, 16–9–29, and 9–11–22. He was named to two All-Star teams. Three times he won more games than any other reliever in the league, and twice he led in saves.

"I was at the top of my game, no doubt about it," Radatz says. "I had the fastball. Good control. I was throwing strikes with something on them. There's really no other explanation. They were outstanding years for me."

The 1963–64 seasons were particularly outstanding. In '63, Radatz won 10 straight games and compiled a glittering 1.97 ERA while pitching in 66 games and going 15–6.

The following year, Dick struck out 181 in 157 innings while posting a 16–9 mark with a 2.29 ERA. His 16 wins, then a league record for a reliever—as was his number of innings pitched—now represents the second highest total for a fireman in American League history.

That year, Radatz was also a central figure in the All-Star Game. On the mound in the ninth inning, Dick gave up a three-run homer to the Philadelphia Phillies' Johnny Callison as the National League came from behind to win, 7–4. Even though he struck out five—giving him a two-year total of 10 strikeouts in four and two-thirds innings of All-Star Game pitching—Radatz was saddled with the loss and a place in history as the pitcher who surrendered one of the game's most dramatic home runs.

"I felt terrible after that game," Dick remembers. "Johnny was one of the great ballplayers for the Phillies, and he hit the devil out of the pitch. I had such good stuff that day, too, and I knew the American League was depending on me heavily. I let them and myself down. It was a crushing blow. It was one of those things you don't get over right away."

While that game was a blemish on Radatz' record, there were plenty of other games with favorable outcomes. "One I remember," says Dick, "came early in my career. I struck out Mickey Mantle, Roger Maris, and Elston Howard on 10 pitches with the bases loaded and with Boston holding a 2–1 lead. That saved the game. It was an outstanding feat for me. Another memorable game came in 1965 when I hit my only big league home run and struck out eight of nine batters against the Kansas City A's."

At the height of his career, Radatz always seemed to pitch well against the Yankees. "I think I got the adrenaline going a little extra when I played against them," he recalls. "It was always a treat to play them. They were so good, so strong. It was a challenge to pitch against them."

And it was a challenge, Radatz says, just entering a game when the outcome was on the line. "Coming into a game in a pressure situation is not something you work on being able to deal with," he says. "It's not like working on a curve ball or learning to hit to the opposite field. I think it's something you're born with. Either you have the mental makeup to do it, or you don't.

"A lot of people call it guts or intestinal fortitude. Maybe that's got something to do with it, but I loved the challenge and I liked the idea that the game was on the line and I had something to say about it. When the challenge was given to me to save the game for a particular pitcher or for the Red Sox, I enjoyed that. It gave me a lot of special responsibility, and I took it."

Radatz says he was never intimidated by the other monster of Fenway Park, the short but high left field wall called "The Green Monster." "It never bothered me," Dick claims. "I never thought about it. The wall sort of evened out, anyway. Guys like Al Kaline would come in and hit balls off it that would've been home runs in Detroit, but Carl Yastrzemski would hold them to a single."

During the 1965 season, when his record was 9–11 with 22 saves and his ERA ballooned to 3.91, Radatz' career started to come untracked. There was a good reason, Dick recalls.

"Ted Williams had said that I needed another pitch. So I tried adding a pitch in '65. It got me into control problems," Radatz says. "I changed my arm position, and came up with a sinker. I started using it when I shouldn't have, and it was all downhill after that. It was a classic case of, if the wheel's not broke, don't fix it. I tried changing something, and it became a nightmare for me.

"It never bothered my arm," Radatz adds. "I never had arm trouble. It was just a mental thing with me. I started pitching defensively, and eventually I just decided to hang it up."

Radatz began the 1966 season with Boston but was traded to Cleveland in June. Less than one year later, the Indians sold him to the Cubs. Dick wound up the 1967 campaign pitching for Tacoma in the Pacific Coast League.

Released by the Cubs in the spring of 1968, Radatz joined the Tigers organization and spent the entire season with Toledo in the International League. He began the 1969 season in Detroit but was sold to Montreal, where he finished the year and his career.

Dick's combined record after the 1965 season was 3–11 with just 22 saves. "I really lost interest after I left Boston," he says. "Some trades are good for people, some aren't. The one that sent me to Cleveland was not good for me. I really had a love affair with the people in Boston. It was beautiful. We treated each other awfully well for about four years. When I left there, it broke my heart.

"It took me a couple of years to get over it. By that time, I'd lost a little bit off the fastball. I didn't have the real good second pitch, so it was pretty much over for me."

While it lasted, though, it was a spectacular career. Few pitchers have ever been as intimidating as Dick Radatz, and few have had as dazzling a four-year run as he did.

When he was right, Radatz was indeed a monster.

Bob Rush

Few Were Tougher or More Durable

THERE ARE ALWAYS two words that come to mind when the name Bob Rush is mentioned: tough and durable.

To the batters who faced him, the 6-5, 208-pound righthander was as difficult to hit as any hurler in the National League. Owner of a sinking fastball that hitters described as a "heavy ball," a nasty curve, and a troublesome change-up, Rush—with a delivery that featured a high leg kick—usually signaled a trying day for opposing batsmen when he took the mound.

He also worked relentlessly, like a finely tuned machine, seldom missing a turn, always getting in his innings, and almost never encountering arm problems. Durability was a word that was synonymous with the name Bob Rush.

Rush toed big league rubbers for 13 years, starting in 1948 and ending in 1960. Ten of those years were spent with the Chicago Cubs and the final three with the Milwaukee Braves and briefly the Chicago White Sox.

Although only two Cubs teams on which he pitched finished higher than seventh place, Rush won in double figures in seven seasons in Chicago (plus one more in Milwaukee), reaching a high in 1952 when he won 17. He pitched in more than 200 innings eight times while starting 27 or more games nine years in a row.

The Battle Creek, Michigan, native, who grew up in South Bend, Indiana, had a career record of 127–152 with a 3.65 ERA while pitching in 417 games. Rush pitched in 2,410.2 innings, allowing 2,327 hits, striking out 1,244 and walking 789. He completed more than one-third (118) of the 321 games he started.

He was also the winner of the 1952 All-Star Game and a member of Milwaukee's National League championship team in 1958. He started the third game of the '58 World Series against the New York Yankees, losing a 4–0 decision.

Overall, it was a splendid career for the towering hurler, even though most of it was spent pitching for losing teams and in the hitter-friendly confines of Wrigley Field.

"In a way, it was frustrating, pitching for the Cubs," says Rush, a resident of Mesa, Arizona, just outside of Phoenix. "Every year you'd figure this is the year we'll do better. But it seldom happened. While I was there, we finished last four times and seventh four times. It was no fun, that's for sure.

"I enjoyed pitching in Wrigley Field, though. It was a great park to pitch in. I didn't mind that at all. I was a sinkerball pitcher, and that was an advantage at Wrigley Field because I could keep the ball down and hitters wouldn't be as likely to hit it out."

Hitters were just as unlikely to find Rush missing a turn on the mound. In his 10 seasons with the Cubs, Bob had arm trouble only once, and he drew the starting assignment more than 30 times in five different years.

"If I didn't pitch every fourth day, I figured I was in the doghouse," he says. "I always felt that you trained yourself to pitch nine innings, and that's what I tried to do. They had no pitch count then. They just knew when you started throwing the ball high, you had probably thrown enough pitches.

"I worked out in the winter," he adds. "I tried to keep active. My theory was, you need strength in the legs. So I ran a lot. It wasn't the arm that usually got you out of a game. Most of the time, it was the legs that went on you."

The only time Rush had arm problems was in 1953. And he still wound up starting 28 of the 29 games in which he appeared. "I had a shoulder problem," he recalls. "Nobody knew what it was. It felt like somebody had stuck a knife in me. I still pitched, but that winter I went to a bone doctor in South Bend. He diagnosed my trouble as weak ligaments. He said I could either get an operation or try to build the shoulder back up. No way I was going to let him cut me. So I went to spring training, and built the strength back up, and everything was fine."

Rush was always a big, strong guy. He began pitching at an early age, and as a teenager began attracting attention. Bob's father played a major role in his development.

"My dad had pitched for Kelloggs back in Battle Creek. We moved to South Bend when I was three or four years old, and there he pitched for Bendix. He had spent a year in the St. Louis Browns organization, but he had decided he could do better playing industrial ball.

"He worked with me and taught me a lot. He was the most influential person in my career. He lived until 1964. I think when I was pitching and he was watching on TV, he worked harder than I did."

By the time Rush was pitching in high school and American Legion, the scouts were following him. A Cleveland Indians scout attempted to sign him when he was a junior in high school, but his father vetoed the deal. Then a Cubs scout picked up the trail.

"He came down to South Bend to watch me pitch," Rush says. "Then I worked out with him. After that, they called me to Chicago to work out, and then they offered me a contract. I signed right out of high school. My dad made an agreement with them that I would finish college, and I got $3,000 toward my tuition."

Rush attended the University of Indiana for one semester, then in the summer of 1944 was called into the military. He spent two years in the Army before launching his pro career in 1947 with Des Moines of the Western League.

After posting a 6–1 record at Des Moines, Rush was promoted during the season to Nashville of the Southern League, where he went 9–7. The following year, after just one season in the minors, he joined the Cubs.

"All the clubs were looking for young players," Bob recalls. "I went to spring training at Catalina Island in 1948 with the Cubs, got a chance and stayed with them. I considered myself very lucky. Usually, you spent three or four years in the minors, but I was at the right place at the right time. The Cubs were rebuilding, and that worked to my advantage.

"I was really surprised to be there, though. I always considered big league players kind of special, and here I was one of them. It was scary. But I was young enough that I didn't know any better, and I had a lot of confidence in my ability."

When the season began, the Cubs threw their 22-year-old rookie directly into the fire. He started the second game of the season. Starting 16 games of the 36 in which he pitched, Rush finished the year with a 5–11 record.

Although his record was hardly spectacular, one enduring experience did emerge from the '48 season for Rush. In September, he, manager Charlie Grimm, and others were the subjects of a Norman Rockwell painting titled "Bottom of the Ninth," which appeared on a cover of *The Saturday Evening Post*. Portraying a somber-looking batboy standing in front of Grimm and several sleepy-eyed players (Rush is on the left), the artwork has become one of the most famous of Rockwell's splendid collection of baseball paintings.

Rush started doing a little artistry of his own in 1949, painting the plate and coming up with a finished work that included a 10–18 record for a club that lost 93 games and finished a distant last in the National League.

The following year, Rush pitched well over the first two months of the season, then fell into a slump and finished the year with a league-leading 20 losses against 13 wins. His ERA, however, was a respectable 3.71, and Bob had supplanted Johnny Schmitz as the bellwether of the Chicago staff.

After an 11–12, 3.83 mark in '51, Rush enjoyed his finest year when he went 17–13 with a 2.70 ERA in 1952. With a few breaks, he would have been a 20-game winner. Two of his losses were by 1–0 scores, two more were by 2–0 counts, and one was a 3–0 defeat.

Rush added to his 1952 laurels by getting the win in the All-Star Game in the National League's 3–2 victory in a rain-shortened, five-inning game at Philadelphia's Shibe Park (the only abbreviated All-Star Game ever played). Bob pitched two innings and gave up two runs, but he got the verdict on the wings of teammate Hank Sauer's two-run homer. He was the first Cubs pitcher ever to win an All-Star Game.

"In 1952, everything seemed to fall into place," Rush says. "The team played good defense, plus it was getting runs for me. And the All-Star Game was really a big thrill. That, pitching my first game, and pitching in the World Series were the biggest thrills of my career.

"Of course, just pitching in the big leagues was a big thrill for me," he adds. "I pitched against some great hitters. Stan Musial was probably the toughest to face. But I probably had more problems with the Phillies than any other team, especially Richie Ashburn, Granny Hamner, and Willie Jones. They were tough."

The shoulder problem held Rush to a 9–14 record in 1953, but he rebounded with seasons of 13–15, 13–11, and 13–10 before posting a 6–16 mark in his last season with the Cubs. On December 5, 1957, Bob was the top name in a five-player trade with Milwaukee.

"The Braves were not too shabby," Rush recalls. "They were one of the better clubs in baseball. Playing for them was like night and day compared to playing with the Cubs. Every time you walked on the field, you felt you were going to win. You figured you could even make a [pitching] mistake and somebody would catch it. When you lost, you couldn't figure out why you had lost."

With the Braves, Rush joined a starting rotation that included Warren Spahn, Lew Burdette, and Bob Buhl. The three had combined for 56 wins the year before to lead the Braves to the National League pennant and victory over New York in the World Series.

With Buhl experiencing arm problems, Rush took over the number three spot in the rotation in 1958 and fashioned a 10–6 record in 28 games. After the Braves captured their second straight pennant, Bob got the nod in the third game of the Series with New York again the opponent and perfect game hurler Don Larsen facing him on the mound at Yankee Stadium.

Rush gave up just three hits in six innings, but a rare streak of wildness cost him. In the fifth inning, he walked three batters, then gave up a two-out, two-run single to Hank Bauer. After Rush departed, Bauer added a two-run homer off Don McMahon to give the Yanks a 4–0 victory. New York went on to win the Series in seven games, but Rush did not pitch again.

"Playing in the World Series was a great feeling," Rush exclaims. "Like all kids, I had my dreams, and my big dream was to start a World Series game against the Yankees at Yankee Stadium. My childhood dream came true. I didn't win the game, but it was sure a big thrill."

Rush pitched again for the Braves in 1959 when the club tied for first place during the regular season before losing to the Los Angeles Dodgers in a special playoff. He appeared in 31 games but started only nine while posting a 5–6 record.

Then, after winning two games during 10 relief appearances the following season, he was released by the Braves in June. Bob was signed by the White Sox, and worked in nine games without a decision before retiring at the end of the season. "I just decided the handwriting was on the wall," Rush says. "It was time to go. I didn't want to hang around."

Soon afterward, Rush took a job in customer relations for a major television manufacturer. Later, he worked for a swimming pool company.

Although he is still a frequent visitor to Cubs' spring training games in Arizona, he views major league baseball with a somewhat jaundiced eye. "There's been a big change in the game," he says. "I don't understand some of the things they're doing. From a fans' standpoint, it was better in the 1940s and 1950s because you were part of the game. You were right on top of the action. The game has lost that feeling.

"When you went to a game, you knew Musial played for the Cardinals. You knew Mantle played for the Yankees. Now, you mention the name of a player, and you don't know what team he's on.

"There used to be more tradition in baseball," Rush adds. "There was more strategy used, too. And good hitters didn't care who was pitching. Whether the pitcher was right or lefthanded, it didn't matter.

"Now, the conditions are so different. I don't know whether the players are better or not; I don't think it's fair to compare them. It's just a different game now."

It's especially different when it comes to pitchers. Those who throw 200 innings year after year and seldom miss a start from one season to the next have all but disappeared from the landscape.

Those like the tough, durable Bob Rush are a dying breed. What a shame.

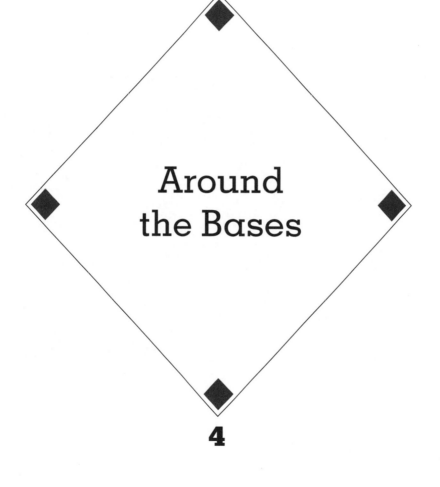

Around the Bases

4

Bill Bruton

The Ideal Leadoff Hitter

THE IDEAL leadoff batter in baseball has always been a solid, high-average line drive hitter with good speed afoot, a good eye, and, most important, a knack for getting on base. He specializes in singles, doubles and triples, can steal a base with ease, has the patience to wait out a walk, and accumulates a high total of runs scored. Usually, he is also an excellent defensive player who more often than not plays center field.

The great leadoff batters always have been players who performed extremely important roles on their teams, and who—because of their ability to perform these roles well—were of exceptionally high value.

If you had to find a guy to fit the description of the ideal leadoff batter, you'd have to look no farther than Bill Bruton. The slender outfielder met the specifications perfectly. He could hit. He could run. He could get on base. He could score runs. And he was a superb center fielder.

At the peak of his career in the 1950s, the fleet Bruton was the man who ignited the offense for some fine Milwaukee Braves clubs, two of which won National League pennants and one a World Series. Later, the left-handed hitter performed the same duties for some high-voltage Detroit Tigers teams.

Bruton's big league career reached from 1953 to 1964. In that time, he won three stolen base titles, led the league in triples twice and in runs scored once, and three times had the most putouts for an outfielder.

His career batting average was .273 with 1,651 hits in 6,056 trips to the plate. Bruton hit .280 or above four times. He scored 938 runs, drove in 545, stole 297 bases, and ripped 241 doubles, 102 triples, and 94 home runs, 12 of which were homers leading off an inning.

During his career, Bruton had three triples in one game (in 1959) and four doubles in one game (in 1962). He hit a grand slam home run in 1956 and another in 1962, both unusual feats for a leadoff batter. One of the hardest men to double up, he hit into just 73 doubleplays in 12 big league seasons. He also had two assists in one inning during a game in 1960.

Overall, Bill—whose father-in-law was Hall of Fame Negro League star Judy Johnson—had an excellent baseball career after coming off the sand-lots of Alabama and making the major leagues as one of the sport's early African-American players.

"It was a career," Bruton said, "that was very satisfying. There have been millions and millions who've played the game the world over, but to be one of only 400 who made the major leagues in any given season gives you a very satisfying feeling."

The soft-spoken, articulate former player had a satisfying career after baseball, too. He spent 24 years with Chrysler Corporation in Detroit, working first in sales promotion and advertising, later owning a dealership, and for the final 14 years—until he retired in 1988—serving, in his words, "as a trouble-shooter for Lee Iacocca."

Bill helped customers solve problems with their cars. For many customers, he was the last step after all other avenues of possible assistance had been exhausted.

Bruton lived his final years until passing away in 1995 in the home once owned by Johnson in Marshalltown, Delaware, just below Wilmington. Bill and his wife—Johnson's daughter—moved there after the great star of primarily the Hilldale Daisies and the Pittsburgh Crawfords died in 1989.

As a player, Bruton was actually older than the record book listed him. "When I went to my first spring training, Bill Yancey, the scout who signed me, told me to say I was 20 instead of 23," Bruton said. "He said I'd get a better look if they thought I was 20. At 23, you're supposed to be in the big leagues already, not just starting out.

"When I retired from the Tigers, they said, 'What do you mean you're retiring? You're only 36.' I said, 'The record book is wrong. I'll be 40 in December.'"

Bruton's late start in baseball was due to a combination of factors that limited his exposure to the game as a youth. Born in Panola, Alabama, a small town near Birmingham, Bill was the oldest of a long, distinguished line of major league players—including Hall of Famers Willie Mays, Billy Williams, Hank Aaron, and Willie McCovey—to come out of that area.

There were no baseball teams in junior or senior high school where Bill grew up. "I was pretty fast as a kid, so I ran track in junior high," Bruton said. "I was usually the number two or three man on the relay teams. But there wasn't any track team in senior high." Bruton learned his baseball from playing on the sandlots and from watching Negro League teams play the hometown Birmingham Black Barons.

"As a kid, I played all the positions," Bruton said. "I even played first base and catcher. But I liked the outfield better. I could use my speed there.

Eventually, center field became my regular position. I tried left field, but I got claustrophobic there. Center field had more room. It was easier to play center field because you looked straight in at the batter. You knew where the pitches were going, and you could move accordingly.

"I lived only about 15 miles from Birmingham. I would go up to see the Negro League teams. I saw all the great players of that day—guys like Satchel Paige, Josh Gibson. There were also a lot of industrial teams in the area, and I used to watch them all the time, too."

At the time, Bruton said, he was a switch-hitter. "I could hit with pretty good power," he claimed. "I had more consistent power from the right side, but I got hit a lot, so I switched to batting lefthanded full-time."

Bruton joined the Army during World War II and spent six months in the Far East. But he played hardly any baseball until getting out of military service.

"After I got out of the service, I lived in Wilmington," Bill recalled. "I had a tryout with the Philadelphia Stars, a team in the Negro League. I had a good spring training with them, and I felt I was going to get a job. But the day before the season opened, they gave me my release. I went back to Wilmington and then joined a barnstorming team called the San Francisco Stars. We played against semipro teams from towns mostly in Canada and the Upper Midwest."

At this point in his life, Bruton was not only courting Judy Johnson's daughter but getting to know the great third baseman himself quite well. "We used to talk a lot," Bruton said. "He had a little store in Wilmington. I saw him every day. He was very supportive. I never saw him play, but from what I heard, he was up at the top [of the list] of great third basemen.

"In 1950," Bruton continued, "Johnson's best friend, Bill Yancey, became a scout with the Boston Braves. He invited me to spring training with the Braves." Bruton went south with the Boston club, was offered a contract, and signed it.

"By this time, Jackie Robinson had broken the color line in professional baseball. I had no big dreams to be a baseball player. But baseball was something I figured I'd pursue if I had the opportunity. I think if I hadn't become a baseball player, I would have gone to school and become a research scientist," Bruton added. "I always liked science."

Bruton was forced like all the other black players of the era to live in segregated housing—a condition that existed not only in Florida but also in places like St. Louis and Cincinnati.

In his first year as a professional, he was sent to Eau Claire of the Northern League. That year, he led the league in stolen bases with 66 and in games, at-bats, runs, hits, and putouts while batting .288.

Over the next two years, Bruton continued on a rampage. He hit .303 with a record-setting 27 triples in 1951 at Denver of the Western League. Then, in 1952, he batted .325 with a league-leading 211 hits, 130 runs, 154 games, 650 at-bats, 22 assists, and a .989 fielding percentage at Milwaukee, then of the American Association. That would be the last season for both Bruton and Milwaukee in the minor leagues.

"I had played in a City Series game in 1952 with the Braves against the Red Sox, but that turned out to be the only time I played in Boston," Bruton said. "In 1953, the Braves moved to Milwaukee, but I didn't really have to move because I had played there the previous year.

"Moving to Milwaukee was pretty exciting," Bruton added. "We had no idea that the attendance would be as great as it was. In 1952, the minor league team had drawn only 280,000 in Milwaukee. In 1953, the Braves were looking for one million, but they got 1.8 million. The team drew fans from all over the Upper Midwest. And when we played the Cubs, their fans would come up from Chicago. We developed a big rivalry with the Cubs. We were big rivals with the Dodgers and Giants, too. We were friendly off the field, but on the field it was dog-eat-dog. It was a great time for baseball in Milwaukee."

It was a great time for the Braves' slender rookie, too. Bill won the first of three straight stolen base crowns, and, although edged out by Junior Gilliam of the Brooklyn Dodgers for Rookie of the Year honors, he had a fine season, despite a .250 batting average that would turn out to be the lowest in his big league career.

"I remember my first game," Bruton said. "We were playing against the Cincinnati Reds at Crosley Field. I got a couple of hits. In those days, Cincinnati used to rope off the outfield for opening day to get more people into the ballpark. I leaned into the crowd and caught a couple of balls that would've been ground-rule doubles.

"Then our first game in Milwaukee that season was against the Cardinals. We must have had 35 or 36,000 people at the game. I had never played in front of that many people before.

"We went into the 11th inning tied at 3–3. In the bottom of the 11th, I hit a leadoff home run against Gerry Staley that won the game. It was the only home run I hit all year."

Although seventh in 1952 as the Boston Braves, the Milwaukee club climbed to second place in 1953. It had begun to discard the excessive number of older players on the roster and were starting to bring in young players who would form the backbone of the club for the rest of the decade.

Along with Bruton, Eddie Mathews, Johnny Logan, Lew Burdette, and Del Crandall were budding young stars with the Braves in 1953. One year later, they were joined by Aaron. With veterans Warren Spahn, Joe Adcock, and Andy Pafko there, too, the Braves had almost overnight been transformed into a team that was definitely on the move.

"We developed into a very close-knit team," Bruton said. "The whole organization was close-knit. It was one for all and all for one. Everybody supported one another. We had good pitching, good hitting, good defense. We had some problems at second base. No one seemed to satisfy the Braves until we got [Red] Schoendienst later on."

Between 1954 and 1956, the Braves finished third once and second twice. And the speedy Bruton was a skilled table-setter at the top of the lineup.

In his sophomore year, he upped his average to .284 while again leading the league with 34 stolen bases. He led the league in at-bats with 636 in 1955, scoring 106 runs while hitting .275 and for the third time in a row topping the league in steals with 25.

"It was always nice to lead the league in anything, but I particularly enjoyed leading in stolen bases," said Bruton, who once was clocked doing 10.1 in the 100-yard dash in a baseball uniform. "I loved to run. Because I could go so fast, it was always more fun to run than anything else.

"Of course, you only stole when you needed to back then. It wasn't like it is today with the big numbers in stolen bases. And it was more of a science. You stole mostly on the pitcher, so you studied all the opposing pitchers very thoroughly. You tried to learn what a pitcher's moves were: what his first move would be, when he would go to first base, and when he would go to the plate. You would study each pitcher and then act accordingly."

In 1956, the Braves changed managers after 46 games. Veteran skipper Charlie Grimm was replaced by Fred Haney. That had a drastic effect on Bruton's stolen base totals, which dropped to eight that season. "Grimm let you run whenever you could," Bruton said. "He used to say, 'You know more about stealing a base than I do.' But when Haney came in, he didn't want you to do anything unless he told you to. So I didn't steal nearly as much."

But while Bill's stolen base totals dropped, his skills with the bat continued to render valuable service to the Braves' lineup. He led the league in triples with 15 in 1956 while batting .272.

Bruton claimed that Robin Roberts, Curt Simmons, and Vinegar Bend Mizell were three of the toughest moundsmen he faced. "I don't know what my average against them was, but they gave me more trouble than the others," he recalled. "Roberts had exceptional control and multiple speeds. Simmons had that herky-jerky motion. And Mizell was tough because of his wildness.

"I hit a leadoff single against Simmons one time [in 1953]. I usually took a couple of pitches against him, but this time I made up my mind I was not going to let him get ahead of me. I was going to swing at the first pitch. So I singled. That was the only hit Simmons gave up that day. I was erased on a doubleplay, and he retired 27 batters in a row [with Bill striking out three times]. That was one of the best-pitched games I ever played in," said Bruton, who did not play in the 12-inning perfect game thrown by the Pittsburgh Pirates' Harvey Haddix against the Braves in 1959.

One other game Bruton wished he hadn't played in occurred on July 11, 1957. With all the pieces finally fitting together, the Braves were headed for their first pennant since 1948 when they played in Boston. The 6-0½, 169-pound Bruton was an integral part of an outstanding Milwaukee team that seemingly had no weakness.

"Felix Mantilla [a utility infielder] and I were going after a little Texas Leaguer," Bill remembered. "We were both running at full speed. Both of us thought we could catch the ball. We collided, and I tore up my right knee and was out for the season."

That meant that Bruton missed the World Series, a thrilling affair in which Burdette won three games and the Braves beat the New York Yankees in seven games.

"I was not only knocked out of the World Series," Bill said. "It was a question whether I would ever play again. They tried treatment, and that didn't work. Finally, I flew to Oklahoma City to see a doctor who had done knee surgery on the Oklahoma [University] Sooners. He put me in the hospital, and on the first day of the World Series, I had surgery. I never saw the game; in fact, I was in the hospital for the whole Series."

Bruton, who was hitting .278 when the accident occurred, underwent a long winter of rehabilitation. He still wasn't fully recovered by the start of the following season and didn't return to action until May 5.

"When I finally came back, I would say I was about 85 percent," Bill said. "I don't think my overall speed was affected, but I lost the spring in my leg. Your right knee is the one you use to push off with when you're on base, and I just couldn't take off as fast. After a couple of steps, though, I would be all right."

Bruton got into 100 games in 1958 and had one of his finest seasons with the bat with a .280 average. And the Braves again won the National League pennant and went to the World Series against the Yankees.

"Playing in that World Series was the biggest thrill of my career," Bruton said. "It was just grand. You can't get any higher than playing in a World Series. That's the top. That's what you play for. It was just a great feeling."

Bruton had an outstanding Series, hitting .412. His single in the bottom of the 10th inning drove in the winning run in the Braves' 4–3 triumph in the opener. He added three hits, including a home run, and scored twice in a 13–5 Milwaukee victory in the second game. After taking a 3–1 lead in the Series, however, the Braves lost three straight with Bob Turley winning two of those games and saving a third for the Yankees.

The 1958 season turned out to be the Braves' last hurrah in Milwaukee. Although they finished second the next two years—losing a special playoff with the Los Angeles Dodgers for the flag in 1959—they won no more pennants and eventually moved to Atlanta after the 1965 season.

"I felt," Bruton said, "that we had a good enough team that we should have won three or four years in a row. We just missed out in 1959, but it always seemed like little things went wrong."

Back to full-time duty, Bruton hit a career-high .289 in 1959. The next year, he hit .286 and led the league in runs (112) and triples (13).

By then, the Braves were managed by Chuck Dressen, a veteran skipper who later became Bruton's pilot on the Tigers. "I could have done without him both times," Bill said. "He always felt that as a lefthanded hitter, I couldn't hit lefthanded pitchers. He platooned me some. I didn't care too much for that or for him."

Despite Bruton's fine season in 1960, the Braves decided that was not as important as finding a second baseman, now that Schoendienst had been relegated to part-time duty after a bout with tuberculosis. On December 7, they traded Bill and three others (Terry Fox, Dick Brown, and Chuck Cottier) to Detroit for second baseman Frank Bolling and outfielder Neil Chrisley.

"I would have liked to have finished my career in Milwaukee," Bruton said. "But it didn't make that much difference. I was still playing ball, and that's what counted. You just make up your mind to play wherever you are."

With the Tigers, Bruton anchored an outfield that included Al Kaline on one side in right field and Rocky Colavito on the other side in left. "They had tried to move Kaline to center, but that didn't work," Bruton said. "That's why they got me. It was nice playing between those two. They were both very good outfielders, although I did break my jaw running into Kaline.

"The Tigers always had good ball clubs," Bruton added. "But they just couldn't seem to win. My first year there, they won 101 games, but we still finished eight games behind the Yankees. The Tigers always had a tough time jelling."

Bruton had three good years as a regular with the Tigers before settling into a reserve role in his fourth and final season in Detroit. In 1961, he hit .257 with a career-high 17 home runs. The following season he hit .278 with 16 homers and a career-high 74 RBI. He batted .256 in 1963 before finishing with a .277 mark in 1964.

"In the American League, I found the strike zone was much higher," Bruton recalled. "I had to make an adjustment to that. They also played for the big inning in the American League. They wouldn't play aggressive ball. They wouldn't steal or bunt much."

By the end of 1964, Dressen, who had replaced Bob Scheffing as Tigers manager in midseason the year before, was playing Bruton less frequently. Bill, with his creaky knee, felt it was time to move on to something else.

He retired from baseball at the end of the season. "I had some reservations about retiring," he said. "But it was a job. You knew it had to end someday. I was going to give the uniform to them. I wasn't going to force them to pull it off me. I thought I could have played a couple more years, but I was playing less and less. It was time to go.

"I was satisfied with my career. I would have liked to have hit .300 and been on an All-Star team. But overall, I think I had a very satisfactory career. One of the most pleasant things about it was I played against some terrific players. I think in the 1950s we saw the best baseball that's ever been played in this country. We had only eight teams in each league. Every team had at least three strong starting pitchers. And the top teams were all very strong.

"It was a great time to be a baseball player."

It was also a time when Bill Bruton established himself as a superb leadoff batter. He was an ideal man for the role.

Alvin Dark

Football Star Excelled in Baseball

IT IS A question that would be perfectly suited for a trivia quiz: Who was an All-American in football, rookie of the year in baseball, and won a World Series as a manager?

Or how about this one: Who played in the same backfield with Steve Van Buren, spent 14 years in big league baseball as a player and 13 as a manager, and later became a golf pro?

The answer to both questions is, of course, Alvin Dark, a brilliant, all-around athlete who blazed a trail across the sports world that was quite unlike any other.

Dark, the rock-solid player with the nickname of Blackie, carved out the lion's share of his success in baseball, where he was one of the National League's leading shortstops before becoming a manager who guided two teams to the World Series.

As a player, Dark was three times a National League All-Star as well as a member of three National League pennant-winners and one World Series victor. He performed most notably with the Boston Braves and New York Giants and also played for the St. Louis Cardinals, Chicago Cubs, Philadelphia Phillies, and Milwaukee Braves in the later years of his career.

In 1948, Dark not only captured Rookie of the Year honors while hitting .322, he helped the Braves win their first pennant in 34 years. Three years later, Alvin was a member of the Giants team that rode Bobby Thomson's home run to a playoff victory over the Brooklyn Dodgers and a berth in the World Series. And three years after that, he was a key player as the Giants swept the powerful Cleveland Indians in one of the biggest upsets in World Series history.

The Giants' captain, who hit .417 in the '51 Series and .412 in the '54 fall classic, batted .300 or above four times during a career that stretched from 1948 to 1960. Three other times he hit .290 or more.

A clutch hitter who specialized in line drives, Dark twice hit more than 40 doubles in a season, leading the league with 41 in 1951, and eight times hit 25 or more two-baggers during the year. He finished with a .289 career batting average, belting 2,089 hits, including 126 home runs in 1,828 games. Dark had 757 RBI and scored 1,064 times.

Alvin's best all-around year was probably 1953, when he batted .300 and had career highs in home runs (23), runs (126), and RBI (88) while leading the league in at-bats with 647. In 1954, he hit .293 with 20 home runs, 98 runs scored, 70 RBI, and a league-leading 644 at-bats.

"Even though 1953 was a good year," Dark says, "I think the best year I ever had in baseball was in 1954. We won the World Series. I felt that as far as winning ball games and putting everything together, that was the best year. I had better years at the plate, but I felt that 1954 was the year I had it all put together."

As good as he was as a hitter, Dark was no slouch as a fielder. Although not flashy, the compact, 5-11, 185-pounder had sure hands and an accurate arm. He led NL shortstops in putouts three times and in assists once. He also led in errors twice.

During his career, Dark was repeatedly involved in big trades. He was swapped for people who became Hall of Famers (Red Schoendienst and Richie Ashburn), an author (Jim Brosnan), and a manager (Joe Morgan). He was even dealt after his playing days ended to a team that wanted him as its manager.

As a manager, Dark skippered the San Francisco Giants, Kansas City A's, Cleveland Indians, Oakland A's, and San Diego Padres. Only one of five managers in baseball history to win a pennant in both leagues (the others are Joe McCarthy, Yogi Berra, Sparky Anderson, and Dick Williams), he won a flag in 1962 with the Giants and led both the 1974 and 1975 A's into the playoffs, winning the pennant and the World Series in '74.

Dark's overall record as a manager was 994–954 (.510). He claims, though, that he liked playing better. "It was always more fun for me to play," he says. "There's more competition. Even if you're on a fifth-place club, if you're a player, you're at least competing and trying to beat the other teams.

"When you're a manager, sometimes you're out of the ball game in the first inning, and you don't manage the rest of the game. That's no fun.

"It was enjoyable managing, don't get me wrong," Dark adds. "There was a lot of enjoyment in it. But managing can't compare with playing."

What sport Dark would play was never a problem—even in his early days as a young athlete and even though he was a baseball, football, and basketball standout and probably could have made a name for himself professionally in any one of the three.

"The choice was made when I was six years old," Dark says. "I wanted to be a baseball player all my life. I played baseball and football at the same time, but baseball was my game. I enjoyed football. But when football was over, my thoughts were entirely on baseball. I played basketball, too. But baseball was my life."

Dark was born in Comanche, Oklahoma, but moved as a youth to Louisiana. He had gone originally to Louisiana State University (LSU) where he encountered Van Buren, who later became the greatest running back of his era with the Philadelphia Eagles and a member of the Pro Football Hall of Fame.

"We were in the same backfield together for one year at LSU," Dark recalls. "I was a sophomore and he was a junior. Steve was a great college football player. As a senior, I don't think LSU ever had a running back who could compete with him. Then when he came into the pros, he really played great."

After his sophomore season at LSU, Dark joined the armed forces. As frequently happened during World War II, athletes in the military were assigned to units at colleges and attended classes as regular students. Dark spent his junior year at Southwestern Louisiana State and was named to the All-American team as a halfback.

Alvin was drafted by the Eagles, but when he was discharged from the military in 1946, he headed right to baseball.

"Ted McGrew was the guy who signed me," Dark remembers. "When I got out of the service, he was in Lake Charles, which was my hometown, waiting for me to come back. He got my dad to phone him and let him know when I was coming home. I had been overseas, and I had told my dad when I'd be there."

Dark signed a contract with a healthy bonus with the Braves' organization and soon afterward was summoned to Boston where he was handed a uniform and told to suit up. Although he had no minor league experience, Dark got into 15 games with the Braves at the end of the 1946 season and hit .231.

Badly in need of some professional seasoning, Dark was sent to the Braves' Triple-A farm club in Milwaukee for the 1947 season. Al proceeded to set the American Association on fire, hitting .303 while leading the league in doubles, runs, and at-bats and at shortstop in putouts, assists, and errors.

The Braves could hardly wait to get Dark back to Boston. With a team comprised mostly of veteran players, the Braves needed some energetic, young talent. Moreover, the club had just acquired Eddie Stanky from the Brooklyn Dodgers to fill a gaping hole at second base, and they had no shortstop to team with him. Alvin was the answer to both needs.

"I'd rather have had a chance to break in without having been in the service for three years," Dark says. "I always felt like that slowed me down. I'd have made the big leagues earlier, had I not gone into the service. But for goodness sake, I can't complain. Ted Williams gave up five years of baseball to the service."

If Dark had trouble adjusting to the big leagues, it didn't show. The 26-year-old rookie was just the sparkplug the Braves were looking for, and—teaming with the veteran Stanky—he gave the club a solid doubleplay combination as well as an exceptional number two hitter in the lineup.

After hitting .322 with 39 doubles, 85 runs, and 48 RBI, Dark was voted the National League's Rookie of the Year by the Baseball Writers' Association, narrowly edging the Phillies' Ashburn, who hit .333. "Your first year in the big leagues, you really don't think about anything except playing baseball," Dark says. "That's all I thought about. I felt, man, I'm in the big leagues. It tickled me to death.

"When the year was over, I finally realized what I'd hit, and I saw that I'd had a pretty good year. Best of all, I was in a World Series."

The Braves had beaten the more powerful Dodgers and St. Louis Cardinals to win the National League pennant, giving the club its first flag since the Miracle Braves won in 1914. Entering the World Series, Boston was a slight underdog to the Cleveland Indians. True to the predictions, the Braves lost in six games with Bob Lemon winning two of the Tribe's four victories, including a 4–3 clincher, the third one-run game of the Series. Dark had just four hits and batted .167.

Dark stayed in Boston just one more year, slumping to .276 in 1949. That winter, he was traded to the Giants in a huge deal for both teams. With the Braves feeling they needed more power and the Giants desirous of a strong middle infield combination, both teams were accommodated in a swap that sent Dark, Stanky, and pitcher Sam Webb to New York for third baseman Sid Gordon, outfielder Willard Marshall, and shortstop Buddy Kerr. The deal stunned fans of both teams.

"People in New York didn't accept Eddie and me too graciously at first," Dark recalls. "But it was a good trade for both clubs. Leo Durocher was the Giants' manager, and he wanted a doubleplay combination. And the Braves had no long-ball hitters and wanted power, which they got with Gordon and Marshall."

The trade turned out to be especially beneficial to the Giants. Dark and Stanky were among the league's doubleplay leaders, and in the second season after the swap, they played key roles in driving the New Yorkers to the National League pennant. Alvin hit .303 and led the league with 41 doubles.

The flag came after the Giants had stormed back from 13½ games behind in mid-August to tie the Dodgers at the end of the regular season, then won the final game of a three-game playoff, 5–4, on Thomson's dramatic three-run homer in the ninth inning.

"In August, we were 13 games behind and were playing for second place," Dark remembers. "But we won about six or seven games in a row, and we started thinking, 'Wait a minute. Let's see what happens. Who knows?' Then the streak got to 16 wins in a row. After that, we were only six or seven games behind, and we felt we had a chance.

"The Dodgers had to win the last game of the season to tie us. We finished our game up in Boston and won, so they had to win, too, and they did. That was the game that Jackie Robinson played a great game against the Phillies [with a game-saving catch in the bottom of the ninth and a game-winning home run in the 14th].

"We won 37 of our last 44 games during the regular season, then we won two of three in the playoffs. At that point, Thomson was one of our greatest competitors. He won a lot of ball games for us all through the season, but all you hear about was his home run in the last game."

In a memorable Series filled with special footnotes—including the last appearance of Joe DiMaggio and the Series debuts of rookies Willie Mays and Mickey Mantle—the Giants lost in six games to the New York Yankees, who were in the midst of five consecutive Series triumphs.

More good times, however, were in store for Dark during his six and one-half years in New York. After hitting .301 in 1952 and .300 in 1953, his .293 mark helped to propel the Giants back into the Series in 1954.

This time, the Giants ascended to baseball's highest plateau. Going against a Cleveland team that had set an American League record with 111 wins, the underdog New York club rode the bat of pinch-hit sensation Dusty Rhodes to a four-game sweep and a stunning upset of the highly rated Indians, owners of one of the finest pitching staffs ever assembled.

"That 1954 team was the best one of the three pennant-winners I played on," says Dark. "We had a better all-around club. We had defense, offense, pitching, everything. We beat Cleveland in four games, and in order to do that, everything had to go right."

Although Dark now had a new doubleplay partner in Davey Williams, he continued to hold the widely diverse Giants together. As captain, Alvin gave the club steady leadership while serving Durocher immeasurably as the team's on-the-field brains.

"I never really thought of myself as a sparkplug," Dark says. "I just did my job. I didn't think about being a holler guy. I just did out on the field what I thought needed to be done to win a ball game."

After hitting .282 in 1955, Dark found himself packing his bags in June 1956 in another major trade. This time, he, Whitey Lockman, and two others were sent to the Cardinals for second baseman Red Schoendienst and four others.

On one of the league's better teams—one that included Stan Musial and Ken Boyer—Dark formed a doubleplay combination with Don Blasingame and put in nearly two workmanlike seasons with the Cardinals, hitting .275 and .290.

Early in 1958, St. Louis swapped Dark to the Cubs for pitcher Jim Brosnan. Al moved to third base, playing in Chicago through 1959 while hitting .295 and .264.

With his career in a decline, Dark was one of three players traded in the winter of 1960 to the Phillies for Ashburn. He stayed in Philadelphia only long enough to play in 55 games before getting sent in midseason to Milwaukee for future Boston Red Sox manager Joe Morgan. Alvin played in 50 more games with the Braves, ending the year with a .265 overall batting mark. After the season, the Braves dealt him to the Giants for Andre Rodgers.

Dark, however, was not going to San Francisco to play. The Giants wanted him to manage. Although noted for his leadership qualities, Dark had not considered managing until late in his playing career.

"When you're a player, you're playing and playing and playing," he explains. "You've been doing the same things all the time out at shortstop—running, everything that a manager does on the bench. You're involved with cutoffs, with relays. You watch the catcher give signs. You pass the signs on to other people on your ball club. Then, all of a sudden, the end of your career is coming, and they say to you, 'Wouldn't you like to manage?' 'Well, sure,' you say. 'I've been managing all these years anyway.'"

Dark brought the Giants home third in 1961. Then in 1962 he found his club finishing in a tie for first place with the Los Angeles Dodgers, 11 years, 3,000 miles, and two transplanted teams away from where they'd been in 1951. Just as the New York Giants did, the San Francisco Giants won a three-game playoff to enter the World Series against the Yankees.

"I'll never forget the '51 playoffs, and I'll also never forget the '62 play-offs," Dark says. "It's ironic, we won both playoffs the same way, beating the Dodgers two games to one."

The '62 Giants lost the Series to the Yankees in seven games with 1960 Series goat Ralph Terry (who served up Bill Mazeroski's Series-winning home run) pitching a four-hitter to beat Jack Sanford, 1–0, in the seventh game. That was the game in which Yank second baseman Bobby Richardson snared Willie McCovey's torrid line drive to end the Series and snuff out a Giants' last-ditch rally.

Dark piloted the Giants for two more uneventful seasons. He then skippered Kansas City for almost two years and Cleveland for nearly four. In 1974, Dark succeeded Dick Williams at Oakland. Alvin led the A's not only to a division title and an LCS victory in four games over the Baltimore Orioles but also to a four-to-one verdict over the Dodgers in the World Series, giving the A's their third straight World Championship. Alvin had the A's back in the playoffs the following year, but they were swept by the Red Sox in three games.

After a dispute with A's owner Charley Finley, Dark departed at the end of the season. His last managing job came two years later when he took over the Padres one-third of the way through the season. He left at the end of the year after finishing fifth in the National League's West Division.

Following that experience, Dark retired from baseball, although his name occasionally continued to surface whenever a managerial job opened. Eventually, he moved to South Carolina and plunged into a new sport—golf. "I went to South Carolina to get involved in golf and a golf course there," Dark says. "It was nice because it let me play a lot."

A resident of Easley, South Carolina, Dark thinks of all the good moments he had in baseball and agrees that it was an exceptionally fine life.

He remembers the time he hit two doubles in one inning in 1952, the time he scored five runs in one game in 1954, and all the playoff and World Series wins, especially the championships of 1954 and 1974.

"You can sit around and think a lot of good things that happened to you," he says. "But the one thing that keeps on coming up was 1951. That final playoff game was the most exciting moment of all.

"All I thought about as a kid was being a big league player," Dark adds. "I'm just so glad that I was able to be one. I played in a wonderful era. It was a time when baseball was king of the street."

It was a time, too, when a guy named Alvin Dark was a pretty high-ranking member of the king's court.

Granny Hamner

Fiery Captain of the Whiz Kids

THERE IS AN old axiom in baseball that a team without a good shortstop is a team that resides in the lower levels of the standings. Good teams and good shortstops go together like bricks and mortar. You can't have one without the other.

Down through the years, good shortstops have come with many variations. Some were tall and sleek; some were short and stocky. Some fit somewhere in between. But they all had several qualities in common: All the good ones could hit, and all of them could field.

One of the best of his era was Granny Hamner. He could hit, and he could field. He ranked as one of the finest clutch hitters of his day, and he was a sure-handed gloveman with an arm like a howitzer.

Hamner was a fiery performer, the captain and heart and soul of the Phillies in the days when they were affectionately called the Whiz Kids by adoring Philadelphia fans. A cocky battler who clawed every step of the way, Hamner typified the spirit of the Fightin' Phils of the 1950s. He was a take-charge kind of player with a quick temper who never took any guff from anybody.

Good shortstops abounded in the post–World War II era. In the National League, Pee Wee Reese, Marty Marion, and Alvin Dark were the ones who got most of the attention. But Hamner was right there with them.

Granny was the shortstop on two All-Star teams in the early 1950s, once as a starter and once as a reserve. And one year when he was shifted to second base, he made the All-Star team as a starter at that position. It was the first time a big league player had ever started at two different positions in the All-Star Game.

Such oddities were not uncommon in Hamner's life. After all, this was a guy who had originally made the big leagues at the age of 17 and one who had a brother play in the majors. Hamner was also briefly a pitcher during his big league career.

"I think probably my greatest asset as a big league player was that I was a timely hitter," said Hamner, who died suddenly in 1993 while attending a Whiz Kids reunion. "If they kept such records, I think you'd probably find that I drove in more runs with two outs than anybody on our ball club."

The records that were kept showed that Hamner hit .262 during a career that spanned 17 years in the majors. In 1,531 games, starting in 1944 and ending in 1962, Granny had 1,529 hits, including 272 doubles, 62 triples, and 104 home runs. He scored 711 and drove in 708.

Although he never hit .300, Hamner hit .299 once and five other times hit over .260 as a regular. Four times he drove in more than 80 runs in a season, a feat that with his other qualities would have commanded a megabucks salary today.

Hamner's crowning achievement as a hitter occurred in the 1950 World Series. Although the Phillies bowed to the New York Yankees in four straight games, largely because the Whiz Kids' hitters stopped hitting, Granny was the one shining light on offense. His .429 batting average was the only respectable figure on his team.

The 5-10, 163-pound infielder had several seasons when he carried an especially big bat. In 1953, he hit .276 with career highs in home runs (21) and RBI (92). The following year, he laced National League pitching for a .299 average with 13 homers and 89 RBI.

Hitting was never easy in those days. With just eight teams in the league, good pitching was in abundance. Even the lowliest teams had at least a few strong arms on the mound.

"Ewell Blackwell was the toughest for me," Hamner said. "I couldn't hit him with a tennis racket. The trouble was, I just couldn't see the ball. His fastball came in on righthanded hitters.

"I remember one time we were playing in Cincinnati and had an off day. Ted Kluszewski [Reds first baseman] asked me if I wanted to go fishing. We went out and Blackwell went with us. We had a nice day together out on a lake. The next night Blackwell pitched, and when I came up, the first pitch he threw knocked me right on my tail. He was mean. [Don] Drysdale was like that, too.

"I used to hit Harvey Haddix," Hamner continued. "I remember hitting two home runs in one game off him one time. He just couldn't get me out. Then we traded for him. That knocked 20 points off my batting average."

Hamner's greatest thrill in baseball is predictable. It came when he was in the dugout on the last day of the 1950 season. That's when Dick Sisler hit a three-run home run in the 10th inning that gave the Phillies a 4–1 victory over the Brooklyn Dodgers and the National League pennant.

"I cried like a baby," Granny said. "I was on the bench, and I saw it go out, and tears just starting running down my face. The ball just made it over the wall in left.

"We had played so hard to get to that point," Hamner added. "But then we had lost a seven-game lead from mid-September on. We knew we could win that last game with Brooklyn, though, because we had [Robin] Roberts pitching. He didn't often lose when it really counted."

For the Phillies it was their first pennant in 35 years. They would not win another flag for 30 more years. "I don't think anybody took us seriously in 1950," Hamner said. "In fact, we were probably only the fifth best club in the league. But we had spirit. That was our strongest asset." No one did more to build that spirit than Hamner, then just a 23-year-old team leader but one of the more experienced players on the young Phillies squad.

Granny, whose real first name was Granville, had been around pro ball since 1944 when he signed an $8,000 bonus to play with the Phillies. The Richmond, Virginia, native joined the wartime Phils immediately,

"I had always played shortstop, although I did a little pitching, too," Hamner recalled. "At the time, Ben Chapman [later to become the Phillies manager] was managing Richmond in the Piedmont League. My brother [Garvin] was playing for them.

"One day I went out to a game with my brother, and he said to Ben, 'How about giving him [Granny] a chance?' So they gave me a uniform, and I worked out with the club. Then they sent me up to Philadelphia to work out.

"I had worked out with four or five other clubs. The Dodgers were interested. But the Phillies didn't have anybody at shortstop. I thought I could get to the big leagues quicker if I signed with them, so that's what I did." Hamner got to the big leagues sooner than even he expected. He joined the Phillies the next day at the tender age of 17.

"We had a very poor club," he said. "The quality of play had really diminished, so coming to the big leagues at that age wasn't as bad as it sounds. There were a few good players still around. But they were all getting older. We didn't get big crowds to watch us. So it wasn't too hard to break in."

Hamner got into 21 games, and in 77 at-bats hit a respectable .247. At the end of the season, he returned to Richmond to start his senior year in high school.

Even in wartime, the youthful Hamner was deemed not yet ready for the big leagues. The Phillies sent him to Utica of the Eastern League for the 1945 season. He hit .258 before returning to Philadelphia for 14 games at the end of the year.

Hamner spent most of the 1946 season in the military. He reported back to Utica in 1947, and there, while hitting .291, he helped to spark a team managed by Eddie Sawyer to the Eastern League pennant.

After returning to the Phillies again at the end of the 1947 season, Hamner was in Philadelphia to stay. At one point, though, the St. Louis Browns tried to pry him away. The Browns thought they had pulled a fast one by drafting a G. Hamner off the Phillies minor league roster. They thought they were getting Granny but instead got his brother Garvin, by then a player in the Phils farm system. Garvin had appeared briefly with the Phillies in 1945. The botched move proved highly embarrassing to the lowly Browns, as well as to the Hamner brothers.

While Garvin went to the Browns—but never played in the majors for them—Granny stayed with the Phillies, and in 1948 launched what would become a string of 10 straight seasons in their starting lineup. He hit .260 in 1948, his first full season in the big leagues in what by then was the start of the Whiz Kids buildup.

In 1949 Hamner hit .263 and led the league in at-bats with 662. Meanwhile, the Phillies under manager Sawyer, who had taken over for Chapman in mid-1948, moved up to third place, their highest finish since 1917.

"You could see us coming," Hamner said. "We kept signing good ballplayers. We had signed Richie Ashburn, Willie Jones, Roberts, [Curt] Simmons, and some others, and had also made some very good trades [landing players such as Sisler, Eddie Waitkus, Russ Meyer, and Bill Nicholson].

"We didn't have much power, but we had good pitching, and we were a fighting, late-scoring club. And we had Jim Konstanty. We had a good chance of winning if we could stay close and get Jim out to the mound. He was outstanding. And Sawyer was the finest manager I ever saw. He was a great psychologist. He knew just how to deal with guys.

"We didn't figure we would win [the pennant] as early as 1950. We were still very young. And before 1950, Curt had been wild as hell. He hadn't really found himself."

Simmons found himself in 1950, winning 17 games before getting called away to military duty late in the season. Many of the other Phillies had spectacular years, including the brilliant Konstanty, who was the National League's Most Valuable Player (the first relief pitcher to win the award), Del Ennis, who led the league in RBI, and Roberts, who won 20 games.

The Phillies won the pennant in dramatic fashion, then went to the World Series where they lost the first three games by one run each and finished with a team batting average of .203.

Despite his high average, Hamner had a somewhat bittersweet Series. In the third game with the Phillies leading, 2–1, after Granny had singled and scored the go-ahead run in the seventh inning, his bobble of a Bobby Brown grounder let in the tying run in the eighth, and the Yankees went on to a 3–2 victory. They then clinched the Series the next day with a 5–2 victory behind Whitey Ford. "Maybe the Series was anticlimactic," Hamner said. "I think we were drained. And we just didn't hit as a team."

The Phillies fully expected to be pennant contenders in the years following 1950, but it never happened. The club's best finish was a tie for third place in 1953.

"Every year we were right in there fighting," Hamner claimed. "But Simmons went into the service, then he hurt his toe [cutting part of it off in a lawn mower accident]. And they started getting to Konstanty. He wasn't nearly as effective any more."

Hamner and others such as Roberts, Ennis, Ashburn, and Jones kept plugging away. Granny had become the Phillies captain, too. "It was a nice honor," he said. "I didn't do much except take the lineup out. I didn't need to keep order or anything like that. We had [catcher] Andy Seminick to do that."

Hamner slipped to .255 in 1951, then bounced back to hit .275 in 1952. That year, he was named the National League's starting shortstop in the All-Star Game played at Shibe Park in Philadelphia. In a rain-shortened contest won by the Nationals, 3–2, in five innings, Hamner had no hits in one at-bat.

"My biggest thrill was winning the pennant and going to the World Series," Granny said. "But making my first All-Star team was a big thrill, too. We had Marty Marion, Pee Wee Reese, Al Dark, and Roy McMillan. I had to beat out some great shortstops. It really meant a lot to me to be voted the starter."

Hamner was named a reserve on the All-Star team again in 1953, a year in which he had one of his finest seasons while hitting .276. He played only briefly in the Nationals' 5–1 win at Cincinnati's Crosley Field.

That season, the Phillies had taken a highly unusual step with Hamner, considering just one year earlier he had been the All-Star shortstop. They moved him to second base to make room for Ted Kazanski at shortstop. Kazanski had been a $100,000 bonus player signed by the Phillies in 1951. By 1953, the club thought he was ready for the majors and called him up during the season. Because Kazanski couldn't play second, Hamner was moved there and Kazanski inserted at shortstop.

"I didn't really care," Hamner said. "It didn't bother me, except that I was never a good defensive second baseman. I had a good arm, but I wasn't quick enough getting rid of the ball. I wasn't a good pivot man. But Kazanski couldn't play second, so they moved me. In those days they didn't ask you, they just told you where you were playing."

Granny finished the 1953 season at the keystone sack, then spent the entire 1954 campaign there. He had a banner season, one that he called his best year in the majors, with a .299 average.

That summer, Hamner was voted the starting second baseman for the National League All-Star team. He was the first major leaguer to make the squad as a starter at two different positions, although others have since done it. No other player, however, has ever been an All-Star starter at shortstop and at second base. Leading off he had no hits in three at-bats in an 11–9 National League loss at Cleveland's Municipal Stadium.

With Kazanski failing to make it though the 1954 season at shortstop (Bobby Morgan finished the season there), Hamner returned to his old position in 1955. Early in the season, he dove for a ball and badly injured his shoulder. He missed a lot of action and wound up playing in more games back at second than he did at short while hitting .257.

Hamner was back at shortstop full-time in 1956, but the shoulder still bothered him and he hit just .224. "Ashburn had a hurt knee, and they were going to send him down to Johns Hopkins Hospital in Baltimore," Hamner remembered. "I asked Bob [Carpenter, Phillies owner] if I could go down, too. He said I could, so I went down with Richie. A doctor came in to look at me. He asked me to take off my shirt. He looked at my shoulder and said, 'You snapped the tendon in your arm.' I came back to Philadelphia and had

an operation. When I came back, I couldn't swing a bat. So I started thinking about pitching."

Hamner pitched in three games in 1956, starting one and losing one. The
following year, thinking he was through as an infielder, he went to spring
training intent on perfecting his knuckleball and making the squad as a
pitcher.

Granny made the squad as a reliever. But three weeks into the season,
Hamner—having pitched in just one game and with the Phillies in the
midst of a slump—was installed at second base. He spent the rest of the
season there and hit .227 with 10 home runs and 62 RBI.

In 1958, Hamner suffered a knee injury. He missed much of the season,
playing in only 35 games and hitting .301. Early in 1959 Hamner and the
Phillies parted company. Granny was hitting .297 in 21 games when the
team traded him to the Cleveland Indians for a nondescript pitcher named
Humberto Robinson.

"I hated to leave," Hamner said. "I didn't want to ever leave the Phillies
organization. But they were breaking up the Whiz Kids. Everybody was
getting old."

Hamner played as a utility infielder with the Indians for the rest of the
1959 season. He hit .164 in 27 games. At the end of the season, at his request,
the Indians released Hamner so he could return to Richmond, then a Yankees farm club, as a coach. After one season at Richmond, Hamner joined
the Kansas City A's organization as manager of its farm team at Portsmouth,
Virginia. Granny spent one season there and the next year as manager at
Binghamton, New York.

"We ran out of pitchers, so I started to pitch again," he recalled. "I had
a great year, and in 1962 Kansas City needed pitching and they called
me up."

Hamner worked in three games for the A's. He retired for good as a player
at the end of the season with a final pitching tally of 0–2 with a 5.40 ERA in
seven big league games. In 13.1 innings, Hamner gave up 21 hits, struck out
five, and walked eight.

Granny returned to Richmond to work in a bowling alley. But eventually, he found his way back to Philadelphia where he sold industrial steel by
day and was playing-manager of a semipro team at night.

In 1972 he rejoined the Phillies organization. Over the next 17 years he worked for the club in a variety of capacities, including minor league manager, coach, instructor, evaluator, and supervisor. After serving as manager of the Class A Clearwater club, Hamner retired from baseball after the 1988 season.

He moved back to the Philadelphia area and lived in New Jersey, playing golf nearly every day and fishing on those days when he wasn't on the links. He remained a popular figure in the Philadelphia area, especially among people who remembered his days with the Whiz Kids.

"We had a bunch of guys who loved to go to the ballpark," he recalled. "When you enjoy the game like that, it makes it so much easier to play. And I did enjoy the game. I loved football and basketball—I was a quarterback in high school. But baseball was where my future was. God, did I love that game."

Jimmy Piersall

Versatile, Volatile Outfielder

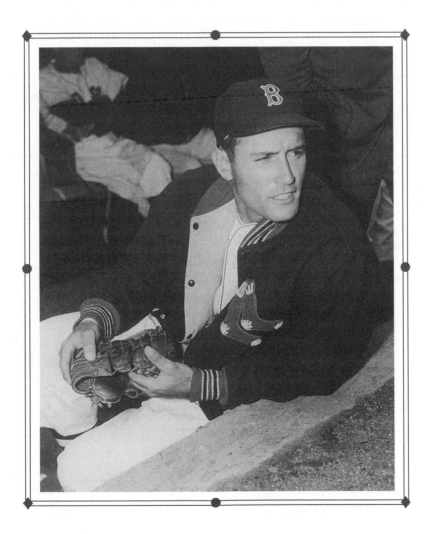

DESCRIBING Jimmy Piersall as a multifaceted individual is like saying that apples grow on trees. Both are truths that are self-evident.

You don't have to be a farmer to know where apples come from. And you certainly don't have to have his memoirs at your fingertips to know that there are many sides to the life and times of the versatile, volatile Piersall.

Baseball player, coach, broadcaster, author, talk-show host, football general manager, social critic, philosopher, and a man who says what he thinks, whether the subject is politics, the economy, or sports, Piersall is a guy who has packed into a lifetime about as many different activities as anybody could imagine.

Most prominent are his days as a participant in 17 major league baseball seasons, beginning in 1950 and ending in 1967, spent with a gaggle of teams, notably the Boston Red Sox but also the Cleveland Indians, Washington Senators, New York Mets, and Los Angeles/California Angels.

Quite possibly, the slender, 6-0, 175-pound Piersall was as good a center fielder as there ever was. He patrolled the outfield with skill and grace, usually playing one of the shallowest center fields in baseball history, a speedy, strong-armed, sure-handed fielding wizard who could track down a fly ball with uncanny ability.

In 1,734 big league games, including 1,610 in the outfield, Piersall made just 49 errors. Eight times he fielded .990 or above, three times leading outfielders in his league in fielding percentage, winning four Gold Gloves, and twice making more than 400 putouts in a season.

Piersall was such a good fielder and corralled so many balls at which normal outfielders would have merely waved that Casey Stengel, the sage manager of the New York Yankees, once said, "I don't like to detract from old-timers like Tris Speaker. So let's put it this way. He [Piersall] is the best man we've seen since the lively ball was introduced."

When he was piloting the Red Sox in the 1950s, Lou Boudreau claimed that Piersall "saved 50 games for us" with his brilliant defense.

Although he had a lifetime fielding percentage of .988, Jimmy was not just a defensive standout. He could hit, too. As a regular, he hit above .280 five times, reaching a high of .322 in 1961. He had a career average of .272 with 1,604 hits, 104 home runs, 591 RBI, and 811 runs scored. Once, during a game in 1953, Piersall slammed six hits in six trips to the plate to tie a major league record.

Jimmy also had some other attributes that had nothing to do with hitting or fielding. He was colorful and controversial. And he could explode at the drop of an umpire's signal.

Piersall had some violent confrontations with the men in blue. He also had a couple of memorable fights with opponents, including one notable battle when he charged Jim Bunning, then pitching with the Detroit Tigers.

You always knew when Piersall was on the field because if he wasn't making a spectacular catch, uncorking a bullet throw, or getting a key hit, he was involved in some other action. There was the time, for instance, when a heckler ran out to harass him in center field at Yankee Stadium, and Jimmy booted the clod halfway to Brooklyn. Of course, who can forget Piersall's 100th home run, which he celebrated, while playing with the Mets, by running backward around the bases?

Piersall was a guy who put everything he had into whatever he was doing. There was never a halfway point for Jimmy; it was either all or nothing. "I just hated to have a bad day," he says. "I only enjoyed the good days. I was great at getting on myself when I didn't play well. But, that's the only way I knew how to play. I had to go all out, no matter what I was doing. I was very demanding. I was a good player because I wanted to be a good player."

Piersall thinks that his kind of player would not be welcome in the big leagues today. "They've taken all the color out of baseball," he says. "Guys like me and Billy Martin and Leo Durocher—colorful guys like that— could never play today. They wouldn't have us."

The once and still handsome Piersall is as trim and fit-looking as he was as a player. A resident of Scottsdale, Arizona, he worked for 14 years as a roving outfield coach with the Chicago Cubs. He worked through 1999 with the parent club during spring training, then hit the road and worked with the minor leaguers during the season.

The job gave him an opportunity to have a firsthand look at the game of baseball as it's presently constituted. It is not necessarily a picture that the outspoken Piersall relishes.

"When I played, we didn't need teachers like me," he says. "We learned things ourselves. Today, you have to teach. That's what it's all about. Kids don't play enough and they don't have the equipment [talent] to be good outfielders. A lot of today's kids are also dreamers, not workers.

"My theory is, if a kid can hit well enough to get signed, I'll show him how to play the outfield. I'm very stern with them. I have to take these kids and first get them to believe in me."

If the student knows anything about his teacher, that shouldn't be hard to accomplish. On the mere basis of his own background and playing ability, not to mention his strong personality, Piersall should be able to command instant respect.

With Piersall, though, being an excellent fielder came naturally. "When I was seven or eight years old, I could catch a ball better than guys who were a lot older," he says. "The outfield was all I played. I lived for baseball, and I loved playing just one position. Kids today don't master their trade, they play all over the place.

"I had God-given ability. I even used to practice throwing behind my back. When I got to the pros, I carried soft rubber balls in my pocket. I would squeeze them constantly to get my hands and wrists strong. The kids use weights today. That's all wrong. I just wish I could've played today with all the padding they have on outfield walls," Piersall adds.

Jimmy ran into more than a few walls in his time, but he played an extremely shallow center field, a trait that was first made popular by Speaker.

"I could go back. I never had any trouble doing that," Jimmy notes. "I played my position according to the situation in the ball game. I didn't play shallow on every hitter. I didn't have superior speed, but I was always moving when the ball was pitched."

Piersall says he avoided doing two things in the outfield. He didn't dive after balls because he didn't believe in it, and he didn't make a big show when he caught a ball.

"I never hot-dogged a ball in my life because I was always afraid I'd drop one and make a fool of myself," Piersall recalls. "That was something that kept me in the big leagues for 17 years: fear. I had this fear of failure.

"But I was very demanding as an outfielder, too. And I never worried about rating my catches. What was important to me was when you had a guy warming up in the bullpen, and you made a great catch and kept the pitcher in the ball game.

"Curt Gowdy [for many years, the Red Sox' play-by-play announcer] once said of the six greatest catches he ever saw, four were by me. Today, the fans don't give you a standing ovation for making a great catch. I used to get them in Boston and New York all the time. That would really give me shivers.

"I guess one of my proudest moments came when I had that great day in Cleveland in front of about 80,000 people. I made five or six good plays. They gave me a standing ovation. One play I remember in particular, I made a catch on Al Rosen, then threw to first to double up Wally Westlake. Bill McKechnie was a coach with the Indians then, and he said to me, 'Young man, I never saw a finer defensive display in my 40 years as you put on today.'

"I used to get really pumped up when we played in Yankee Stadium. One time, I had Joe DiMaggio come up to me in a restaurant. He said, 'Nobody gets them any better than you.' Willie Mays paid me the same kind of compliment once. He said, 'Piersall is looney, but all he ever does is catch the ball.'"

A two-time All-Star himself (1954 and 1956), Piersall grew up in Waterbury, Connecticut, As a youth, he was an avowed Red Sox fan and Yankees hater. "I was always a Red Sox fan, and I hated the Yankees as soon as I came out of my mother's womb," he says. "So it was a big thrill for me to sign with the Red Sox when I got out of high school."

Before then, however, Piersall had been an all-state player in both baseball and basketball. He says he scored 29 points at Boston Garden before 14,000 fans in a New England high school championship game.

Jimmy's first year in the minors was in 1948 at Scranton, where he led the Eastern League in doubles and RBI. He then spent the next two years at Louisville before making a short visit to Boston at the end of the 1950 season.

As a kid, Piersall had worked in a silver factory, loading heavy crates. He continued to work there during the off-season of his first four years as a pro player. "I was throwing those crates and making 95 cents an hour," he recalls. "I used to go to spring training to get a rest."

Piersall divided the 1951 season between Triple-A Louisville and Double-A Birmingham, where he hit .346.

A four-time all-star in the minors, Piersall went back to Boston in 1952. With Dom DiMaggio in center field, however, the Red Sox tried to convert Jimmy into a shortstop.

"I said I didn't want to be a shortstop, but they put me there anyway,"

Piersall says. He wound up playing 30 games there, plus another 22 in right field and one at third base.

By this time, the high-strung Piersall was experiencing problems that eventually resulted in his being hospitalized with a nervous breakdown. Jim, who also spent a short time back in Birmingham that year, missed about half of the season.

In 1953, however, he clawed his way back to Boston and won a starting job in right field while hitting .272. Fans and opposing players, however, razzed him unmercifully.

"When I first came out of the hospital, the other players rode me pretty much," Piersall remembers, recalling some of the cutting epithets that were hurled his way. "But the more they got on me, the better I played. They finally realized that and stopped doing it."

Piersall turned the story of his comeback into a best-selling book, *Fear Strikes Out*. Later, that became the title for a movie starring Anthony Perkins.

In 1954, with Jackie Jensen having been acquired from the Washington Senators and placed in center field, Piersall remained in right and hit .285 for the season. The following year, however, he and Jensen switched positions. Jim hit .283 that year.

Over the next few years, Piersall was the anchorman in an outfield that had Jensen in right and Ted Williams in left. Later, when he went to Cleveland, Piersall was stationed between another redoubtable pair, Minnie Minoso and Rocky Colavito.

"All the guys I played alongside of respected me," Piersall says. "One of the nicest compliments I ever got was from Williams, who said in his book that I was the best outfielder he ever played next to.

"Minnie was a hard worker, but not a good outfielder. Colavito was good because he knew how to play the hitters and had a great arm.

"We had a lot of good outfielders when I played," Piersall adds. "But I wouldn't compare them with today's outfielders. You can't compare today's outfielders and the ones in my day who played·on grass. It's a different way to play today.

"Another thing," adds Piersall, "when I played, the pitchers were better fielders. They all knew how to play their position. And they pitched differently, too. There were more hard-throwers. And they used their fastballs as their best pitch.

"I was a curveball hitter. Allie Reynolds, Vic Raschi, Bob Lemon, Virgil Trucks, Dizzy Trout, and Phil Marchildon all threw great breaking balls, and they had good fastballs, too. The toughest pitcher I ever faced, though, was Hoyt Wilhelm. He had three different knuckleballs. No one ever threw a knuckleball like he did."

Piersall solved opposing pitchers sufficiently that he hit .293 in 1956 while leading the league with 40 doubles and driving in a career-high 87 runs.

Although he hit a career-high 19 home runs in 1957, his average fell to .261. The following year, he broke some ribs, missed some time, and wound up hitting just .237. That winter, the Red Sox traded him to Cleveland for Vic Wertz and Gary Geiger.

"It was a good break for me because I had three pretty good years in Cleveland," Piersall says. "I loved Boston and the fans were great to me. They never booed me because they appreciated the way I played. Ted took care of all the booing. But it was time to go, and I was ready."

Between 1959 and 1961, Piersall hit .246, .282, and .322 with the Indians. But after his sparkling .322 season in 1961, he was swapped to Washington for four players, including pitcher Dick Donovan. At the time, the hapless Senators were an expansion team that had replaced the original Washington club after it had moved to Minnesota. "It was the saddest time of my sports career," Piersall says. "We had lousy teams. It was just terrible."

About the only bright spot in Jim's brief stint in Washington came when Senators' pitcher Tom Cheney struck out a record 21 Baltimore Orioles in 1962 in a 16-inning game in which Piersall played center field.

Piersall hit .244 in his one full year in Washington. Early the next year, he was traded to the Mets for Gil Hodges, who the Senators wanted as their manager. Piersall spent two months in New York, was released, and the same day signed with the Angels.

Reduced to part-time duty, Piersall played a little more than three seasons with the Angels. During that time they changed their name from Los Angeles to California. He hit .314 in 1964 in 87 games.

The end came early in 1967 when, with his body showing the effects of 20 years in pro ball, Piersall decided he had had enough as a player. He became a full-time coach with the Angels, a position he held for two years.

What followed was a winding journey that would take Piersall through an assortment of jobs, marriages, skirmishes with his employers, and another hospitalization.

In the years after leaving the Angels, Piersall worked in ticket sales and on the radio with the Oakland A's, served as a coach under his old pal Billy Martin with the Texas Rangers and as a front office employee with the Rangers, was a general manager for a minor league pro football team in Virginia, ran a hotel in Virginia, worked with Harry Caray broadcasting Chicago White Sox games for six years, and played host for three years to a popular and controversial sports talk show in Chicago.

Controversy has followed the opinionated Piersall almost everywhere he's been. In 1984, he discussed much of that in his second book, *The Truth Hurts*, which gives a revealing look at baseball from the inside while puncturing the balloons of some of the game's most sacred cows and exposing as jerks some of the game's more recognizable figures.

That, of course, has always been Jimmy's style. It has gotten him into trouble at times, but like a cat, he always seems to land on his feet. "I never drank and I never smoked, and I always tried to be honest and to say what I think," Piersall says. "And I would do it all over again the same way only louder."

John Roseboro

Stability Behind the Plate

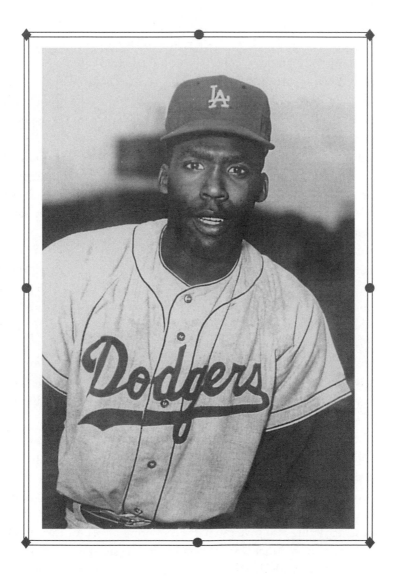

IT CAN BE SAID with a considerable degree of accuracy that behind every good pitching staff squats an excellent catcher. No strong corps of pitchers ever went to battle without someone of substantial ability behind the plate. The great pitching staffs of baseball all had outstanding catchers who could make the right calls, catch their deliveries, boost their confidence, and nurse them through the rough moments.

Bill Dickey and Yogi Berra with the New York Yankees, Jim Hegan with the Cleveland Indians, Johnny Bench with the Cincinnati Reds, and Roy Campanella with the Brooklyn Dodgers were all highly accomplished backstops who played significant roles in guiding talented pitching staffs. And they played major parts in the recurring big seasons enjoyed by those staffs.

In the late 1950s and throughout much of the 1960s, the brilliant pitching staff of the Los Angeles Dodgers had a catcher cut from the same mold. His name is John Roseboro.

While a dazzling array of hurlers, including Sandy Koufax, Don Drysdale, Johnny Podres, and later Claude Osteen, got much of the attention, it was the rock-solid Roseboro who provided stability from behind the plate. Roseboro not only had the talent, he had the brains to hold the staff together and get the best out of it.

"I think I was a knowledgeable catcher," says Roseboro in a bit of understated self-appraisal. "I knew the hitters. I knew what they were probably going to do before they knew what they were going to do. I also analyzed every manager we played against. It got to the point where I could anticipate what the opposition was going to do. I knew the weaknesses of all the hitters.

"I really got paid for my defense," Roseboro adds. "Early on in my career, [Dodgers general manager] Buzzie Bavasi said, 'Kid, I pay you to get behind the plate and catch the ball, keep the runner from scoring, and throw him out at second. Any offense I get is a plus.'

"When it came to keeping the runner from scoring," Roseboro continues, "I was an intimidator. You had to get to that plate before I got to the ball or you didn't get there."

Although he was not exactly built like a linebacker, Roseboro at 5-11½, 190 pounds posed a formidable roadblock for onrushing enemy runners. His muscular frame also gave pitchers an inviting target for their pitches.

Roseboro provided that target for 14 big league seasons, starting in 1957 when he broke in with the Brooklyn Dodgers and advancing through 10 seasons with the Dodgers in Los Angeles, plus two more years with the Minnesota Twins and one with the expansion Washington Senators.

Over the years, Roseboro played in four World Series. He caught two no-hitters by Koufax. He was a member of National League All-Star teams in four different seasons. And he won two Gold Gloves.

In 1,585 games, Roseboro batted .249 with 1,206 hits, 104 home runs, and 548 runs batted in. He had a career high 18 home runs in 1961 and a career high batting average of .287 in 1964. Three other times—1958, 1966, and 1967—he hit in the .270s.

Having caught in 1,476 games, John played a handful of games at first base, third base, and in the outfield, but he ranks among baseball's top 25 catchers in games caught. He holds the major league records for most put-outs (877) and most chances (933) in a 154-game season. Roseboro established both marks in 1961 while catching in 125 games.

Going behind the plate was not an automatic process for Roseboro as a young player. Not only was he originally an outfielder, he was more inclined to be a football player. "I was from a small town in Ohio [Ashland]," Roseboro says. "No scouts ever came by there. So I went to college on a football scholarship."

While he was attending Central State College in Wilberforce, Ohio, Roseboro began to attract some attention as a baseball player. "Somebody from the Dodgers came down to the school because they heard I could play baseball," he notes. "I was offered a chance to go to Cincinnati for a tryout. So I went down there, and as it turned out Campy [Roy Campanella] and Joe Black were my chaperones. I saw how they lived in the hotel, just signing checks for all their food, and I said to myself, 'Geez, this is better than college.' So we agreed on a sum, and they gave me a bonus, promised never to send me to a team in the South, which was one of my conditions, and I became a ballplayer."

In 1952, Roseboro hit .365 in his first pro season while playing at Sheboygan, Wisconsin. He added a .310 mark the next year at Great Falls, Montana, then spent one year in military service before coming back to put in nearly three more seasons in the minors.

"I played the outfield most of my early minor league career," Roseboro recalls. "As a kid, I had played first base or any position that was available. They didn't make me a full-time catcher until I came out of the service in 1955. They told me to get back behind the plate because Campy was getting older, and I had the ability to throw the ball pretty hard, I ran well, and I had some power.

"But in 1957, I was called up to Brooklyn in the middle of June, and the first night Walter Alston handed me a first baseman's mitt and said, 'You're playing first base tonight.' I think that was something they did with young kids at the time to get them over their nervousness. I replaced Gil Hodges, who had been injured and was out for a couple of days. So my first three games in the majors were at first base."

Roseboro's rookie season was relatively uneventful. That winter, though, two major events occurred that had a lasting impact on his career. First, the Dodgers announced that the team was being moved from Brooklyn to Los Angeles. Then Campanella was involved in an auto accident that left him paralyzed for the rest of his life.

Suddenly, and without benefit of much experience, Roseboro was cast into the role of Campanella's replacement as the franchise made a controversial shift to a brand new major league city. It was no easy assignment for the 24-year-old player.

"It was unusual, to say the least," Roseboro recalls. "I had never thought I would really be a catcher, anyway. I thought I would play the outfield. But then Campy had his accident, we moved west, and they put me behind the plate. Just to have to follow Campy, who'd been such a great catcher, was a little bit of pressure.

"As for the move west, I wouldn't say it was traumatic. When I signed, I had never been to the big city before, and I found New York very interesting. The big difference, though, was in Brooklyn. If you made a mental mistake, they jumped all over your tail. In L.A., the fans didn't know what was going on. They were very sedate. They just sat back and watched. That was to my benefit because I wasn't a great catcher my first year. I had a helluva time.

"Early in the season, though," Roseboro adds, "we had another injury. Don Demeter got hurt, and I played center field in the old Coliseum for about a week. I liked it so well and did such a good job that I made the mistake of telling a sportswriter that I'd rather be in the outfield. I got chewed out for that. And from then on, I stayed behind the plate."

Although he was a largely untested youngster, Roseboro did have one advantage. The year before, he had been tutored by Campanella, who, despite his premature departure from the playing field, was headed for the Hall of Fame.

"I certainly benefited from Campy's teachings," John explains. "He taught me some very basic things, such as how to block balls in the dirt, using the face of the glove like a Ping-Pong paddle. He also taught me about throwing the ball to second, getting the ball down there before the runner gets there, and throwing the ball from behind the ear, which most old catchers used to do. I threw it from the side.

"Campy gave me those very important pointers, and I kind of expanded on them. I just kept on working until I got to the point where I became comfortable behind the plate."

Unfortunately, Roseboro never saw his mentor play, except in the closing months of the 1957 season. The one catcher he did see play a lot, however, was Jim Hegan of the Indians.

"He was sort of my idol," Roseboro says. "He was the smoothest catcher I ever saw. My hometown is below Cleveland, and when I was a kid, my dad used to take my brother and me up there to see the Indians. I'd watch Hegan take infield practice and throw to second: It was a beautiful picture. He couldn't hit a lick, and I always thought I could take his place because I could hit better than he could. But he was probably the best defensive catcher I ever saw."

Although a quiet, unassuming person, Roseboro, nicknamed Gabby by his teammates because he didn't talk much, wasted little time asserting himself with a Dodgers pitching staff that was comprised of seasoned veterans and promising youngsters.

"After the first few months, I began calling my own signals," John remembers. "If a pitcher didn't want what I called he'd shake his head. After that first year, there were very few shakes of the head. We learned to communicate with each other. Basically, the pitchers and I learned to think the same way.

"The Dodgers at that time had a game plan of how to pitch to opposing hitters. It was based on what you wanted the hitter to do in that particular situation and how you would pitch to him to accomplish that. Because the pitchers and I were thinking on the same wavelength, we never had any communication problems. If you wanted a ground ball to the right side, everybody knew you had to throw a certain pitch to get that."

Roseboro feels that he really arrived as a big league catcher in 1959. That year, the Dodgers ended the two-year reign of the Milwaukee Braves by winning the National League pennant over the defending champions in a three-game playoff after the two teams had tied for first place during the regular season. In the World Series that fall, the Dodgers faced the Chicago White Sox, a team that had won the American League flag on the strength of speed, defense, and pitching.

"The newspapers were full of comments about how we were the underdogs against the Go-Go Sox because the Dodgers had Roseboro behind the plate and [Maury] Wills at shortstop," John remembers. "They said we were two young guys who hadn't proved ourselves.

"Well, I shot down the White Sox [who stole just two bases], and Wills had a great Series at shortstop, and we won the Series, four games to two. That was when I got over the comparisons to Campanella.

"Of course, there was normally no basis for comparison, anyway. Campy was a power hitter and I was a jackrabbit with a gun. We were two different kinds of players. But after I gunned down the White Sox, I said to myself, 'I'm here now.' After you get that feeling, you get cocky. You become an intimidator. You become aggressive, which I think you have to be to be a good catcher."

Roseboro participated in a key play in the Series when he nailed White Sox Sherman Lollar at the plate in the eighth inning of the second game. Lollar, trying to score from first on Al Smith's double, would have been the tying run in what otherwise became a 4–3 Dodgers victory and evened the Series after Chicago crushed L.A., 11–0, in the first game.

That was to be the first of many memorable moments for Roseboro. Another came in 1962 when John poked a ninth-inning home run off Milt Pappas in a 9–4 National League loss in the All-Star Game at Wrigley Field.

Two other special moments in Roseboro's career occurred when he caught no-hitters by Koufax. John was behind the plate when Koufax threw his first of four no-hitters, beating the New York Mets in 1962. He also caught the brilliant southpaw's second gem, pitched in 1963 against the San Francisco Giants.

What does Roseboro remember about those games? "Those are experiences in which it's hard to remember what went on in your mind at the time," he says. "But it's nice to know you were out there. With Sandy pitching, it was a potential no-hitter every time he went out there. It was just a matter of whether he was on or not.

"But I can't really tell you what went on in those no-hitters. I just remember I didn't want to make a mistake. The pressure comes from not wanting to be the one to have a passed ball with two strikes and let the guy get to first base and have another guy come to bat. Or there's a walk and you let a guy steal second and get into scoring position. Or drop a foul pop and the guy gets another chance to swing the bat, and he might get a hit. It's all defensive pressure. But the real pressure was on Sandy. He was in control of the game. For the rest of us, we just had to do our regular thing."

Roseboro says any pitcher who tosses a no-hitter has a strong element of luck working for him. But Koufax, he says, had a few other things in his favor.

"He would go out, and he had the great fastball, the great curve, and most guys knew they were going to take a comfortable 0-for-4 anyway. They had to be lucky to get a hit.

"There was no special thing about Koufax's no-hitters. He was always capable of pitching one, just like Nolan Ryan [who pitched seven no-hitters] was later. Guys had to be lucky to get a hit off him. They would go up to the plate thinking, here comes that fastball, I better swing before it leaves his hand and hope that the ball and the bat are on the same planes."

Roseboro, who caught Koufax's 18-strikeout game in 1959, also went to the World Series with the Dodgers in 1963, 1965, and 1966. His three-run homer against Whitey Ford led the Dodgers to a 5–2 victory over the Yankees in the first game of the 1963 Series. The Dodgers went on to win that Series in four straight, just as they lost the 1966 Series in four straight to the Baltimore Orioles. They beat the Twins in seven games in the 1965 Series.

"The home run against the Yankees was the only memorable thing I did offensively," Roseboro says. "I didn't hit much during my career. You might say I didn't raise a lot of hell with the bat.

"When I hit the homer, I was thinking just possibly I might be lucky enough to be the World Series hero and win a car. Then the pressure came on. I don't think I got a hit after that." (He had one.)

"You always want to be a hero in an All-Star Game or World Series. I think that's why a lot of guys who are the stars have a hard time, and a lot of guys who are the Punch-and-Judy hitters come up with big games. It's usually somebody like Bobby Richardson who becomes the Series hero. Look at Larry Sherry. When we won the 1959 Series, he pitched like no man has ever pitched in his life. And he never did it again. It's just that God taps some of those guys on the shoulder and lets them have a little of the limelight."

Despite all the thrilling events in which he participated, Roseboro says the moment he remembers most distinctly "is a negative." He refers to the celebrated fight he had in San Francisco with Giants' pitcher Juan Marichal. "That memory really sticks out in my mind," he says.

"The battle," Roseboro explains, "began over some knockdown pitches. He knocked down a couple of our guys, then I knocked him down from behind the plate. He reacted and we had a little fist fight. Actually, it was a helluva fight. He hit me with a bat, and then we really went at it. It was one of those things that happen in baseball where you have to retaliate, and you expect somebody else to react to it. He reacted, and we just had a big fight." Roseboro says that he holds no grudge against Marichal. In fact, he says, "We're good friends. After that year, it was all forgotten."

Roseboro played with the Dodgers through the 1967 season. That fall, with the Dodgers desperate for a shortstop, Roseboro was shipped with pitchers Ron Perranoski and Bob Miller to the Twins for shortstop Zoilo Versalles and pitcher Jim (Mudcat) Grant.

John played two seasons with the Twins, helping them to the American League's Western Division title in 1969, after which the club lost to Baltimore in the first year of the League Championship Series. Following that season, Roseboro was released by the Twins and signed by the Senators.

Roseboro played one year under manager Ted Williams, then retired at the end of the season. The following year, he began a four-year sojourn as a coach with the California Angels, then left baseball after the 1974 season.

In the late 1980s, though, he returned to the game as a minor league catching instructor with the Dodgers, a position he held into the 1990s.

"I stayed out of baseball until Al Campanis made his little boo-boo [statements on Ted Koppel's *Night Line* TV show that many considered to be racial slurs] a few years ago," says Roseboro. "When that happened, I thought maybe things would open up a little bit, so I got back into baseball. The boo-boo was most definitely to my benefit. I think the doors started to open a little more after Campanis made those statements."

Roseboro's son, Jaime, also spent some time in baseball as a center fielder in the New York Mets' farm system. "The Dodgers were kind of negligent in their scouting procedures, and I didn't really want him to come into the organization that I was in, anyway," says Roseboro. "I didn't want him to have that pressure. So I was happy he went with the Mets."

Roseboro says he enjoys seeing old friends and opponents. "But it's nice not to be playing and to meet your old opponents, especially at old-timers games, and find out they're just like the guys on your own team," he says. "They're nice guys, too. But in our day, there wasn't a lot of love between teams because we were the best. We had a lot of pride and that pride meant that you didn't associate or become overly friendly with your opponents. You had to be businesslike in your dealings."

No catcher was more businesslike than Roseboro. And when he looks back on his career, John realizes that baseball was a good business to be in.

"I would say, I was a very lucky boy from Ohio," he reflects. "I could've been a high school football coach somewhere. I don't know if I'd have made it playing football. Or I could've been working in a foundry back home with some of the kids I grew up with.

"But I've traveled all over the world. I have some property in L.A. That's nice. I'm doing all right. I've been very, very lucky. And I would do it again in a minute. I wouldn't change a thing."

Neither would all those outstanding Dodgers pitchers who got where they did in part because of the standout receiver they had behind the plate.

Roy Sievers

From Top Rookie to Top Home Run Hitter

HARD AS IT may be to believe, in the long and illustrious history of the American League, only three players have captured both the Rookie of the Year award and the home run crown.

Numerous players have won Rookie of the Year honors and home run titles in the National League, and several players have won one award in one league and one in the other. But only Roy Sievers, Eddie Murray (who shared the home run crown with three others), and Mark McGwire have earned that distinction in the American League.

In 1949, the first year the award was presented to players in each league, Sievers, a powerful righthanded slugger, captured Rookie of the Year honors while playing for his hometown team, the St. Louis Browns. Eight years later, by then an enormously popular player in the nation's capital, he slammed 42 home runs for the Washington Senators to win the American League home run championship. Sievers also led the league that season with 114 runs batted in.

Winning the two awards was a special distinction for Sievers, one of many that marked the outstanding career of the outfielder–first baseman.

It was a career in which Sievers ranked as one of the premier sluggers of his era. Mostly noted as a long-distance clouter, Roy hit 318 homers during his 17 years in the big leagues, which included 12 seasons in which he homered in double figures. In one 10-year stretch from 1954 to 1963, Roy's home run totals read 24, 25, 29, 42, 39, 21, 28, 27, 21, and 19.

Sievers hit 10 grand slam home runs and eight pinch-hit homers. He leads the defunct Senators in career home runs with 180, and his 42 in 1957 held the club record until it was equaled by Harmon Killebrew.

In a career that also saw him play for the Chicago White Sox and Philadelphia Phillies, Sievers had a lifetime batting average of .267 with 1,147 runs batted in. He had 1,703 hits in 1,887 games.

A four-time American League All-Star, Sievers had numerous other memorable experiences in addition to his batting exploits. He was there the day Bill Veeck sent up the midget, Eddie Gaedel, to pinch-hit for the Browns. He was on hand to witness the demise of the Browns. He played for the original as well as the expansion Washington Senators. And he took part in the movie, *Damn Yankees*, in which a film clip of his hitting a home run was used.

What's more, Sievers is an avid collector, specializing in autographed baseballs. He also owns a nice collection of his old uniforms. He has some

300 autographed balls, including ones signed by most of the living Hall of Famers. His uniform collection consists of eight full uniforms, including two from the Browns and two from the Senators.

All in all, it has been an enjoyable association with baseball for Sievers, and Roy has fond memories of his days in the game. "I would say, if I were to go tomorrow?" he muses, "I think I would have had a helluva life. I'm very fortunate to have gotten the chance to play baseball and to meet all of the people I did.

"There is no greater way to make a living than by being a professional athlete. You meet people from every walk of life—sports celebrities, movie stars, politicians. Where else would a kid like me from St. Louis have been able to have lunch with four presidents of the United States and to play with so many great ballplayers? It's been a great life, and even now I still get goose bumps when I put on the uniform at old-timers games."

Sievers still lives in his native city of St. Louis. After his playing days ended, he was a coach with the Cincinnati Reds, then tried managing in the minor leagues in the New York Mets and Oakland A's farm systems. Roy managed at Williamsport (Pennsylvania) in the Mets' chain and at Burlington (Iowa) in the A's system.

"I was making $8,000, and you can't live on that," Sievers says. "So after four years, I got out and went to work for a trucking company. I worked there for 16 years, and then they fired me. So now, I just relax. I golf, fish, play in old-timers games, and do a couple of baseball card shows a year.

"I also go to about eight to 10 Cardinals games a year," he adds. "And I try to keep in touch with some of my old friends from the game like Whitey Herzog, Tommy Lasorda, Pete Rose, Don Zimmer, and Bobby Wine."

Herzog was a roommate of Sievers when the two were players. Later, when Roy decided to go into managing, Herzog was farm director of the Mets and hired him. He also fired him, Roy laughingly points out.

Sievers made many friends during a career that had its origins in north St. Louis where Roy was a football, basketball, and baseball star at Beaumont High School. The school has produced 15 major league players—more than any other high school in the country. Beaumont alumni include Pete Reiser, Lee Thomas, and Buddy Blattner as well as former Baltimore Orioles manager Earl Weaver.

A big youngster who grew to be 6-1, 195 pounds, Sievers was an all-state selection in basketball and baseball at Beaumont. He also did well as a football player, but Roy's father decided that he had to choose between the gridiron and the diamond. Sievers, who picked up the nickname "Squirrel" during his high school basketball days because somebody said he always hung around the cage, like a squirrel, selected baseball.

"That was really my sport," he recalls. "As kids, we used to play all the time. From six or seven o'clock in the morning until it got dark, that's all we did. And we lived close to Sportsman's Park, so we used to go to a lot of baseball games. We'd watch both the American and National League.

"I didn't have any particular favorites, although I kind of liked Joe Medwick the best. But I remember watching all the great players—Gehrig, DiMaggio, Williams, Greenberg, Musial. We had a knot-hole gang as kids, and we were at the park early in the afternoon every afternoon in the summer, watching either the Browns or the Cardinals."

Sievers played third base in high school. His coach was a scout with the Cardinals, and the Redbirds tried hard to sign him after his senior year. But the Browns also pursued the hometown boy, and Roy eventually signed with them.

"I decided I'd have a better chance of making it with the Browns," Sievers explains. "So I signed. I got a pair of baseball shoes as a bonus. When I called the Cardinals' scout to tell him I had signed with the Browns, he said, 'Why didn't you tell me what you were going to do? I was willing to give you a $5,000 bonus.' But really, when I think about it, signing with the Browns was the best thing to do."

Sievers signed in 1944, but had to serve two years in the military before joining Class C Hannibal (Missouri) in 1947. That year, Roy tore up the Central Association, hitting .317 and leading the league in home runs (34), RBI (141), hits (159), and runs (121). He played mostly third base but also pitched in two games when the team was shorthanded on the mound.

"That year got me invited to spring training with the Browns in 1948," Sievers remembers. "I had a great spring, too. But they sent me down to their Triple-A club, and then they told me they were sending me down to Double-A. I wound up in Single-A with Elmira of the Eastern League, but after a couple of weeks, they sent me to Springfield, which was Class B."

Sievers wound up hitting .309 with 19 home runs and 75 RBI in the Three-I League. That earned him a promotion back to spring training the following year with the Browns. "This time, I had a helluva spring," Sievers says, "and I made the team. When the season started, I didn't play for a couple of weeks, then I finally pinch-hit and struck out. Then I struck out the second time. I thought I was gone.

"I was thinking, boy, what a league this is. But I had had a good spring, so I knew I could hit big league pitching. The third time up, I hit a double and drove in two runs. Zack Taylor, our manager, said, 'Starting tomorrow, you're going to be in left field.' We had a doubleheader, and I went seven-for-eight. That put me in the lineup to stay."

Sievers went on to hit his first big league home run against Fred Hutchinson of the Detroit Tigers. He finished the season with 16 homers while driving in 91 runs and hitting a lusty .306. That made him a leading candidate for Rookie of the Year honors. "It was between Gus Zernial, Johnny Groth, and me," Sievers recalls. "I squeezed them out to get the award. It was a big thrill for me, and it made my folks very proud."

It also gave Sievers' neighborhood buddies something to cheer about. "They were always in the stands, all season long," Roy says. "Sometimes, they would really razz me. A lot of times I got abuse from my three brothers up in the stands, too. Playing in front of the hometown crowd put a lot of pressure on me. But I tried not to think too much about it."

There were enough other things to think about, anyway. The 1949 Browns lost 101 games and finished 44 games out of first place. They still finished seventh, ranking ahead of the forlorn Washington Senators. But they hardly drew enough fans to fill a laundromat, despite the promotional genius of Browns owner Bill Veeck.

"Veeck was really good for baseball," Sievers says. "He was a great promoter and a helluva man to play for. If you had a good year, he treated you well. He was good for the players and good for the fans. He appreciated what you did.

"Some of his promotions were unbelievable. One time, he put cards under every seat in a section, and the winning card got a fur coat. Another time, he had Taylor hold up signs that said either bunt or steal or hit and run, things like that. The fans would decide what strategy the team would use.

"Of course, I guess his crowning achievement was when he brought in the midget, Eddie Gaedel, to pinch-hit in 1951. Nobody knew what was going on. We were all sitting in the dugout, and they brought out this big cake. Out popped the midget. He said he was a new Browns player.

"When he went up to the plate to hit, Red Rolfe, the Tigers manager, raised hell. Veeck was up in the press box waving a contract. It was all legal, so they let him bat, and Bob Cain walked him on four pitches. We were having trouble getting men on base and we weren't winning that much, anyway, so all of us players figured we might as well go along with it."

After his outstanding freshman year, Sievers tapered off considerably in his second season, hitting just .238 with 10 homers and 57 RBI. "I hit the sophomore jinx, all right," says Roy. "They wanted me to hit to right field, and that threw my natural swing off. After that season, I vowed to go back to the old way of hitting."

The old way of hitting, however, did nothing to save Roy from the disaster that was to be the 1951 season. First, after hitting just .225 with one home run in 31 games, Sievers was sent down to the Browns Double-A farm team at San Antonio. There, after playing in 39 games and hitting .297, Sievers separated his shoulder while making a diving catch. The injury put him out for the rest of the season.

Sievers decided not to have an operation and reported early to spring training in 1952. "I had worked out at first base all winter, and I decided that if I could throw 90 feet, I could play," he says.

But in late February, Roy dislocated his right arm at the shoulder while making a throw. This time, he had the operation and was out of the lineup until September, when he returned as a pinch-hitter and hit .200 the rest of the way while playing in 11 games.

Sievers spent the 1953 season as a part-time first baseman for the Browns. He hit .270 with eight home runs in 92 games. That fall, the Browns moved to Baltimore. Four months later, Sievers, bad arm and all, was traded to the Senators for outfielder Gil Coan.

"The arm never got strong until I did construction work after I got to Washington," Sievers says. "That built it back up again. But before that, it wasn't too good. The secret for me was that I got rid of the ball quickly. But I was beginning to think my career was over until I went to Washington.

"It was tough leaving St. Louis because I had grown up there," Sievers says. "But playing for the Browns was never easy. We liked to win just like anybody else, but we'd go into the sixth or seventh inning with a lead, and end up losing. It was no fun losing so much. And we never had any more than four or five thousand people in the stands. One time we had 500.

"So, it was really a big break for me when I was traded. They had Mickey Vernon over there [at first base], and he had just won a batting title the year before. Bucky Harris, the manager, said to me, 'I want your bat in the line-up. You'll play left field. The shortstop will come out for relays, so don't worry about your arm.'"

Even though they were a second-division team, too, the Senators gave Sievers a new lease on life. In 1954, he hit .232 with 24 home runs and 102 RBI and began what would become a 10-year home run binge. Over the next four years, he would also rack up consecutive RBI totals of 106, 95, 114, and 108.

Sievers had his finest overall season in 1957, when he led the league in home runs and RBI (114) while hitting .301. That year, he hit six home runs in six consecutive games.

"I started off the season fairly well," Roy remembers. "All season long, I battled Ted Williams and Mickey Mantle for the home run lead. Finally, in the last couple of weeks, I pulled it out. I never hit well in Baltimore, but I had a great series there, hitting three home runs. I finished four ahead of Williams and eight ahead of Mantle.

"That year was my greatest thrill," remarks Sievers. "At the end of the season, they had a night for me. I had said I didn't want it, but they insisted on it. My mother and father, my wife and kids, and all my brothers and their wives were there. They had a home run hitting contest, which I won. And Vice President Nixon presented me with an automobile, a new Mercury. When I looked up in the stands and saw all those people, I just broke down. Pretty soon, there wasn't a dry eye in the place.

"It was an especially big thrill for my father to see his son make good in the big leagues," Roy adds. "He had a chance to pitch in the big leagues, but his dad had told him to stay home. So the night I was honored was a very special night for my dad as well as for me.

"Ironically," Sievers continues, "after the season, I battled Calvin Griffith all winter for a raise. I had to go back to Washington four times. Finally, I got an 80 percent raise. The only thing that helped was that I had President Eisenhower on my side. He spoke up for me.

"But the next year, I hit 39 home runs and had a .295 batting average with 108 RBI, and Griffith wanted to cut me $10,000. He said, 'You didn't win any hitting titles this year.' I finally signed, but I didn't take a cut.

"It was great, though, playing in Washington," Sievers adds. "I met a lot of people you'd never get a chance to meet otherwise. I had lunch with four presidents. I met a lot of Congressmen and dignitaries from other countries. I even met Nikita Khrushchev. It was quite a thrill playing in Washington. You never knew who was going to be in the clubhouse or up in the stands."

Sievers' honeymoon in Washington ended after the 1959 season when he was traded to the Chicago White Sox for Earl Battey, Don Mincher, and $150,000 in cash. "We were in spring training, and our manager, Cookie Lavagetto, called me in and told me I'd been traded," he recalls. "I was really surprised. But apparently Veeck, who was now in Chicago, wanted a little more power, and Griffith needed the money.

"So I packed my bags and drove over to Sarasota. When I got there, [manager] Al Lopez said, 'Boy, am I glad to see you. But I don't know where I'm going to play you.' Nellie Fox grabbed me and said, 'I can't believe he said that.' But I just bided my time. When the season started, they had Ted Kluszewski at first. I pinch-hit, but pretty soon they just left me in the lineup."

Sievers had two strong seasons in Chicago, hitting .295 in both 1960 and 1961 while driving in more than 90 runs each year and blasting 28 and 27 home runs, respectively. At one point in 1960, Roy also had a 21-game hitting streak.

And, for the first time in his career, Sievers was playing for a first-division team. "It proved to me that I could play on a first-division ball club," he says. "I was beginning to have my doubts. When you're last all the time, you start to wonder about yourself. You think, 'Am I the kind of player who's just a second-division player?' I was tickled to play and play well for the White Sox. Of course, I always thought I could play for a first-division team."

Sievers' stint in Chicago turned out to be much more brief than he would have liked. An up-and-coming Phillies team, desperately in need of a right-handed power hitter, had cast a covetous eye in Sievers' direction. Soon, a trade was engineered in which the Phillies gave up pitcher John Buzhardt and third baseman Charlie Smith for Roy.

Over the next two years, Sievers hit 40 home runs for the Phillies, including the 300th of his career. He also drove in more than 80 runs each season while hitting .262 and .240.

In 1964, Roy got into only 49 games before a knee injury knocked him out of action for 30 days.

"I was ready to come back, but John Quinn, the general manager, sold me to Washington," Sievers says. "I couldn't believe it. In fact, neither could anybody else. I was talking a few years ago to Gene Mauch, who was our manager back then, and he said to this day he didn't want to get rid of me. He said, 'I knew we could use you in September.'"

Sievers went to the expansion Senators and watched from a distance as the Phillies blew the National League pennant, losing 10 games in a row and erasing a lead of six and one-half games with 12 games remaining.

Roy finished the 1964 season in a reserve role. He began the 1965 season in the same capacity, but he was released after playing in 12 games. He worked out with the White Sox and the Cardinals and, he says, never hit the ball better, but each team turned him down. With 17 seasons under his belt, Sievers decided it was time to retire.

He did so not only with the feeling he could still play but with the notion that he had played in a glorious era of baseball. "I think I played in the best time in baseball," Sievers says. "There were so many good ballplayers back then. And there were four or five clubs that each had four or five good pitchers who all went nine innings. It was a great era for baseball, and I'm proud to have been a part of it."

And a mighty big part of it he was.

Gus Zernial

A Real-Life Ozark Ike

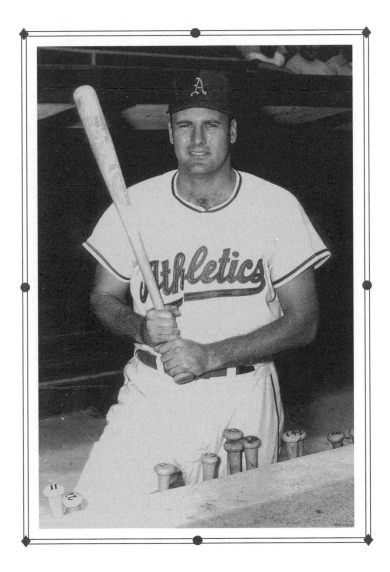

AT THE PEAK of his career, the mere sight of Gus Zernial standing in the batter's box was enough to make most pitchers wish they'd undertaken another line of work. A huge, strapping guy with great bulging muscles, Zernial would stand menacingly at the plate, a bat the size of a wagon tong in his hand. On any given at-bat, he was a threat to send a pitched ball crashing far away into some distant bleacher.

With his massive frame and the rugged good looks of the proverbial All-American boy, it was no wonder that Zernial was nicknamed after the wholesome, baseball-playing comic strip character Ozark Ike.

Both Gus and Ozark loved to hit. And in real life as well as in the fantasy world of cartoons, they were forever slugging home runs and winning games. "I never was a great outfielder," says Zernial. "But I could hit the ball. It was a God-given talent. Oh, how I loved to swing the bat."

The 6-2½, 220-pound righthander swung the bat with such skill that in just 11 big league seasons he cracked 237 home runs while batting .265. In 1,234 games with the Chicago White Sox, Philadelphia and Kansas City A's, and Detroit Tigers, Zernial collected 1,093 hits, drove in 776 runs, and had a slugging average of .486.

Zernial won two legs of the triple crown in 1951 when he led the American League in home runs and RBI. He was second in the league in homers twice, fourth once, and fifth another time. Once, he hit seven home runs in four consecutive games. Thirty-two times he hit two or more four-baggers in one game. He hit three grand slams in one season (1952). And he had 10 career pinch-hit homers.

Home runs were indeed Zernial's specialty, and between 1950 and 1957, only twice did he hit fewer than 27 homers, both times when he missed major parts of the season because of injuries.

"I operated on the philosophy that I wanted to drive the ball," Zernial says. "I always figured that I was big enough to make the ball go. I was strictly a pull-hitter. I hit with my hips and tried to drive the ball at the third baseman."

Of course, despite his proclivity for hitting home runs, there were other dimensions of Zernial's career. Twice he was involved in stupendous trades, one involving 13 players. He was on hand to watch the death of the A's in Philadelphia and their rebirth in Kansas City. And he played an indirect role in the introduction of Joe DiMaggio to movie star Marilyn Monroe.

"That story was always a little exaggerated," Zernial relates. "It was always written that I had introduced Joe to her, but that's not quite the way it happened.

"In the early 1950s, Marilyn Monroe was a popular, young movie star on the way up. I never met a more beautiful young lady or one with any more intelligence," he recalls.

"We were playing in New York, and someone wanted Hank Majeski, Eddie Robinson, and me to pose with her for some publicity pictures. She was there making her first movie. We met her, and they took a lot of pictures, and that was pretty much the end of it.

"But then DiMaggio made the comment to one of the reporters, 'Why does a guy like Gus have the chance to meet her, and I can't?' After that, somebody introduced them, but I had nothing to do with the introduction. Later, of course, they got married."

At that point in his career, Zernial was a big name in Philadelphia, having come to the A's from the White Sox on April 30, 1951, in a mammoth trade that sent tremors throughout the American League.

Badly in need of offensive help, the A's had obtained Zernial, outfielder Dave Philley, catcher Ray Murray, and pitcher Sam Zoldak in a three-team deal in which Chicago landed outfielders Minnie Minoso and Paul Lehner and the Cleveland Indians received pitcher Lou Brissie.

"Frankie Lane was the general manager in Chicago, and he was always trading the biggest names he could find," Zernial says. "Chicago was really after Minoso. They wanted speed. They were a young, improving team. I would have liked to have stayed with them because Paul Richards was coming in as manager. [Nellie] Fox was there, and Billy Pierce was coming along.

"But I think I went to a good ball club, too. If [Dick] Fowler and [Joe] Coleman hadn't fallen apart, we would've had a real good club. We had good hitters, strong defense, and pretty good pitching.

"When I went there, I looked at the lineup with Majeski at third, [Eddie] Joost at short, [Pete] Suder at second, and [Ferris] Fain at first. I said to myself, 'This club can win it.' But we just didn't put it together."

It has been nearly 50 years since that trade, but Zernial delights in recalling those days when he was known as Ozark Ike, a guy who sent chills shivering up and down the spines of opposing pitchers.

A resident of Fresno, California, Zernial worked in recent years as a financial counselor with a bank. Prior to that, he had been involved in radio and television. "After I retired from baseball in 1959," he says, "I spent one year with an investment firm in Los Angeles. But what I really wanted to do was come back to the big leagues as a broadcaster. I talked to a couple of guys, and they suggested I go into a small market and learn the business. So I went to Fresno and started out doing a little five-minute sports show in the morning and at night."

From there, Zernial graduated into being a play-by-play man, covering all sports at Fresno State College. He did that for 10 years while also spending several years doing sports on the six and 11 o'clock news for a CBS television affiliate. Along the way, he also had a tryout as a White Sox broadcaster, but a subsequent job offer, he says, got bogged down in red tape, and he wound up returning to Fresno.

"At that point, I decided to get out," Gus says. "I went into the financing business. I didn't have any aspirations of being a millionaire, but I was involved with a lot of major deals."

An extremely amiable fellow, Zernial still does freelance broadcasting in the Fresno area. He also works informally with young players, ranging from those in a local youth program to students at Fresno State—a major college baseball power—to area residents who play in the minor leagues. Always willing to lend a hand, Gus is a ready volunteer whenever somebody needs a lesson in hitting.

Working with youngsters reminds Zernial of his own boyhood days and dreams growing up in Beaumont, Texas. "I started playing when I was about nine years old," he says. "Very quickly, I developed a great desire to be a baseball player. I played everything in high school, but I just loved baseball. Somehow, I learned to drive a ball, and by the time I was 15, I was playing in a semipro league with older men.

"My senior year in high school, Branch Rickey and the St. Louis Cardinals held a tryout in Houston. A bunch of us got in a car and drove 90 miles. There must have been 400 kids there. I was a first baseman at the time, but one of the kids with us wanted to play first base. I said, 'Well, give me your glove, and I'll play the outfield.' I'd never played there before. But that day, they offered me a contract as an outfielder.

"They asked me if I'd go to Hamilton, Ontario, to play. I'd never been out of Beaumont. I said Hamilton was too far. So I didn't go, but the next year—1942—they called and asked me to go to Albany, Georgia. I said, 'Okay.' I knew where that was. I went to Albany, and they had Red Schoendienst and Chuck Diering on the club.

"After a couple of weeks, I was playing center field and hitting .336," Zernial remembers. "The manager called me in and said he was releasing me. They wanted to keep a guy named Hal Bowen instead. I don't know whatever happened to him. I went home, and a little later I got a call from the Waycross team in the same [Georgia-Florida] league. They asked me to play for them, so I went back to Georgia and became a 6–1, 170-pound leadoff batter."

Zernial hit .286 with just three home runs at Waycross, then a Class D team owned by the Atlanta Crackers. At the end of the season, he enlisted in the Navy. He served three years in World War II, and when he was discharged in 1945 and reported to Atlanta, his weight had ballooned to 225.

"I was really green," Gus recalls. "So Atlanta sent me to Burlington, North Carolina, and I had a big year there. [He hit .333 with a league-leading 41 home runs and 111 RBI.] I was really tickled. I'd become stronger, more mature."

That winter, Zernial was drafted by Cleveland. He reported to the Indians' spring training base in Tucson, Arizona, the following spring. But with 15 outfielders in camp, Zernial was assigned to Baltimore. He played one game for the International League Orioles, then was abruptly claimed by the White Sox because the Indians had failed to adhere to a technicality in the waiver rules.

Chicago sent Gus to Hollywood of the Pacific Coast League where he had two huge years, hitting .344 and .322 and in his second year belting 40 home runs while leading the league in RBI with 156 and in hits with 237.

While at Hollywood, Gus picked up the nickname that would stick with him the rest of his career. "Fred Haney, who later became a big league manager, was broadcasting Hollywood games," he says. "He's the one who gave me the name. I guess it was because I was big and had blonde hair and blue eyes. He thought I looked like Ozark Ike."

Zernial finally made the big leagues in 1949, breaking in as the left fielder for the Chisox.

"I'll never forget my first game," he says. "It was opening day. We were facing the Detroit Tigers and Hal Newhouser. I had seen Newhouser and a lot of the other Tigers before because Detroit had a farm club in Beaumont, and they had all played there. My first time up, Newhouser threw me three pitches, and I never saw one of them. But I ended up going two-for-three. We got only three hits, and I drove in [Luke] Appling with a double. We lost, 4–1.

"I had never seen a big league park until that day," Zernial adds. "I had played in the Coast League with a lot of ex–big leaguers, and some of their experience had rubbed off on me. But I was really impressed with the big league parks."

Early in the season, however, Zernial suffered the first of two crippling injuries. In the ninth inning of a tie game with Cleveland, he raced across the outfield to make a catch of a line drive off the bat of Thurman Tucker, but in the process he stumbled and fell on his shoulder. The result was a broken collarbone that put Gus out of action for two months.

Told he might not play again, Zernial had a steel pin inserted in his shoulder and surprised the medics by returning to action in late July. Swinging gingerly the rest of the way, he finished the season with only five home runs but a .318 batting average.

"I just tried to meet the ball," he remembers. "I made up my mind guys weren't going to strike me out. Actually," he adds, "I never thought too many guys could throw the ball by me anyway. I was a big, flat-footed hitter. I had more trouble with the deceptive pitchers than the hard-throwers. If they wouldn't throw the ball hard, I'd get overanxious.

"Probably the toughest guy for me was Bob Lemon. He was deceptive, and he was smart enough not to throw the ball over the plate. He knew I'd get impatient. I'd always grit my teeth when he was pitching. I never had as much trouble with [Bob] Feller as I did Lemon. Alex Kellner used to drive me nuts, too."

In 1950, it was Zernial who was driving the pitchers nuts. Gus exploded with 29 home runs while collecting 93 RBI and a .280 batting average. At the end of the season in a doubleheader against the St. Louis Browns, the big slugger slammed four homers, including three in one game.

Although he had become a favorite of Comiskey Park fans, Zernial was stunned to learn early in the 1951 season that he had become part of a bone-jarring, three-team trade. Reluctantly, he packed his bags and headed for the City of Brotherly Love.

Less than three weeks after reporting to the A's, Zernial endeared himself to the tough Philadelphia fans by clouting two home runs in each of three consecutive games and a seventh homer in the fourth game. Both feats not only tied American League records but also convinced hero-starved A's fans that Zernial was surely the greatest thing to come to town since Jimmie Foxx.

"It's funny, but I don't remember a big deal being made out of it," Zernial says. "After I'd hit the sixth home run, a newspaper guy came out to take a picture of me with six balls taped to my bat. But there was no big thing made of it, and there certainly wasn't any pressure on me.

"Actually, I hit the seventh home run against Detroit, but it should have been eight that day. I hit a line drive that hit the barbed wire above the wall and bounced back on the field. The bullpen signaled home run, but I only got a double out of it."

Zernial continued his hot-hitting streak, and by the end of the season he had 33 homers and 129 RBI, leading the league and beating Ted Williams by three in both categories. That same year, teammate Fain topped the circuit with a .344 batting average, giving the A's a clean sweep of the triple crown.

"It was a big thrill to win the title, and especially to win in only my second full year in the majors," Zernial states. "To me, it was worth about $5,000 because that's how much my salary was raised. But it was also important beating out Williams because he was the premier hitter in the game."

Zernial, who had also led American League outfielders in assists in 1951 with 18 and topped the league in strikeouts for the second straight year, slammed 29 home runs and drove in 100 the following year. In 1953, he zoomed his home run count to 42 while collecting 108 RBI and hitting a career high .284. Zernial went down to the final weekend of the season before losing the home run title by one to Al Rosen of Cleveland.

"We went into Washington that final weekend," Gus remembers, "and I was thinking home run title. We both hit homers on Friday night, so I had a 42–41 lead. The next night, though, Rosen hit two more homers. On the final day, I got three or four hits but couldn't get one out."

By then, Zernial, who had played in his only All-Star game that year, had built a strange love-hate relationship with the fickle Philadelphia fans. While they loved to see the big left fielder bust home runs, they showed no mercy when he didn't, raining a chorus of boos down from the stands in his direction.

"The fans were tough," Gus says. "They were good fans, though. In 1951, we were a good team, and they left us alone. In 1952, we weren't as good because we'd made some changes [including the trading of Fain]. I had the big year in 1953, but the club was going downhill because we had no pitching. Then 1954 was a total disaster.

"The fans used to give me a hard time, but I would egg them on. I talked to them a lot when I was out in left field, and got them all riled up."

During his first three years with the A's, the team was managed by Jimmy Dykes. But the club was still under the thumb of the octogenarian Connie Mack.

"You really admired him," Zernial says. "By that time, he didn't know a lot of players by name. He'd always look at me and say, 'I know you, you're number 30.' One day in spring training, he said to me, 'Have a good game, Gus.' It almost knocked me over.

"The guy who really helped me on that club," Zernial adds, "was Al Simmons, who was then a coach with the A's. He got me to move up to the front of the batter's box against off-speed pitchers. He used to let me use his bat, too. It was a 39-inch model. I normally used a 36–36 to start the season, then I would drop down to a 35–35 later on in the season."

Frequently, Zernial would uncork prodigious clouts atop the left field roof of Shibe Park. His years were filled with memorable home runs that many old A's fans still talk about.

"I remember one time we were playing Chicago, and Billy Pierce was pitching," Zernial recalls. "He and I were good friends. I hit two home runs off him, and then we went out to dinner together after the game."

The 1954 season was not a pleasant one for either Zernial or the A's. The club finished a distant last under unpopular manager Eddie Joost, hardly drew enough fans to fill a hot dog stand, and ended the year by announcing the sale of the club and moving to Kansas City.

For Zernial, 1954 meant another broken collarbone and an abbreviated season in which he hit just 14 home runs.

"We were playing the Boston Red Sox, and they were beating us something like 18–0," Zernial remembers. "The fans were really gnawing on us. I was mad. I was probably 0-for-4, and as I went out to left field, I said to myself, 'I don't care where they hit it, I'm going to get it.'

"Billy Consolo hit a shot, and I went racing after it. But I stepped in a hole in a spot where there was no cap on a drain. The ball hit me in the leg, and I hit the ground. I felt the bone crack."

He missed one and one-half months of the season. By the time he got back, Mack and his sons had decided to sell the franchise. "We were glad to get out of Philadelphia and go to Kansas City," Zernial says. "We needed to make a change. Philadelphia had always been the A's town, but after the Phillies won the pennant in 1950, things started to change. By 1954, there wasn't much left for us."

Zernial bashed 30 home runs in his first year in Kansas City, 16 the next year, and 27 in 1957. He drove in 84 runs in 1955 and 69 in 1957. Then, much to his surprise, he was traded to Detroit in a massive 13-player swap that also sent second baseman Billy Martin to the Tigers.

"I don't know why Detroit wanted me," Gus says. "They had an outfield of Al Kaline, Harvey Kuenn, and Charley Maxwell. They wanted me mostly to pinch-hit. Then when Dykes became manager in 1959, he asked me to play first base. I played a couple dozen games there and hit seven home runs. I remember my first game at first base was on my birthday. We were playing Baltimore. I went 4-for-4 and hit two home runs, one in the upper deck."

Zernial led the American League in pinch-hits in 1958 with 15. Seeing limited action, he hit .323 that year. His average sloughed off considerably in 1959, and at the end of the season Gus decided to call it quits.

"I didn't want to give up the game; in fact, I had an offer to go to the Dodgers," he says. "But I saw no reason just to hang on. I had a good job offer, and I decided to take it.

"I would've liked to have gone to Boston," Zernial adds. "I always wanted to play there. If they'd have offered me a job or if the designated-hitter had been in, I would've stayed.

"As it was, though, I had a pretty good career. I always enjoyed baseball so much that even when I was striking out, I enjoyed the game. Every day was a challenge between you and the pitcher.

"There's no doubt about it, I was happy that I was a big league player. I was a good player but not a great one. But I sure did love to hit."

And hit he sure did. For the better part of a decade, there wasn't anybody quite like the big slugger they called Ozark Ike.

Photo Credits

RICH WESTCOTT has served as a writer and editor for a number of newspapers and magazines during his 40 years in publishing. He is the founder and for 14 years was the editor and publisher of *Phillies Report,* the nation's oldest, continuous team newspaper. He's also the author of eight other books, including both the original and the updated editions of *The Phillies Encyclopedia* (with Frank Bilovsky), *Phillies '93, An Incredible Season, Mike Schmidt, Philadelphia's Old Ballparks,* and *No-Hitters* (with Allen Lewis). *Splendor on the Diamond* is the third in Westcott's highly acclaimed Diamond series of interviews with former major leaguers, the previous two being *Diamond Greats* and *Masters of the Diamond.* Westcott lives in Springfield, Pennsylvania.